All of Me

All of Me

Patient-Centered Spirituality for Holistic Caregiving

Rev. Dr. Helen T. Boursier

BLOOMSBURY ACADEMIC
NEW YORK • LONDON • OXFORD • NEW DELHI • SYDNEY

BLOOMSBURY ACADEMIC
Bloomsbury Publishing Inc
1359 Broadway, New York, NY 10018, USA
50 Bedford Square, London, WC1B 3DP, UK
29 Earlsfort Terrace, Dublin 2, Ireland

BLOOMSBURY, BLOOMSBURY ACADEMIC and the Diana logo are trademarks of
Bloomsbury Publishing Plc

First published in the United States of America 2025

Copyright © Bloomsbury Publishing Inc, 2025

For legal purposes the Acknowledgments on p. xii constitute an extension of this copyright page.

Cover design: Diana Nuhn
Cover image Left: Freezing Cold in ER: © Helen T. Boursier;
Top right: Digital image of mother/daughter: © Lee F. Estridge;
Bottom middle: New Father: "It's All New to Me Too" © Helen T. Boursier;
Bottom right: Labor of Love: © Helen T. Boursier

All rights reserved. No part of this publication may be reproduced or transmitted in any form or by any means, electronic or mechanical, including photocopying, recording, or any information storage or retrieval system, without prior permission in writing from the publishers.

Bloomsbury Publishing Inc does not have any control over, or responsibility for, any third-party websites referred to or in this book. All internet addresses given in this book were correct at the time of going to press. The author and publisher regret any inconvenience caused if addresses have changed or sites have ceased to exist, but can accept no responsibility for any such changes.

Library of Congress Cataloging-in-Publication Data

Library of Congress Control Number: 2025944491

ISBN: HB: 978-1-5381-9341-9
PB: 978-1-5381-9342-6
ePDF: 979-8-8818-6320-3
eBook: 978-1-5381-9343-3

Typeset by Deanta Global Publishing Services, Chennai, India
Printed and bound in the United States of America

For product safety related questions contact productsafety@bloomsbury.com

To find out more about our authors and books visit www.bloomsbury.com and sign up for our newsletters.

*To the research participants who so graciously shared their experiences.
Thank you.*

Contents

Illustrations ix
Preface xi
Acknowledgments xii

Introduction 1

1 Essence (of Spirituality) 5

2 Misconceptions 15

3 Cognitive Dissonance Nets Spiritual Disjuncture 25

4 Systems, Protocols, and Procedures 39

5 Risk and Vulnerability 57

6 Dignity 69

7 Spiritual Distress 83

8 Intersections: Spirituality as *All of Me* 95

9 (Reducing) Death Anxiety 111

10 (Attitude) Reorientation 123

11 Sacred Space 137

12 Caring Presence 149

13 Advocacy for (Patient) Agency 161

14 (Spiritual) Call to Action 173

Notes 181
Bibliography 206
Index 221

Illustrations

2.1	*Historical Hospital Ward* graphite pencil sketch of the Ft. Davis Army Hospital at the Ft. Davis National Historic Site, Texas. It could accommodate up to twenty-four patients circa 1884. Artwork © Helen T. Boursier.	16
2.2	*All of Me* patient example of the contributing factors to their spirituality. The underlined words contribute in general, and the circled words are the contributing factors when this patient is in an ER or hospital context.	20
4.1	*Freezing Cold in ER* pastel (self) portrait based off of a photograph by Michael L. Boursier; shared by permission. Artwork © Helen T. Boursier.	41
4.2	*Intimidating* digital image of the entrance to an ICU. Photo © Helen T. Boursier	46
5.1	*Inpatient 09* stacked journaling art-reflection of their admittance from ER to ICU. © Helen T. Boursier	60
9.1	*Get Me Out of Here* pastel painting of Morro Bay, California, reflects a patient's urgency to be released from ICU and prepare to relocate (back to) the West Coast. The artwork was her post-release spiritual selfcare. © Helen T. Boursier	114
10.1	*New Father: "It's All New to Me Too"* graphite pencil portrait of a new father holding his newborn daughter. © Helen T. Boursier	132
10.2	*Labor of Love* pastel portrait on Toned Tan of a toddler resting on his mother as she labors to deliver her second child. Artwork © Helen T. Boursier based on a digital image by the mother's birth photographer Janae Boyter; shared by permission.	134
11.1	*Lee and Maxx* posterized digital image "selfie" of mother and daughter. © Lee F. Estridge; shared by permission.	142
11.2	*Goodbye Mommy* pastel portrait of a five-year-old daughter saying goodbye to her mother. Artwork © Helen T. Boursier based on a	

	photograph by the father/grandfather Mark McNeese; shared by permission.	144
12.1	*Holding Hands* digital image of a 96-year-old mother holding on to her son's hand. © Helen T. Boursier	155
14.1	*Sunflower in Bloom* watercolor with ink example of art as spiritual (self)care. © Helen T. Boursier	180

Preface

The experiential research for this book began when I found myself, unexpectedly, admitted from the Emergency Room (ER) to an Intensive Care Unit (ICU) at a mid-sized suburban hospital in the southern Midwest. Other than the occasional sinus infection or round of the flu, I'd had no health issues or conditions, and I hadn't been admitted to a hospital since I'd had an emergency C-section when my son was born in 1981. Meanwhile, I've taught college courses to nursing and social work students for nearly a decade about the intersections of spirituality with patient-centered care, including Introduction to Spirituality at the College of St. Scholastica. Even though I was debilitated enough to be admitted to the ICU, I remember thinking almost immediately upon arrival, "Oh, my nursing students so need to know what Dr. B's thinking here," as I reflected on my interactions with the various caregivers. It quickly became evident that hospital caregivers needed to know what's going on *inside* their patients while they are taking care of their *outsides*. Physical care isn't a separate thing that's apart for the rest of a patient. The physical body is the container for the spiritual and emotional, which are framed in each patient's particular social context. Our bodies are intersectional: body, mind, spirit. They're not a compilation of separate parts.

Within days after I'd been released from the ICU, I began collecting the experiential stories of other former patients and their families. Thirty days later, I submitted a book proposal, and I completed this manifesto of patient-centered spirituality for holistic caregiving a year later. As the collective experiential patient-centered witness confirms, physical care needs to address *all of me*, not part of me.

Rev. Dr. Helen T. Boursier
California, June 2025

Acknowledgments

First, I appreciate the candid conversations with the research participants who generously shared their experiences. Thank you all. I'm also grateful for the many contributing voices, particularly the students in my Introduction to Spirituality course at the College of St. Scholastica, who graciously shared their insights and observations about spirituality in a healthcare context. I've learned so much from each one of you. Thank you. I'm also grateful to Meredith Patterson, a registered nurse with nearly four decades of experience, who thoughtfully reviewed an early version of this manuscript. Her feedback was extremely helpful. I also appreciate hospital chaplain Anjeanette Allen for sharing her chaplaincy experiences, along with the chaplains, clergy, and nurses who participated but who preferred to remain anonymous. Thank you all.

Rev. Dr. Helen T. Boursier, California, June 2025

Introduction

What unfolds emphasizes spiritual care (not religiosity) from the perspective of (former) patients about when they'd received physical care in a hospital, emergency room (ER), or urgent care setting. Based on the data from these research participants, spirituality is each person's holistic essence of being. Spirituality is who they *are*. Through the testimonies of patients and their families, *All of Me: Patient Centered Spirituality for Holistic Caregiving* seeks to correct an erroneous prevailing medicalized definition and understanding of spirituality as "meaning in/of life," shifting it to how patients and their families describe spirituality as *essence of being*. The redirected understanding will facilitate holistic caregiving, which encompasses a patient's physical, mental, spiritual, and social intersectionality (see Chapter 2).[1] The patient-centered data confirms patients want and need attention to their entire being, even when they can't, haven't, or don't articulate this need while they're in a hospital or ER context. All of these research participants described how their physical care had harmed what they specified were the contributing factors to their spirituality. They described the bad things that had happened physically first, and then explained how these were detrimental to their spirituality. Patients said their spirituality is inseparable from their physicality. Spirituality isn't part of me, it's *all of me*.

Conversation Partners

All of Me documents thirty-five adults (and/or their families) who've experienced direct patient care in a hospital-type facility, either as an ER patient for traumatic/crisis healthcare intervention or due to a scheduled operation or treatment. All of the participants responded because they had a story they wanted to share related to an aspect of their experience in an urgent care or hospital. By mutual agreement, their testimonies are on the record for content, but off the record for privacy. These participants are from across the continental United States, including the East Coast, West Coast, Midwest, and South. Respondent diversity includes race, ethnicity, age, gender, sexual orientation, marital status, religious affiliation or disaffiliation, and medical conditions.² Despite a wide range of socio-economic-racial, etc., differences and varying medical conditions, there are intersecting commonalities regarding how these former patients experienced a disconnect between their spirituality while they were being cared for physically. All of the research participants are privileged in the sense that they had some form of health insurance or a benefactor (i.e., a parent of a young adult), which gave them access to healthcare.

The research doesn't compare similarities or differences between types of illnesses and/or health emergencies. Rather, it focuses on patient understandings, expectations, and experiences of spiritual care integrated with their physical care, not as an add-on extra, but included togetherwith. The interviews uncovered any misconceptions or false assumptions about the meaning and/or nature of spiritually informed direct patient care in a hospital setting *from the patient's perspective*.³ In addition to the interviews, the qualitative data includes reflections of nursing, social work, and clinical pastoral education students in various clinical settings, shared anonymously and by permission, most notably from the Introduction to Spirituality course I taught at the College of St. Scholastica. Conversation partners also include experiential reflections of seasoned nurses, chaplains, and clergy, with a brief analysis through a practical theology lens, with its emphasis on moving from idealized theory to contextualized praxis (practice).

Content Overview

Chapter 1: "Essence (of Spirituality)" explains the differing characteristics of spirituality versus religion and why these distinctions are relevant for healthcare workers. It addresses why spirituality in a healthcare setting matters, including what's at stake.

Chapter 2: "Misconceptions" refutes healthcare's standardized view of spirituality as the "meaning in/of life," arguing instead for spirituality as *all of me*.

Chapter 3: "Cognitive Dissonance Nets Spiritual Disjuncture" addresses when spirituality isn't factored in with physical well-being, including the various ways caregivers don't respect patients during physical caregiving, and how the "black box" mentality of a medicalized view of spirituality hinders patient-centered caregiving.

Chapter 4: "Systems, Protocols and Procedures" discusses how policies, protocols, and procedures interfere with holistic patient well-being. Patient examples highlight experiences in maternity, ICU, transgender top surgery, and a misdiagnosis after a slow journey through multiple hospitals.

Chapter 5: "Risk and Vulnerability" discusses how these core aspects of a patient's care experience contribute to (or not) spiritual well-being. Patient examples include a young adult diagnosed with stage four melanoma, his older brother who almost needed to have his hand or finger amputated due to a delayed or inaccurate assessment in urgent care, and the added familial challenges caused by being estranged through distance, Covid-19, and HIPAA.

Chapter 6: "Dignity" addresses testimonial and hermeneutical injustice in a healthcare context, including power differentials that demonize patients by labeling them as *frequent fliers* or "drug seekers." Arguing for a *spirituality of dignity*, it addresses the intersections of gender, race, ageism, sexual orientation, and psychiatric patients.

Chapter 7: "Spiritual Distress" explores this diagnosis from a healthcare perspective, comparing nursing, chaplaincy, and pastoral perspectives with patient experiential documentation, which includes pain and medication mismanagement, how extended fasting leads to spiritual distress, and ICU delirium.

Chapter 8: "Intersections: Spirituality as *All of Me*" addresses spiritual assessment, spiritual care, medicalized spiritual care interventions, "crossing the line" into what's a chaplain's role, and how patient-centered care from the patient's perspective also can be spiritual care. Experiential data raises an awareness of the intersections between the physical, psychosocial, and spiritual.

Chapter 9: "(Reducing) Death Anxiety" considers human finitude, death, and death anxiety. It explains the concept of "dying well" in order to care well. It also addresses "to tell or not to tell," and includes chaplain and clergy reflections on dying and death, preparing for death, and insights on spiritual maturity in a healthcare context.

Chapter 10: "(Attitude) Reorientation" documents the experiences of former patients who explain their (spiritual) care disconnects. It recommends cultural humility, deep listening, and compassion for professional caregivers to embrace the physical, psychosocial, *and* spiritual with compassionate care through empathy.

Chapter 11: "Sacred Space" explains the role of hope in creating liminal space in a secular place of healing as former patients share their experiential witness in the ICU, maternity, and at the bedside of a dying adult daughter. It compares hope with hopelessness and shows how hope can be present amidst secularism and a/religious spirituality.

Chapter 12: "Caring Presence" discusses what it means to be a healing presence with the dying and offers a father's reflections on the morning after his adult daughter's death. By being a practical, caring presence, spiritual care flows through exceptional, compassionate attentiveness to the whole patient.

Chapter 13: "Advocacy for (Patient) Agency" discusses how caregivers can find their voice for "defiant spirituality" and "holy boldness," which advocate for patient agency and freedom of choice.

Chapter 14: "(Spiritual) Call to Action" recommends a caregiver's self-assessment of what spirituality looks like as ~~part~~ *all of me* which becomes a guidon for spiritual humility and personal growth, which moves toward cultural humility. It includes recommendations for caregivers to find their spiritual center in order to live a considered life, which then fosters a compassionate, caring presence with all patients.

1 Essence (of Spirituality)

We're living in a time of spiritual reorientation.[1] Spirituality is becoming more and more "in" as religion is becoming more and more "out."[2] With the increasing disaffiliation from religion, spirituality often doesn't have a connection with any religious authority, making it free-floating from any moral parameters expected by a Higher Power. Hence, spirituality often [incorrectly] means whatever anyone wants it to mean, with a tendency to focus on the inner self and inner feelings. For example, a middle-aged white female who'd had to retire early from her job as a police detective due to poor health described spirituality as "feeling comfortable within my heart." A Black octogenarian male and former professional musician who's now physically disabled said, "Spirituality means the inner still part of you that nobody knows but yourself."

Spirituality might begin within, but it's more than the personal voice that speaks deep inside each person. Kurtz and Ketcham explain, "Spirituality points, always beyond: *beyond* the ordinary, *beyond* possession, *beyond* the narrow confines of the self, and—above all—*beyond* expectation."[3] Spirituality often isn't exactly what we expect, and it also isn't externally controllable. Someone can't tell *me* what *my* spirituality is. A student in Introduction to Spirituality proposed, "The search for spirituality is, first of all, a search for reality, for honesty, for true speaking and true thinking."[4] A conservative rabbi and board-certified chaplain explains, "For me, spirituality is not just religious, nor is it bound to a belief in a higher power. Rather, it entails everything that makes us breathe and breathe freely, everything that defines us and identifies us." This rabbi adds, "Hence, I believe everyone has a form of spirituality, whether it be related to something sacred or something profane; even the profane becomes 'sacred' if it makes us feel alive and gives us the power to go through challenging situations."[5] Spirituality becomes an empowering inner guidon during good times but also, and perhaps especially, when bad things happen.

Spirituality encompasses the transcendent, the range of intangible experience that goes beyond what's touchable, perceptible, or definable.[6] It's a dimension within and without that can't quite be named, explained, or defined. Sometimes it intersects with religion, but more often spirituality encompasses much more than what's understood or defined by any particular religion.[7] In the opening moments of his TED Talk, when social scientist Jonathan Haidt asks his audience to raise their hand if they consider themselves to be religious, about three or four percent do. He immediately responds by asking the audience to raise their hands if they consider themselves to be spiritual "in any way, shape, or form," and the majority raise their hands.[8] His simple survey highlights an important distinction between religion and spirituality.

Spirituality

All of Me examines spirituality through a theological-philosophical lens which understands spirituality connotes what it means to be fully human.[9] It's the very essence of beingness for what otherwise would be bodily fluids held together with skin and bones. Or, as one of my students commented, "We're spiritual beings having a human experience." The spirit is what gives a corpse its life and makes it fully human. Without this spiritual effervescence, each person would be a mere shell of a body. A Black female retired U.S. Army nurse who shifted careers to vocational ordained ministry said, "Without spirituality, your very being is nothing more than a carcass walking around. Your spirituality is all of you, and it shouldn't be separated into subsets, parts, or pieces." In their initial post in a course on introduction to spirituality, a nursing student said, "Spirituality is characteristic of what it means to be human. We create art and music. We seek beauty. We ask questions like how can I make a difference? What is the meaning of life? What is the purpose of life? What is life after death?" Spirituality encompasses a person's interior yearnings, feelings, emotions, desires, and the very essence of being as it intersects with their exterior world, including people, places, and events.

Spirituality is the *something more* that speaks to the inner self while also pulling outwards toward an ineffable something that's not quite named or defined. It includes identifiable and unidentifiable personal values that intersect with people, places, nature, the environment, and life.[10] It's an individualized personal connection that's nurtured through "interconnectedness with internal and external forces."[11] It's very personal, but spirituality also necessarily is connected with the world around. It's nurtured in community. Instead of spirituality being "me, myself, and I," it enjoins with family, friends, neighbors, colleagues, and more to become an intersecting "us."

In healthcare, spirituality can be known, at least in part, by listening to patients as they describe what helps or hinders their spirituality. It also can be known through the words and witness of family and friends who participate as caregivers with their beloveds. Spirituality can be known through descriptive language in academic literature, particularly theology, religious studies, and philosophy. It also can be understood through the experiential observations made by chaplains, clergy, and other caregivers in a healthcare context who are a caring presence with patients. For however much spirituality as essence of being can be known, much of it remains a mystery, which moves us into the uncomfortable place of not being able to fully define and control spirituality as essence of being. It's this same indescribable mystery that points to the sacredness of spirituality as what it means to be fully human.[12]

Describing the Indescribable

In some regards, the term "spirituality" doesn't seem like it would need to be explained. It's such a common word that's frequently used in everyday conversations. Once a conversation ensues about what spirituality actually means, it quickly becomes evident that it means different things to different people, and much of that meaning is derived from the particular context of each person sharing. This seemingly simple term takes on, absorbs, and then reflects back the worldviews surrounding it, making it mean very different things from one person to another.[13] For example, in the introduction to their essay on spirituality, a white female social work student in her mid-twenties wrote,

> *It's not possible to hold spirituality in our hands. We cannot see, taste, or even hear it. Spirituality is a feeling that usually comes in times of despair or great need. Spirituality is hope, when there could not be a single hope left in the world. It's an essence or an understanding that life simply is, in all of its imperfections. Spirituality doesn't come in a universal size; it just simply is.*[14]

A nursing student in her early thirties said,

> *Spirituality includes an understanding of not just yourself, but those around you. Spirituality is the essence of caring, including the decision to care for one*

another no matter the differences, caring with love, compassion, and the moral desire to do right. Spirituality is fighting for what's right and helping others to understand. Spirituality is a deep connection with yourself and those around you.[15]

Another student highlighted, "Spirituality can foster good, positive traits/actions, but it also can produce bad/negative actions such as Manifest Destiny when its spiritual or religious belief system crosses the line from being just, to unjust; from empowerment to oppression; and from helpful to harmful."[16] Another student specified spirituality is "an emotional connection to things that you can't see, but you can *feel*. Being spiritual means being present, recognizing what's going on around you and connecting on a deeper level with people." Occasionally, a student defines spirituality as being "a personal quest for meaning in life," but the student would quickly follow up with this being connected to believing in "a higher power of some sort" which provides moral guidance.

Spirituality can only be discovered through what Haidt calls "the longer story."[17] It's a long-term gig that includes our past, our present, and our future.[18] Spirituality is the *is*-ness of life in this moment, but it overlaps with what brought us to the present and what's before us in the future. Regardless of the place or point along the journey, spirituality serves as the rudder to steer us along the uncertain paths of life.[19] Roger Gottlieb proposes, "at the center of the spiritual journey is the search for a peaceful heart."[20] Spirituality isn't a separate "thing," like a black, brown, or white box with a carefully and tightly closed lid that keeps this ineffable, inexplainable, transcendence separately and securely locked inside. Rather, spirituality has a pervasive intersectionality.

It's who we are. It's our very essence of being, the invisible and intangible artery of life that permeates who we are and what we do.[21] Kurtz and Ketcham propose, "The question is not whether we 'have spirituality' but whether the spirituality we have is a negative one that leads to isolation and self-destruction or one that is more positive and life-giving."[22] Put simply, they propose, "Like 'love,' spirituality is a way to 'be.'"[23] Spirituality becomes heightened when people are feeling vulnerable. Hence, it's particularly important for caregivers to recognize the all-inclusive intersectionality of spirituality. It's not a separate "thing" to manage. It's who each patient *is*. When spirituality is dissected, separated, and removed apart from the whole person, that person's full humanity is harmed because it's been segmented, sliced, diced, and amputated away from its fullness of being.[24]

Religion Versus Spirituality

Religion and spirituality are sometimes used interchangeably, but they're not synonymous. Religion is typically understood as being a set of beliefs, practices, doctrines, and rules that are prescribed from the top down, with the people sitting in the pews or kneeling on the floor having little say in any of these beliefs and practices.[25] Some religious beliefs are off-putting for the a/religious or disaffiliated. For example, a nursing student said, "I find it interesting—actually infuriating—how often religion is used as an excuse for prejudice." Where spirituality often goes it alone; religion functions in community, particularly for seniors whose closest friends and connections (outside of immediate family) often are from their religious places of worship.[26] Religion is associated with doing "religious" actions like attending worship, praying, giving alms, and studying sacred texts. Religion is an organized response to an internal sense of call to an external Supreme Being, which draws a practitioner's religious response to be better than what they otherwise would or could be. Religion does overlap with spirituality, as Harold Koenig explains religion seeks to "provide answers to the big questions in life that are outside the realm of medicine and science: Where did I come from? Why am I here? Where am I going?"[27]

Religious Spirituality

It's a misnomer and false supposition to suggest that religion necessarily excludes spirituality. Religion has been the home base for spirituality for thousands of years.[28] Spirituality's separation from religion is a moderately new innovation. First and foremost, there's been spirituality in a diversity of religions through the centuries and around the globe. Spirituality isn't a new thing. It's as ancient as prehistoric humans who first carved sacred symbols on the walls of caves, and religious spirituality is as varied as the people, place, and religion being expressed.[29] Spirituality is so pervasive that philosopher Martin Heidegger describes the history of the world as being comprised of spirit, which has been expressed over time through spirituality, including by people who consider themselves to be spiritual (*not* religious).[30]

*Spiritual (Not **Religious**)*

Interest in generic spirituality, unattached from any religion, has been growing among people who can't, don't, or won't accept orthodox religious beliefs and practices. The religiously disaffiliated don't necessarily discard every aspect of whichever religion was part of their upbringing or cultural heritage. In fact, some might be more spiritual and have a stronger belief in their Supreme Being than those who remain religiously affiliated. Many who are spiritual but not religious may disagree with religion-supported ideology, but they continue to believe in Allah, God, Jesus, or Buddha.[31] For example, a white male nursing student who was raised Catholic but who rarely if ever attends any religious service said he prays and reads his Bible daily as expressions of his spirituality. He just doesn't attend Mass, other than the occasional high holy day like Christmas and Easter. His story is typical of the disaffiliated who separate their spirituality from religion.

A white female nursing student in her mid-thirties said, even though she's spiritual and not religious, she acknowledges the many religiously affiliated schools, universities, social services, healthcare facilities, etc., which are available to anyone, regardless of any religious affiliation (or not). She said, "Religion may have played a positive role in who you are, and where you've gotten to today because of these various religiously affiliated organizations," adding, "I know this is true for me."[32] Some disaffiliated say they haven't "found the right church," and others don't want to associate with religion because of its inattention to issues of contemporary social concern.[33] Instead, they opt to self-identify as spiritual (*not* religious).

Disaffiliation doesn't necessarily mean the disaffiliated have no knowledge about or connection with religion. For example, a conservative rabbi and board-certified chaplain whose context is Israel, where patients and hospital staff are Christian, Christian-Arab, Jewish, and Muslim, explains their religious context is ever present in all its multiplicity because religions are everywhere. The chaplain said:

> *For almost anyone growing up in the Middle East, religion is part of their lives. Even people who describe themselves as secular do so with a large cultural background in any or all of these religions. . . . Religion is everywhere: on the street, in the politics, in the history and in pretty much every publicly discussed topic. It is impossible to escape it. Personal religiosity or spirituality still is chosen, even though many more people adopt it simply by living in this environment."*[34]

This context parallels religious spirituality in America, on a somewhat tamer scale, because growing up in America means some intersection with religion. Someone might be technically disaffiliated, but they've still had interaction with something religious.

Spirituality in a Healthcare Setting: Why It Matters and What's at Stake

Health must address the entire person, without isolating a physical ailment from the rest of the patient.[35] Based on the professional and academic literature, there's clearly "a growing consensus that spirituality is part of a holistic patient-centered approach to healthcare."[36] The World Health Organization (WHO) includes spirituality in its understanding of holistic healthy well-being.[37] In addition, "The American College of Physicians has convened two consensus conferences and concluded that physicians are obligated to address all dimensions of suffering—the physical, psychosocial, spiritual, and existential."[38] Even secular entities, including "most governments recognize the importance of the spiritual part of life for the health and wellbeing of their citizens, particularly when facing life-challenging events such as birth, illness and/or death."[39] Similarly, a nursing student in her initial self-introduction explained that when she'd told her husband she was taking Introduction to Spirituality as part of her final semester course requirements in the accelerated BSN program, she said:

> My husband immediately said, "So that really seems like a waste of time." And I replied to him, "It's not a waste of time at all. It's actually really important." I gave the example in my current job where I frequently take care of people who are dying. I said, "It's really important that we understand what people's religious beliefs are, and what's important to them."

She added, "When my patients are dying, I want to meet their spiritual needs, and I want to honor their customs and practices."[40] Spirituality is more likely to be attended to when a patient is in hospice or palliative care, but all patients have spiritual needs.

While debriefing after a pastoral care visit with a young woman in hospice, a chaplain said, "When I see someone in great physical pain, with great discomfort and a mounting frustration and confusion about not being able to do simple things, it validates that the spirit, body, and mind are tightly interconnected. They're three in one physical being. To attend to one aspect, while disregarding the others would be a disservice in every way." The chaplain said a patient clearly has physical needs, including being comfortable and having pain management with a pathway toward healing and wholeness to the fullest possible, adding, "But it's equally clear the physical care needs to be done in harmony with what the patient's spirit wants and needs." Ultimately, spirituality in a healthcare setting must matter for caregivers because it matters to patients.[41] Patients don't leave their essence of being at home when they go to the ER or urgent care. Their whole selves come with them.

A recently retired Black female nurse with a master's in hospital administration who also pastors a nondenominational church said," If you don't take care of the whole patient, you run the risk of exacerbating whatever it is that you're trying to address." Giving a hypothetical example of someone with heart disease, the retired nurse/now clergy said, "If the health care team has decided that my spirituality isn't valuable, rather than doing anything to help me, to guide me, they'll have me just stick with the pills or whatever other medical intervention." She added, "Rather than doing or saying anything that would foster holistic caregiving, the medical profession practices avoidance medicine." She explained, "In a *whole-person* approach to caregiving, every aspect of health is a part of my life," adding, "When you take the body only as the definition for health, when you ignore my spirit, you automatically do me harm."

A Black male nurse manager in his early fifties who said they focus on the interconnection of whole health where he works, which he specified includes spiritual, physical, and mental, emphasized, "Including spirituality in the healthcare equation prioritizes *healing*, instead of overly focusing on *curing*." Distinguishing between these terms, Barbara Ganim explains in *Art and Healing*, "Healing restores balance and harmony to the body, mind, and spirit. Neither surgery, medicine, nor time can do that. Surgery merely removes the cancer from the body, but if the emotional stress that brought the body into disharmony in the first place is not relieved, the cancer will return. The same is true for all disease and illness."[42] Holistic caregiving includes the whole human.

A recently retired nurse in her late sixties said how much spirituality and spiritual needs are recognized "can vary according to the healthcare setting and the culture of that setting," adding, "In acute care hospitals, it's relegated largely to the chaplains because the medical staff keeps score of getting tasks done quickly so that ultimately the patient can be discharged." This retired nurse noted there's also "lots of pressure to not 'waste' a minute doing otherwise." The nurse noted that in other settings, such as long-term care, "They're "somewhat more understanding in this regard." Notice how this nurse's explanation separates physical care from spiritual and/or emotional care instead of recognizing the overlap of physical care with *all of me*. What helps or harms one aspect helps or harms the others.

The Spirituality All of Me Doesn't Address

All of Me doesn't address spirituality as a nonreligion, what social scientists and philosophers of religion examine to categorize various "types" of spirituality and the different ways of living out or embodying "spiritual" behaviors, practices, and ideals,[43] much like studying New Age religions as spirituality becomes its own formation of a *non*religious religion.[44] For the purpose of the following chapters, spirituality is what it means to be fully human. It's *all of me*; not part of me. When spirituality is ignored, dismissed, or misunderstood, it harms patient care and hinders their overall well-being.

2 Misconceptions

The spiritual and religious care of the sick and dying was integral to caregiving in previous centuries (see Illustration 2.1), something that's been set aside in recent years in favor of focusing on the physical aspect of healthcare.[1] Because the medical profession has embraced a "preoccupation with the secular,"[2] instead of treating *all of me*, "the innovations and advances in medical and surgical treatments have patients fragmentalized, compartmentalized, and in some instances dehumanized by being divided into function mechanistic units."[3] Rather than whole-person care, typical treatment follows "the biological, reductionist approach to health care in which the concept of spirituality plays little or even no part."[4] Professional caregivers need to reclaim the more integrated spiritual ↔ physical care of the past to enhance the medical (only) excellence of the present to actualize patient-centered care, which includes attention to *all of me*.[5]

Medicalized View of Spirituality as Meaning in/of Life

Spirituality in much of the healthcare literature, particularly in nursing, defines spirituality as being someone's meaning in life, based upon a skewed interpretation of Viktor Frankl's landmark book, *Man's Search for Meaning*.[6] Part of the medicalized misconstrual of spirituality arises from its myopic view, which reiterates the same (mis)understanding without considering views beyond the realm of medicine.[7] Frankl wasn't writing about spirituality. Rather, he was writing about what it took to survive in a Nazi concentration camp, what he describes as "the immediate task of keeping oneself and one's closest friends alive."[8] Frankl explains, "Once an individual's search for meaning is successful, it not only renders him happy but also gives him the capability to cope with suffering."[9] He was writing about the survival strategies undergirding a prisoner's will to live, or their search for *life*.

Illustration 2.1 *Historical Hospital Ward* graphite pencil sketch of the Ft. Davis Army Hospital at the Ft. Davis National Historic Site, Texas. It could accommodate up to twenty-four patients circa 1884. Artwork © Helen T. Boursier.

Freedom to Choose How to Respond to Suffering and Loss

Frankl's much more relevant and helpful point for healthcare is his argument on what he calls "the last of the human freedoms," which is choosing how each person responds to suffering.[10] For Frankl, it's in the choosing, the will to live, which helps suffering people to press on when they otherwise would give up. Frankl argues, "Suffering ceases to be suffering at the moment it finds a meaning."[11] The freedom to choose how to respond to the bad stuff that happens in life is an exhilarating spiritual practice because it reshapes what otherwise could be a negative, cynical, or fatalistic response. Meaning in/of life is *one* contributing factor to spirituality, but it isn't spirituality.

Gold Standard

Spirituality as meaning in/of life based upon a misconstrued interpretation and application of Frankl's work frequently originates from within healthcare and then becomes the *gold standard*, which is repeated again and again by everyone else within healthcare. A literature review indicates redundancy through a tunnel view. A Black female who's been a nurse for nearly forty years said, "It's too easy to restate what someone else has said rather than to "get out of the silo and think for yourself."[12] One of the reasons patients don't receive spiritual care is because of this misunderstanding of what spirituality is, *from the patient's perspective*.[13] When healthcare professionals begin from an incorrect premise on what spirituality is and then sanctify it as a gold standard, it becomes an untouchable *black box*.

Black Boxes

Janet Shim, who researches the sociology and inequalities of health, helpfully highlights ethical concerns that arise when medicalized exoneration of esteemed theories, processes, elements, and/or ideas becomes sacralized through the metaphor of a black box. In her research with people of color who live with heart disease, which she documents in *Heart-Sick: The Politics of Risk, Inequality, and Heart Disease*, Shim explains, "science studies scholar Bruno Latour argues that black boxes are created when many elements and processes are made to fit together into a machine or assembly that in fact acts as one."[14] Furthermore, "The black box metaphor is often used in situations wherein scientific claims and procedures are perceived as facts and routines, despite their often having a whole history of debates and controversy."[15] Shim's summary points that the "factness, ritualization, and taken-for-grantedness are actually achieved" parallels the medicalized view of spirituality that validates the erroneous standardized definition of what healthcare has decided it wants spirituality to mean and be. In addition, there's a medicalized obsession with commanding unilateral agreement on defining spirituality and any related terms, which is an unhelpful and often misguided rabbit trail. The quest for a universal definition also begs the question of which voice or voices "should be" included in this conversation.[16] Most importantly, the standardized healthcare definition differs exponentially from how patients describe and experience their spirituality.

(More) Missing Voices

In addition to the missing voices of patients, the medical literature on spirituality barely (if ever) engages the academic disciplines that have been discussing, examining, reflecting, and writing about spirituality since the beginning of time, most notably philosophy, religious studies, and theology. Instead, as Bradshaw observes, "writers cobble together an approach to spirituality taken piecemeal from various writers as diverse as Sarte, Maslow,

Frankl, Kierkegaard, and Heidegger. The result is a mess of ideas taken out of context."[17] These concepts are quoted in subsequent journal articles and taken as evidential documentation that's been grounded upon inaccuracies.[18] As the patient testimonies and theological-philosophical conversation partners confirm, meaning in/of life contributes partially to spirituality, but it isn't in and of itself spirituality. This *mis*interpretation or *mis*application of Frankl's focus means a caregiver can't hinder or harm someone's spirituality because they're not doing anything personally that would harm or inhibit someone's meaning in life.[19] However, when spirituality encompasses *all of me*, then there are multiple ways medical professionals at all levels could help *or* harm a patient's spirituality.

Professional Nursing Perspective: Theory Versus Actual Practice

A white female nurse in her mid-sixties who's worked much of her thirty-plus years in nursing in neurology said, "In theory, nurses are to address the whole person, including their spirituality, and respect their culture and religion." She said, "Ours has the role to listen and to be supportive, but not to convert them to our way of thinking or certainly to question their beliefs and values. You are to remain an impartial, but willing-to-listen person." She added, "So that's in theory. What you do for the most part is *practice*," by doing the practical work of a nurse. She said there's a wide range of people in the healthcare profession, with some being kinder and more compassionate and others remaining more aloof or detached." She said, "Sadly, probably the biggest complaint that nurses have more than anything is that they don't have time to give complete patient care because they're too busy doing medical tasks." She added, "This is certainly true in hospital-based ones. The sicker your patients are, the less time you have to spend listening and talking to them and holding their hand because you're so busy managing critical tasks." Notice how this nurse's explanation differentiates and separates physical care from spiritual care without seeing the intersections and overlaps.

All of Me: **More than Meaning in/of Life**

The self-explanation of patients about what contributes to their personal understanding of spirituality significantly differs from the medically sanctioned definition of spirituality, which emphasizes it is the meaning in/of life. Initially, I began each interview with a detailed set of questions, starting by asking how they defined or described "spirituality." Most responded with a blank stare or a comment like, "I'll have to think about that a moment." Early on, I shifted from asking this question to inviting participants to identify what their contributing factors are for their spirituality, and I offered a set of some 140 suggestions, plus the option to add additional factors (see Illustration 2.2). I used this as a "warm-up exercise" before the formal conversation began. After they'd underlined all of the contributing factors for their spirituality in general, I invited them to go back and circle their top ten factors that impacted their spirituality while in a healthcare context. These could be the same or different from what they'd indicated contributed to their spirituality in general. After they'd made their choices, I asked one open-ended question: "Tell me about your healthcare experience . . ." which opened a floodgate as each patient shared their experience in an ER, urgent care, or hospital and how this had helped or harmed their spirituality.

A Patient's Perspective

A white transgender male in his mid-thirties who was raised in a Christian home and later disaffiliated due to his sexual orientation laughed out loud when he was halfway into the first step of the self-assessment on what contributes to his spirituality. He joked, "I could just about highlight all of these words." He highlighted seventy-five words or phrases which contribute to his spirituality, either for the good or for the bad (see Illustration 2.2). Then he underlined what most contributed to his spirituality in a healthcare context, including trauma, chronic illness, truth, abilities, dignity, sex/gender, respect, disabilities, assumptions, exclusion, and healing. He said he was initially thinking of his top surgery, but explained these words continue to intersect with his spirituality each time he goes in for any sort of healthcare, including ER or scheduled direct patient care.

During the subsequent conversation, he repeatedly emphasized that truth, truthfulness, and living and being truthful are central to his spirituality. He explained that before and after the top surgery, he'd had multiple trips to various urgent care clinics and doctors for stomach and urinary tract infections related to his hormone treatments to transgender. He said he'd love to think that all the disrespect and mistreatment he's experienced in various hospital and healthcare contexts was "just a coincidence." He explained it's been "very, very awkward" each time he's gone to *any* healthcare setting, urgent care or

Contributing Factors to Spirituality as *All of Me*
Internal/External: Individual or Personal Spirituality Lived or Embodied Internally or in Community

Physical Comfort/Discomfort   Distress: Physical, Emotional, Psychological, Spiritual   Meaning of [My] Life   Regret
Self-respect   Pain: Physical, Emotional, Psychological, Spiritual   Solitude   Political Beliefs   Autonomy
Abilities   Chronic Illness   Choice   Healthy/Unhealthy   Transcendence   Dignity   Acceptance   Truth   Anger
Trauma   Gratitude   Fears   Physical Fitness   Faith   Citizenship Status   Delight   Freedom   Mystery
Finitude ("Life is Short")   Loneliness   Unfinished Goals/Projects   Religious Beliefs/Values/Practices   Ethics
Culture   Stress   Abuse: Verbal, Physical, Emotional, Psychological   Values   Morals   Peace
Death of a Loved One   Abilities   Joy   Nationality   God/Higher Power
Adversity   Physical Comfort/Discomfort   'All of Me'   Language(s)   Family   Spouse/Partner
Trust: Implicit/Explicit   Anxiety   Hope   Spirituality as   Relationships   Community   Neighbors
Memory/ies   Emotions   Age   Essence of Being   Geographic Location   Colleagues
Race   Moods   Feelings   Respect   Social Location   Classmates   Abilities
Sex/Gender   Being Kind/Considerate   Silence   Safety   Optimism   Friends   Unresolved Conflict   Housing Insecurity
Solitude   Feelings   Recognition   EcoJustice   Plants/Landscapes   Travel   Exclusion
Sexual Orientation   Estrangement   Compassion   Social Media Connections   Nature   Animals   Music   Enlightenment
Self-esteem   Marital Status   Personal Agency   Disabilities   The Arts   Beauty   War   Education   Vocation/Job
Justice/Injustice   Substance Abuse   Sights   Smells   Assumptions   Pessimism   Self-identity   World Peace
Rape   Eating Disorders   Happiness   Sounds   Equity/Inequity   Contentedness   Self-Understanding
Spiritual Practices   Unresolved Conflict   Healing   Personal Maturity   Cynicism   Dignity   Self-transcendence
   Self-actualization   Acceptance

Illustration 2.2 *All of Me* patient example of the contributing factors to their spirituality. The underlined words contribute in general, and the circled words are the contributing factors when this patient is in an ER or hospital context.

otherwise since he began the transgender process to the present. He said, "It's like each time I have to 'come out' all over again." He said his queer wife "can just see the anxiety on my face" when he needs to go to an urgent care or MD appointment of any kind. His angst isn't about the treatment itself. Rather, his anxiety rises because he knows his spiritual and emotional well-being likely will be harmed by how he's (mis)treated as a transgender male.

Hip Replacement Reflection

A Black heterosexual female in her early seventies who pastors a conservative Black church and who had hip replacement surgery included the following as contributing to her spirituality, either pro or con: self-respect; meaning in life; regret; age; ethics; joy; culture; God/Higher Power; trust; relationships; expectations; self-esteem; silence; self-identity; plants/landscapes; vocation/employment; education; spiritual practices; personal maturity; and self-understanding. She marked ten totally different terms or phrases for what impacted her spirituality during her hip replacement experience in a hospital: pain; aptitudes; religious beliefs, values, and practices; language(s); family; friends; recognition; optimism; disabilities; cynicism; and healing.

When I asked this patient, who'd served nearly forty years as a nurse before becoming an ordained minister, if she was surprised that she'd chosen ten totally different contributing factors for her spirituality as a patient compared to her spirituality in general, she exclaimed, "Initially, my response was because I love the Lord and I'm saved, and I'm living as holy as I can. But when I go into the hospital as a patient it's completely different." She emphasized, "It's *a completely different* set of circumstances than when I'm walking around in life. I have full control. I'm not dependent on another human being." She added,

> But as a patient, you give up your independence. Everything depends on the caregiver, the provider, the nurses, the person who's taking care of you. I had a hip replacement, so I didn't have the option to just get up and go to the bathroom, which is something I would take for granted and not even give a second thought to normally.

She remembered a "very pleasant individual who was a very astute nurse who was doing a lot of other things," and when this patient asked to be helped to the restroom, the busy nurse asked, "Do you have to go *right now*?" The patient explained, "Being a nurse myself, I understood that she had other patients, but from a patient's perspective, I wanted to say 'Are you kidding me?!' Sorry, but if I didn't have to go *right now*, I wouldn't have said I had to go. I needed to use the restroom!" Then she added, "But because I am a spiritual person, and I always think of the other person, I thought maybe it's somebody down the hall who this nurse needed to see before me. So, I stretched my bladder a little bit more and waited for the nurse to come back."

Spirituality as meaning in life had nothing to do with this former nurse's stressed-out experience as a patient. Being at the mercy of a caregiver when she needed something as basic as help going to the bathroom was physically uncomfortable, but even more so, it was spiritually distressing. The patient explained being at a caregiver's mercy and being made to wait, "that's a different position. That put me in a very different place. Now I'm feeling abandoned. I'm feeling lost. I'm feeling out of control, and my pain grows." She clarified, "My emotional and spiritual pain begin to grow along with my physical pain." She said she already knew she'd have to endure some pain just getting up to go to the restroom, "so I waited as long as I could before I asked for help to go." Defending her former colleagues, this patient added, "I would hope no caregiver, no nurse especially, and I'm very partial to nurses, would put someone purposely in pain, but we don't think like the patient when we're doing the job."

Logically she realized that someone down the hall had asked for something, and the nurse had stopped in the hip replacement's room to drop off or pick up something, only to be asked for something else. She postulated, "How do you work that out? I've been there. Choose your words. Words matter. The words 'Of course I will get you to the bathroom. I'm going to drop this off, and I'll be right back'" are much more comforting, compassionate, and helpful. The spiritual, emotional, and wounding came when this nurse asked, "'Do you have to go *right now?*'" This seemingly innocuous question also discounted the intersectionality of the patient's body, mind, and spirit. Discomfort in one aspect contributed to pain in the others.

A Nurse's (Slow) Epiphany

I asked this hip replacement patient how her training and experience as a pastor contributed to what she understood about spirituality in a healthcare context during her nursing career. She responded,

> *Well, I'm sitting here, and I'm smiling. Nobody else will know that I'm smiling. I'm smiling because, when I got out of nursing school, I was super nervous. I had the science down. I was a good student. I'll brag a little: I was a very good student, and I got it right. I knew the anatomy and physiology of the human body, and how to fix, or how to aid in the repair and recovery. I was always kind to my patients. My spirituality was shown through how I lived. My "Good morning!" was one that people really felt that I cared about them. However, I stuck with the science. And if I had three people that I was caring for, I cared for those three people, and I followed the doctor's orders. I gave the medicine. I performed the treatment. I never asked, "How are you?" I did **not** work with the ministry of touch and presence. I didn't have time for those things while I was moving through caregiving.*

She said, in retrospect, "What was missing was what I call *caring*. It's either there or it's not there. Some people can practice it and learn to do it better. There's a spirituality of knowing when someone just needs a touch, knowing when someone needs to be heard." She said it's the busy-ness of caregivers that interferes with their being fully present during their physical care with patients.

The patient/clergy/nurse said, "I know we're busy going about and doing the work. I worked in the ICU, so the machines were going off, and I was busy." She said the difference now is, "I can hear the machines going off and *still know* that this patient is a human being. Although they have tubes and everything coming out of everywhere, I can see them first as a human being. Sometimes as I wash their face, I can touch their hand, and I can say, 'You're not alone.'" She explained, "That's the growth in my spirituality. I'm no longer afraid or ashamed or feel that it's wrong to say to a person, "Someone cares about you."" Instead of what she termed a "mechanical approach," attending to spirituality means caring about a patient's humaneness, and this shows through the caregiver's compassionate interactions with patients, treating each one as a human being and not a faceless, personless, room number, illness, condition, or situation.

When she mentioned she'd discovered this aspect of caring while she was still a nurse, I asked how she'd figured out something was missing in her caregiving, she responded:

> *I was working in the intensive care unit. And my patient was sedated and on a ventilator. I was doing the work that needed doing, and then I saw a tear run down her face. This woman was a mother. She had three children. She'd been in an automobile accident and was critically ill. The doctors were doing everything that they could, and nursing was doing everything we could. Everybody was doing their job, and I knew she needed someone to touch her and say, "I'm here for you, not just the machines, not just for doing, but I'll be a person being present with you for a second, for just a nanosecond."*

She emphasized she chose to "be a human *being* rather than a human *doing*." Explaining she could still remember this patient's face, she said, "That was a spiritual awakening for me." After pausing briefly, she added, "I am embarrassed to say that happened twelve years into 'good nursing.' Wow!"

The technically proficient nurse turned caregiver said she knew that forever after she couldn't and wouldn't separate her spirituality from her vocational calling. Nor would she separate the spirituality of her patients from their physical and mental/emotional well-being. Spirituality isn't a separate entity. It's intricately interconnected with the full human being and virtually every aspect of direct patient care. Misconceptions about these intersections create disjunctures in how the patient perceives, receives, experiences, and forever after remembers how they were cared for in an ER or hospital setting.

3 Cognitive Dissonance Nets Spiritual Disjuncture

Historically, prior to the 1900s, health care and its various institutions were under the auspices of religion, and spiritual care was an integral component of physical care.[1] Now, there's a cognitive dissonance in contemporary medicine around the role (if any) of spirituality in healing and wholeness. Medicine, once directly connected with religion, became surgically separated during the Enlightenment and following. Medicine became conceived as "secular" because it's facilitated in public institutions, including many that originated with specifically religious roots. When biomedical science arrived, it was "focused on cure or fixing an identified problem," with "fixing" concentrating on the particular illness or broken part of a person's system at the expense of "the broader concept of healing," which includes the entire human being.[2] This separation created a spiritual disjuncture.

In her acclaimed classic, *The Spirit Catches You and You Fall Down: A Hmong Child, Her American Doctors, and the Collision of Two Cultures*, Anne Fadiman proposes medical students quickly have learned to be emotionally detached from their patients. She explains, "The desensitization starts on the very first day of medical school, when each student is given a scalpel with which to penetrate his or her cadaver: 'the ideal patient,' as it is nicknamed, since it can't be killed, never complains, and never sues."[3] What she terms "the emotional skin-thickening" is required "because without it, doctors would be overwhelmed by their chronic exposure to suffering and despair. Dissociation is part of the job."[4] Of course, anatomy, dissection, and physiology are critically important. The point is to recognize how this *de*synthetizes future medical professionals from the live human beings they're preparing to care for. Cognitive dissonance further arises from spirituality's role (if any) in an era of increasing secularity.

A/religious Secularity

Since the Enlightenment, separating physical care from the rest of a human being evolved from modernity's gradual yet forceful separation of the sacred from the secular, from religious spirituality to a/religious secularity.[5] Modernity brought in the strong distinction or separation between what's supposed to be nonsectarian, neutral, and *a*religious space, which of course includes public institutions like hospitals, which once had a religious affiliation and were extensions of compassionate spiritual care, which included physical and spiritual well-being.[6] Society changed from being religious or sacred-centered to being fully secular. Where in an earlier age it wouldn't have remotely been possible *not* to be religious or to have separation from public/religious space, now the differentiation is absolutely accepted and expected. Not only is it okay to not have anything to do with the sacred, it's preferred and even demanded, particularly in public or secular places and spaces.[7] Secularity further plays out in a medical context because institutions that once were founded with religious affiliations to engender compassionate physical care as an extension of spirituality, particularly hospitals, are now considered secular public places.[8]

Secularity and disenchantment, philosophical terms that personify disaffiliation from anything sacred or religious, which historically had contributed to making life meaningful, are moving America to follow the secularity trail that's been blazed in Europe.[9] Despite the effort to (forcefully) separate medicine from being anything religious or spiritual, MD Mark Sullivan insists medicine actually "straddles this divide between public and private spheres of society"[10] because it interacts very personally with human beings during their most intense times of birth, pain, dying, and death. The more spiritual well-being is separated from strictly physical care, primarily because it's so misunderstood about what spirituality is and how it intersects with literally every aspect of physical care, the more patients will suffer.

It's not just in healthcare that spirituality has been missing. This disconnection with anything sacred has been pervasive in the *post*modern West, the timeframe in history that immediately follows the earlier modern period. Contributing to the cognitive dissonance of caregivers and also of patients, the DNA of the secular age begets internal tension (God is ↔ God isn't) with an external tension (the sacred is/should be present in a secular hospital context ↔ the sacred isn't/shouldn't be present in a secular hospital context). A caregiver might assume spirituality isn't important (because it isn't important for this caregiver) when it actually matters very much to a particular patient. This dissonance arises, again, because of the misunderstood medicalized view of spirituality as meaning in/or life instead of as each person's essence of being.

Proliferation of Specialization

The Enlightenment also fostered the specialization and then differentiation of professions, particularly in medicine. Where a patient once went to their family doctor and their family dentist, now the list of annual or semi-annual visits to different specialists can easily be six, eight, or even ten different medical professionals. The number increases with age and each new chronic illness that's added to a patient's list of ailments. Given this specialization in medicine, it's easy to see the lack of connection between systems within one patient because their different "parts" are farmed out and treated by numerous specialists.[11] Overspecialization, compounded with a detachment from anything spiritual in the secular age, intersects with medicine's all-out focus to save a patient physically, including a treatment or procedure that might be beyond what a patient desires. During the 1970s, spirituality and spiritual care started to become part of a return to caregiving for a renewed and improved *whole-person* patient experience.[12] (See Chapter 7.)

A Doctor's Reflective Perspective

After nearly forty years as a medical doctor and using a pen name, Patricia Grayhall writes a frank memoir based on her journals of her life experience of coming out as a lesbian in the 1960s and going to medical school when both aspects weren't considered socially acceptable, being a lesbian or being a female MD. She recalls when she did her residency in a Boston teaching hospital, explaining:

> *Even when there was no hope, the attendings and senior staff urged us to do procedures on patients just so we could learn. In this macho culture, my male colleagues vied for the opportunity to put a central line in the jugular vein in the neck, a large-bore needle into a distended abdomen to tap off excess fluid awash with cancer cells, or into the chest to drain bloody fluid in the pleural sac between lung and chest wall.*

She adds, "Sometimes these procedures relieved suffering, but in dying cancer patients they often just added to it. I would steel myself and do what they ordered me to do."[13] After one of these forced-on-a-dying-patient procedures, she remembers, "I would go into the supply closet and bang my fist on a blanket or cry a few tears of frustration. I questioned the rationale for some of these invasions with the senior residents when it felt unnecessary and wrong."[14]

She describes a terminal patient who didn't want any more labs drawn and who pleaded, "'Don't do this,'" but this doctor-in-training had been ordered to do so by the senior resident, so she drew the blood, including a particularly painful stab in the patient's groin."[15] She asked herself, "To whose benefit was all this?"[16] These unnecessary and painful labs, tests, and procedures inflicted tremendous spiritual pain in addition to the obvious physical pain and emotional trauma. The resident reflected, "To me, 'doing all we could' would have been to leave her to peace and keep her comfortable while we let nature take its course.'"[17] This aging patient was prepared and ready to die, but the medical staff wasn't ready to *allow* her to do so. Instead, the push for more medical activity extended her physical life a modicum while unnecessarily exacerbating her emotional and spiritual distress.

A Nurse's Reflective Perspective

A recently retired white female nurse in her late sixties who'd worked at several large metropolitan hospitals in the southern Midwest said, "In reality, the biggest problem that I've found, especially as a new nurse, is that you tend to spend more time with the sickest people. If I had someone on my floor, or maybe a few people who were very sick and required extra attention, then you ended up in that room, on the phone with their doctors, and doing things to manage those people. Others may have been less critical, but they still had needs, even though they didn't get much attention at all."

She highlighted another concern, explaining, "Now that hospitals are being bought out by larger companies and hospitals swallow each other," there's a focus on the bottom line, with things like finding more effective means of staffing, which usually means that your staff is shorter. Doing without trained people becomes more important than the actual care." She said her nursing colleagues "have complained very loudly about staffing levels, and this has gone on for years and years and years." She added, "I've worked in only one setting in my three-plus decades of nursing where I felt like I had adequate staffing, but that was the exception. The rest of the time, I felt like I was running like a chicken with their head cut off. There literally would be some shifts when I would just pray that all my patients would be alive because I hardly looked at any of them." She said, "Of course, from a patient's perspective, this isn't what they expect. It's not right for them. It's not fair for them."

Overtasked Caregiving Scenario

The RN said, "Even when you're caring for a particularly critical patient who's requiring more of a nurse's time, mind you, all of your patients are still critically sick. They've got a bunch of medical problems, or they've just had surgery, and they can't safely get out of bed, or they could fall on the floor. Or, in my case as a neuro nurse, maybe they just had brain surgery, and if things go wrong, you have to be there to do something about it." She explained, "It's one of the myths of healthcare that you've had your surgery and you go into recovery, and then you just recover on a linear basis, so every day is better." She clarified, while this may be the case for some people, it's more likely that a patient has good days and bad days. She said, "As a nurse, you're supposed to assess their pain," adding, "and we were taught pain is what the patient says it is because everybody's got a different threshold." She continued:

> So as a brain injury nurse, or working with someone who'd had a stroke or has dementia, it's not so easy to give them a chart and ask, "What is your pain level on a level of one to 10?" Someone who has confusion cannot answer that question. But if they're writhing in the bed and screaming and moaning, well then, I'm guessing they probably have pain, but they can't tell me where it is, or how bad it is, or if something seems to relieve it. I have to be a detective and figure that out, which requires having the time to use your observation and to rule out what could be causing the pain, but that's time-consuming. Depending upon the model of care and staffing, you may or may not have time to accurately assess what's going on.

She added, "In a perfect world, every patient would have adequate care but that doesn't always happen."

When I asked how her examples intersected with a patient's spirituality, the nurse responded, "So, let's put ourselves in the patient's room, and you're lying in a bed, and maybe you've put your call light on fifteen minutes ago, but there's nobody for a while, and you're hurting. You need something, or you want to go to the bathroom. You're lying there in those terrible hospital gowns, which dehumanize everyone." She paused and asked, "Why do we have to put them in that particular little blue number and make them all look the same?" The nurse continued:

If you're in the patient's shoes, you're gonna feel dehumanized. You're gonna feel like nobody cares about you. You're already physically uncomfortable. Perhaps you're stressed out, or you have a new diagnosis, or you just had surgery, or you're finding out that you need to have other procedures. You're not getting any sleep, because we come and take your blood or take your vital signs at all hours of the day and night. So this patient would either be drawing heavily from their spirituality to help get them through this, or they would feel perhaps just downright despondent. Many people in the hospital appear depressed and anxious, and rightfully so. What a difference it would make if they had someone to listen and hold their hand and dispel their fears.

She believes nurses can make that difference and be there for them, "but if you don't have time, if you're putting out fires for eight to twelve hours nonstop, then the lovely things that you could do to make their stay better, don't get done."

Task Bunny

This RN reflected, "When I graduated from school, I could be as compassionate as Mother Teresa, but none of that would count. What counted was, did I get that vein on the first stick? Did I hang all my IV meds on time? Did I complete my tasks? That was the measure. It mattered not if my patient outcome was successful, if they were miserable and in pain. What mattered was that I navigated a maze and completed tasks and just kind of kept my cool for the whole shift." She said she agreed her description is "a gargantuan disconnect from patient-centered care," but she also said it's possible to "buck that trend" by spending an extra minute with a patient to treat each as a human being instead of as "just" a patient. She said, "The disconnect between what you expect in nursing school and reality is like the Grand Canyon," regarding the patient-centered care they teach nursing students to do, and the reality of not having the time or staffing to actually do more than being what this retired RN termed "a task bunny." She added, "It's easy to get to the point of feeling like the system is rigged against us—nurses—so why bother? Why care?" She pointed out, "There's a reason that burnout is so high. I think there will always be a nursing shortage because of this." A patient or client isn't just a broken thing to fix but an independent, thinking, feeling, autonomous agent who wants caregivers to care.

Patient Perspectives

A patient in ICU room eleven who'd been diagnosed with extremely low sodium following a particularly intense round of flu said she found herself getting "angrier and angrier" with her frustration in being "abandoned and alone" in ICU because she couldn't do even the simplest of tasks without permission and supervision. She explained she was ambulatory enough so she could "unhook things and shuffle over to the commode" if no one responded to her call button, noting, "The nurse didn't like it and would fuss at me, but in an emergency, I could get up and take care of myself." She said her frustrations mounted at the inattention to her full system—physical, spiritual, and emotional. She was in the ICU for four days and nights, and no one ever offered, suggested, or helped her to brush her teeth. She said, "My teeth could rot off and fall out, but as long as my sodium was slowly increasing, then they were doing their job." This seemingly simple example is one of the consistent contributing factors to medical ↔ spiritual disjuncture *from the patients' perspective.*

Medical ↔ Spiritual Disjunctures

A patient's perspective on how medical care helps or harms their spirituality differs significantly from what's discussed or represented in much of the medical-related literature on spirituality and spiritual care (see Chapter 2). When they're at the mercy of caregivers, a patient's view of what helps or harms their spirituality always includes how they're treated *or* mistreated. Their spirituality isn't a separate "thing" that's carefully bracketed off all by itself and safely tucked away until a patient is back outside of a hospital or urgent care. Their spirituality comes right into that the ER, ICU, and the recovery room with them. Even when a caregiver thinks they're "just doing labs" or "just administering meds," or just whatever it may be, each interaction, large and small, touches a patient's spiritual essence of being. The following scenarios briefly explain some of the key contributing factors to spirituality in a healthcare context *from the patient's perspective*, beginning with agency.

Agency

A Jewish American breast cancer and double mastectomy survivor in her mid-seventies described herself "as an enlightened young thinking wise woman who's incredibly spiritual." She defined spirituality as "her essence," and she lamented the lack of agency, autonomy, and respect when she's been a hospital patient. She said, "It's scary to get sick," explaining it's not only the illness itself but the care you'll receive on the journey to healing and wholeness. She added, "When you disrespect a patient, when a caregiver doesn't give a patient any agency, when they don't listen, when they don't hear what a patient is saying, and when they don't really *see* you, they're harming this patient's spirituality."

I asked how she claimed her agency when they wouldn't give it to her, she responded, "One night, when they thought I had C. diff (clostridium difficile)," she'd been isolated in a single room because it's highly contagious. She remembered:

> *In the middle of the night, this nurse came in and said, "We're moving you," at like two o'clock in the morning. First of all, I had no gas in my tank, and I'm thinking, "They're moving me in the middle of the night?!" I looked at the nurse and I said, "I'm advocating for myself. I don't want to be moved right now. I'm not ready to be moved right now." The nurse said, "Well, somebody has Covid, and we need your room . . ." She did this whole guilt trip on me.*

The C. diff patient told the nurse that she appreciated the dilemma and that, of course, the Covid patient needed to be isolated, but not in the middle of the night. Despite her objection, they moved the C. diff patient to another room. She said what irked her spirit was, "They didn't come in and talk to me like I was a human being. They didn't say, 'We have a problem, and we need your help.'" Instead, they barged in in the middle of the night and demanded and commanded without respecting her agency. She said they didn't give her the courtesy as a human being. She added, "So to me, it goes back to, 'Do unto others as you would have others do unto you.' If that nurse had been in that bed, I doubt that she'd want somebody to do that to her in that way. You can do the same thing in a nice way." Poor bedside manner harms spirituality.

Not Seeing; Not Respecting

Recalling a similar dismissal and disrespect of human agency, she described a doctor's interchange she'd observed with a roommate in a metropolitan hospital in the Northeast. She said, "We named ourselves Thelma and Louise," adding, "One day this particular doctor came in, and intimidated this young woman. It's *her* body, and she'd been through hell and back, and was only in her thirties." She said when the male doctor left, the young patient "was an emotional and spiritual mess." The elder patient clarified, "I was a witness to what happened. This doctor absolutely didn't *see* her. He didn't *hear* her. It was almost like she was beaten up by the time the doctor walked back out of the door." In their conversation following this doctor's departure, the elder patient said she encouraged the young woman to share with her regular doctor how she'd been treated and how she felt. The wise older woman said, "Thank God she did tell her regular doctor because that other doctor should *not* be practicing. He did more damage to her internally, emotionally, and spiritually, and that contributes to our wellness." Spiritual and emotional harm hinder healing and wholeness.

Not Listening; Not Hearing

Aloofness can be expressed in many ways, but it's most often recounted by patients who describe it as caregiver arrogance because medical people "know so much more" than a patient about their medical condition.[18] A young adult white male melanoma patient said he generally received exceptional care, except once, when he was having migraine headaches. The senior doctor overseeing his care was concerned because a small tumor had metastasized behind an eye in this young man's head. The patient said, "My doctors were worried that potentially it would become something heavy, like a stroke, so they threw the book at me with an MRI, CT, and everything like that." During the process of tracking down the source of his migraines, this patient saw an ophthalmologist three times. He recalled, "The first time the ophthalmologist was so condescending." He said he'd described when he'd had similar moments a few years earlier during high school when he'd have a "pounding headache and was super sensitive to light and sound." Instead of accepting his parallel health experience from a few years prior, the young adult cancer patient said this doctor corrected his misuse of terminology, saying things like, "'Well actually what you're calling a migraine isn't.'"

After this initial encounter with the ophthalmologist, the patient said, "I remember walking out of there thinking, 'Wow, I don't think that person believed me.' I recognize that, as a white male, I'm probably the best demographic group to have people believe me and give me the treatment." But this doctor hadn't. The patient explained that he'd taken medical ethics courses where he'd learned about the dismissal of minorities by the medical industrial complex, and it stunned him to experience it firsthand as a white male. He said, "I've never experienced anything like that before. It was like, 'Wow, you're my doctor, but also, 'fuck you!'" He added it was clear the attitude was, "'You're the patient here. I'll be the doctor. Thank you very much.'" He said this doctor was "a little bit better" the next two times he saw them, commenting, "So I don't know if they were having a bad day, or maybe going through a divorce, or something, but I definitely felt the effects." He immediately added, "Let me summarize: For me, my spirituality is my autonomy, my ability to function, my ability to think." He said this was encroached upon when this ophthalmologist didn't listen, didn't hear, and didn't respect his explanation of his symptoms. He emphasized this experience was in striking contrast to virtually every other aspect of his care at a prestigious cancer research hospital. This reserved young man added, "I really can't thank them enough for the truly brilliant care that they gave to me."

Being Ignored

Two years after the Covid-19 pandemic lifted, a Hispanic male and practicing lifetime Catholic in his late seventies who was hospitalized for Covid in a large metropolitan hospital said he was "really disappointed" during his six days there, particularly in the doctors "who seemed to be acting or staging." His spouse interjected and said, "Some doctors didn't even know who he was or why he was in that room, which was crazy." The elderly Hispanic male described the time these doctors spent in his room as "just an act." When he commented that he didn't feel like he'd been treated badly because of his age or his racial heritage, his Anglo wife interjected, "He was ignored." The couple talked back-and-forth about their mutual frustration, with the husband lamenting, "I couldn't get a straight answer from the doctors." This retired college professor said the doctors didn't know exactly what illness he'd had, and they also wouldn't make any conjectures or give him any specific information about what it might be. He exclaimed, "I knew I had Covid!"

Convalescing at home after this recent hospital stay, he said, "I thought I was going to die for several days."

Describing the scene in his hospital room, his wife said, "Once there were too many doctors in the room at the same time. They would bump into each other. They also would contradict each other." She paused, then added, "It was like they didn't have enough to do, or something." The retired professor said, once they finally figured out he had Covid, they were to start him on a treatment, but then "they waited two days before they actually started," which delayed his release because he was required to do this treatment each of four days. The couple agreed there hadn't been any explanation about the delayed treatment. It just was what it was. From a patient's perspective, who sees their spirituality as intersecting with all of who and what they are, these irritants harm their spiritual, emotional, and physical well-being.

"Look at Me..."

A white female in her late sixties who's spiritual/not religious and who'd had a scheduled hip replacement at a suburban hospital in a bedroom community of a metropolis in the southern Midwest said the doctor appointments leading up to her surgery were making her increasingly uncomfortable because the surgeon never looked at her. She said, "I decided when I went for the final visit, if I didn't have eye contact with the doctor, if he didn't *look* at me, then I'd find another doctor." She explained, with both of the earlier visits, the doctor entered the room and went straight to his computer to make notes. She reiterated, "The doctor never *looked* at me." During the third visit, when she was there to schedule the surgery, the doctor and patient were seated directly across from each other. She said, "Finally, we had eye contact, so I decided to go through with the hip replacement surgery." Seeing the patient, looking into their eyes, recognizes them as being fully human and not just another procedure to be performed on a cadaver that happens to still be alive.

Condescending

Interview participants frequently expressed that condescension in any form was an insult to the patient, not only an affront to their basic intelligence as mature adults but also to the spike that dug into their emotional and spiritual morale. A fifty-year-old white female described her experience in having her first colonoscopy at an outpatient surgical center in a mid-sized suburban community in the Midwest. After the procedure, she wanted to speak briefly with the anesthesiologist to ask about their experience because this patient's niece was planning to go to school for this profession. She explained her initial encounter with the anesthesiologist had been very brief while she was being put under for the procedure, and she wanted to ask a couple of quick questions afterward. When she asked the attending nurse if that would be possible, the nurse ignored her request and spoke to the patient's spouse, who was seated beside the bed. She said they both started speaking to her in a patronizing fashion each time she reiterated that she wanted to speak briefly with the anesthesiologist. She exclaimed, "They were both treating me like I was an invalid! I said, 'Excuse me, I'm awake, and I know exactly what's going on, and I'm asking a very valid question. I'm not wanting to talk to somebody who doesn't exist.'"[19] She added she was very aware of what was going on, fully cognizant, yet she was brushed off. She said it was *how* she was responded to that irked her spirit. Had someone politely explained that this nurse anesthetist already was with another patient, she said she would've understood. Instead, they were condescending and brushed her off like she was a child. She said she also felt like they were saying, "'Get dressed. Go! We need the bed for another patient.'"

The colonoscopy patient said, ultimately, it's about "just respecting each other. Patients respect the caregivers, and caregivers respect the patients." She reflected, "Being in this medical situation for a routine procedure was eye-opening. When you're lying in a hospital bed at their mercy, *at their mercy*, and they're the ones taking care of you." She added, "I was treated like an imbecile, like I had no brain. They talk over you, and they treat you like you're a doped-up imbecile, and that's if they respond to you at all." She added, "It's like the medical people are on the top step of a ladder, condescendingly looking down on the patient."

Not Doing Their Job

A middle-aged white female who spent four days in the ICU for extremely low sodium said, once she'd been stabilized, the time between anyone being in her room was so long, she said she'd forget what it was she wanted to ask, so she started writing down her questions with the time, date, and name of the RN on duty. Most of the questions were simple enough to answer, such as "Please write the current sodium number on the white board. When do I get my new water quota?" Other queries might have required input from the supervising physician, such as "Is the result of the brain scan in yet? What are my new release date possibilities?" The ICU patient said a nurse on an overnight shift was so offended at seeing their name at the top of the patient's list of questions, along with the date and time for each request, that this nurse walked over and erased their name from the whiteboard. The patient concluded, "I guess that RN sure showed me!" Spirituality is all-encompassing.[20] Because spirituality is *all of me*, medical systems, processes, and protocols (inadvertently) harm holistic caregiving, *from the patient's perspective*.

4 Systems, Protocols, and Procedures

Hospitals, including those with a faith-based name in the corporation's sign above the entrance, are structured to adhere to secular protocols, procedures, and practices, many of which are government-mandated and regulated. Systems make it easier for individuals to blame their unkind, unhelpful, unwanted, and/or unnecessary actions on the policies etc. that were established by the Powers-That-Be where they're employed.[1]

Overcoming any innate systemic barriers for patient-centered holistic care moves forth from a caregiver's spiritual centeredness. As a nursing student said, "When our connection to our spirituality is severed, we tend to *not* make the best decisions for ourselves or towards others."[2] When care moves forth primarily from healthcare's systemic structures of protocols, procedures, rules, and regulations, patient well-being can become lost in the very policies and practices that are supposed to be formulated with patient care in view.[3]

The Rhythm of a Hospital (Inadvertently) Harms Patient Spirituality

Sometimes it's the rules and rhythm of a hospital that hinder, rather than help, a patient's holistic well-being, including the physical attributes, such as climate control.

Freezing Cold in ER

A patient who arrived shortly before midnight in late May at an ER in a mid-sized suburban hospital located in the South lamented, "As expected, ER was COLD! I was huddled up lying on my side trying to get warm on the skinny hospital gurney. They didn't have the sides up (probably should have). Eventually, someone covered me with a paper-thin blanket that didn't even begin to keep the bone-chilling cold at bay." The patient added, "Every single employee who came in-and-out of my cubicle was wearing a winter coat *inside* when it was nearly one hundred degrees outside." (See Illustration 4.1)

Whatever the medical rationale that justifies a freezing cold temperature in the ER, patients experience it as punitive and debilitating.

Long Delays in ER

Suffering through a long delay in the ER was a common patient lament. A recently retired Latina female professor in a small city on the West Coast who'd had surgery on her neck said, as soon as the local hospital was finally completed, it already was too small for the regional population growth. She advised, "If you can hold off going until 7:00 a.m., the wait in ER isn't as bad." Similarly, womanist chaplain Anjeanette Allen described a system's glitch that chaplains are caught up in to mediate the long delays for patients in an ER waiting room. Allen explained, "There's a status called *patient recovery*. If a patient decides to leave without being seen and returns within thirty days, it dings the hospital for not providing the care it should have." Allen said these extensive waits are particularly true in poor areas with predominately Black and Brown clientele who are "just sitting there waiting for somebody; waiting." She explained, "It's become part of a chaplain's job to go out there and talk to them, maybe take them a warm blanket, but that's all pacification." The chaplain emphasized, "The most important thing a patient can do is bring somebody with them as their real advocate. Period." She added, "Chaplains have crucial roles to play, but they've got to be willing to understand who they really serve," which she said for her is "God, who is a God of justice."

Shift Change

Every urgent care, ER, or hospital has its own rhythm for things like who works when, shift change procedures, and schedule rotations. These normal aspects can be emotionally and spiritually distressful for patients. An ICU patient who'd been admitted after waiting for eight hours in the ER said, "When I'd asked the night shift nurse in ER for something to eat, I was assured they'd get me something. They didn't, and my request got lost in the shuffle when the day shift arrived. Then I'd arrived at the ICU too late for breakfast, so I couldn't get anything to eat until lunchtime." The patient continued,

Illustration 4.1 *Freezing Cold in ER* pastel (self) portrait based off of a photograph by Michael L. Boursier; shared by permission. Artwork © Helen T. Boursier.

The shift in ICU runs 7:00 a.m. to 7:00 p.m. and then 7:00 p.m. to 7:00 a.m, so you have twelve hours with the same nurse, which could be a very good thing, or a very bad thing, depending on the nurse. They also rotated the ICU nurses, so you never had the same one twice. Each twelve-hour shift was with another stranger who was responsible for your care. You could be blessed with a kind, compassionate, efficient, excellent nurse for twelve hours or you could be stuck with a mediocre one for what feels like an eternity, particularly when it was an overnight shift. It makes for a super-long, tedious, spiritually distressing, sucky night with no sleep that exacerbates feeling scared shitless, isolated, and alone.

The patient added, "You definitely don't want to need to push the call button when it's nearing shift change because the nurses are all into doing their own thing." Similarly, a white chaplain in her mid-fifties said she's experienced multiple instances when call buttons were ignored. Explaining she'd try to intervene where she could, she said, "I'd go in one room, and they'd sing the praises. Then I'd go into another room, and it'd just be, 'This is a shit show.'"

Making the Rounds

Making the morning rounds with the lead physician includes another set of protocols. An ICU patient recalled, "When a team of people were making the rounds in the morning, my RN opened the sliding glass door a crack, pulled the curtain back, and said, 'You can listen in if you want to.' I sent my husband to the door to listen in, but the conversation was a low mumble, so he couldn't hear much." The patient added, "Yes, the doctor came back by for a one-on-one an hour or so later, but if you're welcome to listen in, then make it so we can actually *hear*." Also, when this ICU doctor returned an hour or so later, it was after her spouse had left to go to work. She said, "I didn't have anything to write with, so it was up to me to pay careful attention and then to quickly text the update to my spouse." She said it was very distressing to be forced to "take notes on myself" while she was in such a vulnerable position in the ICU, but there wasn't any other way she could transfer the information to her spouse. She said she regretted that it hadn't occurred to her to record the conversation on her cell phone so she could've more accurately relayed the doctor's update to her husband. Much later, after this patient was released, she said a nurse mentioned that she could've asked to see the doctor's notes, which, the patient said, would've been helpful for the ICU nurses to have mentioned. They didn't.

Impossible to Sleep

It's pretty common knowledge that it's impossible to sleep in a hospital for a variety of reasons, some related to a person's reason for being there, but much of the sleeplessness is due to a hospital's policies and practices. For example, a white female in her early sixties shared a text she'd sent to her older sister, "It's a typical evening for me in ICU. As usual I can't sleep. This place is like trying to sleep in an airport." The patient explained:

> *Someone comes to draw blood every four hours around the clock. The tech would say, "This is going to pinch." Then they'd stab me. Some got the needle right in on the first attempt, but others missed. They also tried to stab me in the big vein on the inside of my right arm where I already had a two-inch long bruise from the ER nurse who'd missed on two attempts. Every single time I'd say, "It's already clearly bruised and tender there. Please choose another spot."*

When this patient asked why she "had to get a fresh stab every four hours; why couldn't they put an IV port in so it would be painless," she said the technician replied, "'Because you only get a second port if you have a second med. You don't two meds, so we poke you for each lab draw.'" The patient added, "So they flipped on all the lights every four hours around the clock. And then the nurses wondered why I couldn't sleep?!" Meanwhile, it's well-documented "that impaired quality of sleep resulting from a severe disease, sedation, and an unfriendly ICU environment can be associated with the occurrence of delirium," with contributing factors including "sleep fragmentation caused by noise, bright light, lack of quality nocturnal breaks, and drugs."[4] Caregivers at all levels need to recognize the intersections of policy with patient (dis) comfort and spiritual distress (see Chapter 7).[5]

The Kitchen Is Closed Twelve Hours a Day

A patient in ICU room #11 of a mid-sized suburban hospital said,

> *I'll always remember my first night in ICU as the night I was so hungry my stomach HURT. I was trying to think warm thoughts (in the freezing cold!) and wishing away my hunger pains. I finally rang the call button at 3:00 a.m., and the kind male nurse promptly responded. I begged him for something to eat. "Anything!" He was very nice about explaining that the hospital kitchen closes at 6:30 p.m. and that it didn't reopen until 6:30 a.m. so there were no food options.*

The patient said the nurse offered to look in the staff lounge to see if there was anything in the fridge there. He returned with a small single serving of applesauce and a few packages of stale saltines. The patient remembered, "I knocked back the applesauce and had one or two crackers." She said the daily twelve-hour fast was long and painful, particularly since she'd had the flu for six days prior to going to the ICU. She said, "Finally, I could eat, but there was nothing *to* eat." She shared a text she'd sent to her husband at 4:25 a.m.: "I'm starving. I had supper eleven hours ago and the kitchen doesn't open for two more hours, so it'll be at least three more hours before I can eat. ICU is complicated!!!" The structural issue of the hospital kitchen being closed from 6:30 p.m. to 6:30 a.m. contributed to her physical, emotional, *and* spiritual distress.

The patient explained, "I was more stressed out by the spiritual and emotional internal trauma from the overall experience of being in ICU, much more so than any physical discomfort." Contrary to the medical definition and understanding of spirituality that an "essential element of spirituality is finding meaning and purpose in life,"[6] this patient wasn't worried about any infringement on their meaning of life. Rather, this patient was traumatized because she was cold, hungry, awakened every four hours with a sharp needle, and unable to sleep for the duration of their four days in the ICU due to systemic protocols and procedures.

Maternity Floor Protocols

A Black female in the Pacific Northwest who'd had pregnancies with three deliveries and one miscarriage spanning age twenty-nine to age forty, described what she remembers as her worst maternity experience, which was with her third child. After an unexpected C-section, when she'd had limited physical movement because of the incision and how much it hurt to get in-and-out of bed, she said her most negative experience was the hospital's policy that her newborn couldn't sleep in bed with her. She said:

*With both of my previous babies, we'd been allowed to co-inhabit in the hospital bed and sleep together. For whatever particular reason, this nurse would **not** let me sleep with [my third child] in my bed. Whenever she did rounds and saw me sleeping with the baby in my bed, she scooped up the baby and put her in the incubator. Then the nurse would leave the room. Of course, as soon as the* *baby was separated from me, the baby would start crying. Then I had to slowly get myself up and out of the bed, with the pain from the C-section, scoop the baby back up, and then get back into the bed. Then this nurse would see me sleeping with the baby in my bed, and she would scoop her up and put her back in the incubator. Then it started all over again. By the time it was time for me to go home, I was starting to hallucinate because I hadn't been able to get any sleep.*

She paused briefly, then added, "You know, this isn't my first rodeo. I've done this twice before." She said she didn't understand the nurse's logic for separating the baby from her and repeating the cycle over and over again. She'd slept side-by-side in the same bed with both of her previous babies, at two different hospitals, but at this third place, the rules disallowed her from having her baby sleep in bed with her. She said it was particularly distressing because the nurse never explained why. She simply scooped up the baby and ceremoniously placed her daughter back in the incubator "where she belonged."

Meanwhile, she was in the hospital alone, due to the Covid-19 pandemic, without the support of her husband or her extended family, which she'd had with her two previous births. She said, "My spirit was plummeting. I called my husband and said, 'Please get me home.'" She said, "It's not serving the patient, neither me nor the child." She explained she'd slept with a newborn and a two-year-old in her hospital bed when their second child was born, adding, "I know that there are better ways to do things." She said she also felt zero compassion for her desire and need to cohabit with her newborn (which she would soon be doing once she was released and allowed to go home).

Her spouse, a male nurse supervisor at a large metropolitan hospital, interjected, "If my wife was too tired and they were worried about the risk of her smothering the baby, they could have explained that to her so my wife would understand the hospital rules and regulations are there for a reason. It's also possible that this nurse could have consulted with the doctor who might have asked the nurse to round on her a little more often." The nurse/father said, "It is helpful and important to explain the rationale behind the rules." Expecting unilateral submission or compliance to hospital rules and regulations isn't helpful for a patient's spiritual well-being. The nurse/father emphasized, "Nurses have got to look at the whole picture," including the patient's physical, mental, and spiritual well-being.

Illustration 4.2 *Intimidating* digital image of the entrance to an ICU. Photo © Helen T. Boursier

Welcome to ICU: No Privacy

Just *being* in the ICU is intimidating for patients and their families. (See Illustration 4.2.) ICU room eleven patient said her welcome to ICU included the immediate reality that there's zero privacy. She'd spent overnight in an ER cubicle while waiting for a room to open up in the ICU. She said she'd planned to ask to use the restroom before being hooked up to the equipment in the ICU. She explained,

> As we pulled up in the wheelchair to the ICU room, I mentioned, "I need to use the restroom before I get hooked up." The nurse in my room pointed to a toilet in the corner of my room—open with no curtain around it—and said, "Well you're ours now." I immediately responded, "I didn't realize I was going to put on a show."

The two orderlies who'd brought her up from the ER immediately responded, "'We're leaving.'"

After the orderlies helped her to stand, she walked to the corner of the room where the toilet was located in open view. The orderlies left the room and pulled the exterior room curtain closed, but the nurse in the opposite corner across from the toilet remained in the room "fussing with her things on the machine." The ICU patient recalled the conversation as she sat down on the toilet:

    Patient: I cannot do this with an audience, and I really need to go.

    ICU nurse: You have to understand that, in here, you are *my* responsibility.

    Patient: I appreciate that. However, I still can't go with someone standing there watching me. I really need to get my body back on track.

    ICU nurse: I'll be just outside the door. Pull the cord if you need anything.

The RN left the sliding glass door open a crack so she could hear the patient, but she pulled the room curtain closed for privacy. The ICU patient said, "A few minutes later, the RN hollered in, 'Are you okay?' I said, 'Yes, but this isn't going to be quick.'" The patient said she texted her spouse, "I'm finally in the ICU room but on the hopper. Feels like I'm putting on a show, but the last one did finally leave. Geeze!"

Communication (Disconnects)

For an ICU patient who spent most of their time alone, without family or friends physically present, being able to recharge their cell phone to communicate was the Big Glitch and ongoing challenge throughout their ICU stay. Even though they'd brought their charger, the ICU bed was situated in the middle of the room, so this patient couldn't reach their phone when it was plugged in to charge. They also couldn't reach the wall socket to plug it in when the phone needed recharging. This patient explained, "When I was unable to reach my phone because it was plugged into a wall socket, or it was beside me but dead, it felt very threatening to have no way to communicate with anyone outside of the hospital. When I said something about this early on, my RN responded, 'We're not exactly used to having people in ICU who can talk on their cell phones.'" The dismissiveness didn't help because this communication frustration added to the patient's spiritual anxiety, which also contributed to why they couldn't sleep. An ICU nurse later commented, "The ICU room design isn't necessarily patient-friendly."

Internal (Medical) Miscommunication

The wife of a leukemia patient who was "at his bedside almost 24/7 for ten months" said, "As I sat in the hospital, I found myself asking 'Why are they giving him Lasix at 8:00 p.m. when he can't get out of bed to go to the bathroom at night?" Then when they realized her husband "was almost 99 percent terminal, we couldn't get the physician to talk to him about his outcome." When she realized that it was going to fall to her to tell her husband his leukemia was terminal, she said, "I was livid that I was the person who had to tell him what his future looked like."

The internal medical miscommunication she experienced at the hospital bedside of her late husband became the catalyst for her to earn a bachelor's degree and then a master's degree in health communication. She now teaches electronic health records to all of the hospital roles, including oncology, home health, and hospice, to the clinical staff at a 900-bed trauma one hospital in the Midwest, which serves seven states through smaller critical access hospitals. She explained there are elements of electronic health records where it's possible to integrate communication with medical documentation, including adding a personal note. She said she promotes this aspect during training sessions with staff to let the patient know caregivers are "giving them the dignity of individualism." She emphasized personalizing the notes makes it clear to the patient that they're being treated as a full human being and not just another specimen.

How Efficiency and Productivity Harm Spiritual Well-being

A white male young adult stage four cancer patient who was diagnosed early in the Covid-19 pandemic and received his care at a prestigious cancer research hospital said his experience with the systems, protocols, procedures, and overall process, other than the glitches that were part of the pandemic, was generally exceptional. He said, "Pretty much everybody that I dealt with on a regular basis was really, really incredible, and clearly very invested in my health and well-being." He said an important aspect of the care process at this facility is that it intentionally clusters treatments and surgeries together. He explained, "Their whole *modus operandi* is to cram everything in a really short amount of time, so that the patient can go back to their normal life until they have to come back the next time." He went in every three weeks for two or three days, depending on the required procedures. He said, "They follow the principle of getting it all out of the way super quick." Religiously disaffiliated, this young adult said his spirituality is informed by personal agency. The patient reflected, "I felt good enough to go rock climbing on days that I got the immunotherapy infusion, which is pretty impressive," adding, "I really lucked out in terms of that." The "get in/get it done/get back to your life" honored his personal agency inside the hospital, and rock climbing helped him remain spiritually centered and grateful.

Just a Number

Patients frequently lamented they felt like they were "just a number," either being pushed through the system by the facility itself or by the providers who had another patient (quickly) coming next in the queue, what's been called "an era of turnstile medicine."[7] Cranking through patients from diagnosis through treatment harms patient spirituality because this dismisses who each patient is as a human being. Their "owie" might get treated, but the rest of who they are too often isn't considered. In fact, it's likely to be dismissed, disregarded, and/or ignored.

Transgender Top Surgery

A white transgender male in his mid-thirties compared the experience of when he'd traveled fifteen hundred miles from the Midwest to the Southeast in solidarity and support to be with a friend who'd had top surgery to his own experience at the same location a year or two later. The trans male said when he'd been the support caregiver for his friend, the waiting room was nearly empty. When he returned as a patient himself, the notoriety of this doctor had spread, and the waiting room was packed. This doctor's popularity contributed to turnstile medicine and a mediocre surgery, which has continued to haunt this patient nearly a decade later.

His queer wife with Latina heritage in her mid-thirties was his support caregiver. After they'd returned home, they contacted the doctor's office with concerns and questions about the healing. The transgender male said, "One of the worst things was the second or third time we called the surgeon's office, they were like, 'Oh, it's supposed to be bad. It's supposed to look bad.

It's gonna look bad for a while.'" He paused and added, "And then my nipple fell off." His wife interjected, "We even emailed them pictures, but they were like, 'No, just keep doing what you're doing. It's fine.'" Her husband added, "I'm over here freaking out because I'm like, 'Dude, I have a fucking pepperoni on a napkin that's supposed to be my nipple, and it's not on me right now.'" He added, "So I stuck it back on in hopes that it would just take, and thank God it did."

Through the referral of a friend, they located a local surgeon, who the trans male said, "was mad about what the other surgeon had done, pointing out where the other surgeon had screwed up." The local surgeon did some necessary aftercare at no charge. The top surgery patient said, "It was amazing and incredibly validating because I was respected as a person and not just another thing that goes through another procedure, like in a factory or something." His wife added, "Instead of them gaslighting you and telling you, 'Oh, it's fine.' Instead, they acknowledged there's a problem here." The patient said, "The original surgeon implied I was just being a big baby about it, and then my nipple falls off, and I'm pretty sure I'm not being a big baby." The patient's wife said, "Both of us were having panic attacks when that happened. It was so awful." The patient said, "The nipples did take, but they didn't take very well, so they don't look right," clarifying, "They're not normal looking." The top surgery also was supposed to factor in shaping male breasts, which would become enhanced through building muscle. The transgender male explained, "The way they make the incision is so that it lines up more naturally with male pectoral muscles," which defines the shape and direction of the muscle." Instead, his muscles are misshapen because the doctor incorrectly positioned the incision, and the subsequent scar doesn't correctly align as it should have. He said, "It's painful to think about, and it's there in my mind all the time." The misplaced scar is a lingering physical visual of the rush job, which includes ongoing spiritual and emotional harm.

The trans patient, who said his spirituality revolves around living and being truthful, explained, "I felt like I wasn't being heard or believed. I knew it was bad, but nobody heard or believed us or took it seriously until we went to the second surgeon." The patient added, "Being taken seriously relates to truth, which I believe is very, very spiritual." His wife interrupted, speaking to her husband, "You can confirm or correct me, but I think it also really impacted your body grief, what you'd already been dealing with, with how you feel about your body. And then to have that happen, added additional grief." Her husband agreed, adding, "It's not the top surgery that I regret. It's that I wasn't treated as a human being who deserves dignity, respect, and truth." If you're not respected, if you're not validated, if your very sense of who you are is dismissed out of hand, it's devastating spiritually. His wife added, "After all the denigration and invalidating treatment, then to not even have the results he had hoped for." Her husband said, "There's a big difference in the results from my friend's surgery," adding, "With me, I definitely became a number."

Misdiagnosis After a Slow Journey Through Multiple Hospitals

A white female police detective who, after seven years of symptoms and multiple trips to the ER and various hospitals, was diagnosed in 2004, in her early forties, with a mixed connective tissue disease that's a crossover of connective tissue disease and skin discoid lupus. She explained that shortly before she was diagnosed in a southern city where she'd worked as a police detective, an infectious disease doctor said they didn't know what was going on with all her various symptoms. The patient recalled, "The doctor walked in and looked at me and asked, 'Would you mind if I admitted you to the hospital?' And I said, 'No, I think I'm dying.'" She said she remembers thinking, "Finally somebody sees that something's wrong." The doctors were so concerned, they had the patient's mother fly in from out of state. After five years of flare-ups, she said it "regrettably led to my retirement with 25 years in the police department." She also relocated back to her Midwestern hometown.

Medical Paternalism

She said, "The most distressing episode started in 2018," when she began having extremely bad headaches and the back of her head had a huge knot with more lumps in her neck. She explained she saw a variety of specialists over several months and told each one of them to "just feel my head and neck." She added, "Each time I left I was so angry because they wouldn't put their hands on me and feel my head or my neck." She quipped, "My hair's not dirty. I shower." She said her physical symptoms were becoming more severe, but "nobody, *nobody* would feel my neck or my head where all these bumps were." She said, in fairness, her illness is so rare that it's not very well-known, commenting, "I don't know why they would think that I would be putting myself through something like this. When you looked at me, you could see that obviously I was sick." She continued seeing various doctors, but her escalating symptoms were ignored, dismissed, or dumbed down. She said she remembers at one point raising up her hand and saying, "There's a fucking problem here!" Not listening to the patient is a form of medical paternalism.[8] The patient doesn't know what the doctor knows, which becomes a justification for the doctor *not* to listen to the patient.

Misdiagnosis

Finally, eight months later, she went for six hours of neurological testing. A month later (November 2019), she was diagnosed with "frontotemporal dementia." The retired police officer said, "The first question from the doctor when she came in was, 'Are all your personal effects in order?' And I looked at my brothers [who went with her to this appointment] and I'm like, 'I don't believe they are,' and the doctor responded, 'Well, I think you have three months.'" She added, "I was told to sell my four-bedroom house on the lake; to downsize, and to make sure that I had people who could handle my finances." She recalled the doctor saying, "'The good news is, you won't lose your memory completely. The bad news is you won't completely lose my memory.' That was it. Oh, and, 'There's not a lot we can do.'" The lupus patient continued, "And so we did everything that the doctor said to do. We sold my four-bedroom, three-bath house that sat on the lake where there were all my ducks that I fed twice a day. We sold pretty much all of my belongings. Everything's gone."

"Oops We Misdiagnosed"

When this lupus patient returned a year later for a follow-up appointment, she said, "The doctor looked at me and said, 'I'm really sorry, but it looks like we misdiagnosed you.' I looked at [my childhood friend] who came with me and I'm like, 'You've got to be fucking kidding me. The good news is I'm not going to lose my mind and start licking people's ankles [like a puppy] or behaving erratic, but do you know what you just caused me?'" She said nobody listened to her, and nothing was done until that point eight months later, "when they tell me 'I've got dementia and go ahead and enjoy your life that's over, and then I ended up with 'Oops, I'm sorry, but we misdiagnosed you.'"

After several years and various episodes that included numerous trips to the ER and/or the hospital, she said when she'd mention these earlier episodes, because of this prior medical history, she said, "I was just dismissed as a hypochondriac." She explained, with lupus, which was her initial diagnosis, "patients suffer from a wide constellation of symptoms that are just unexplainable." Her attending specialist made a reverse assumption about this patient's lack of autonomy and effectively made the decision for her without due diligence.[9]

The retired police detective who's now living in an apartment said, "The damage this did to my whole life, is *huge*, particularly by them being so flippant. Just because someone's never seen this illness or these symptoms before doesn't mean that they don't happen or that they aren't real." She added, "My spirituality really took a nosedive." This demoralizing experience occurred after she'd moved back to her childhood hometown. Previously, she said her doctors understood her condition and respected and treated her full humanity.

She said it wasn't until she relocated back to her hometown that the dismissiveness began with her new set of doctors. She explained her original doctors had offered to consult with the new ones after she moved, but the patient said the new doctors "wanted to start from scratch and come up with their own conclusions and their own diagnoses." She said her new doctors "questioned, challenged, dismissed, and disbelieved" the conclusions from her previous medical tests, which caused an exponential downward spiral that was unnecessary had they had the courtesy to respect the work of their colleagues who'd gone before them.

Second Opinion?

When I asked, "Why didn't you go on your own accord to seek a second opinion?" she replied, "*I did!* I saw two more neurologists." In addition, she said when she asked her original neurologist to go over the scans which showed the different white matter areas, he said 'We don't do that.'" When she returned with an advocate, hoping to get a better explanation, she said, "They just dismissed me. They said they'd send me to a speech therapist, to see if they could help." She saw three different neurologists, but "nobody would explain it to me. It was like I didn't have a right to know." She added, "They'd show you where your leg was broken, or where you had cancer in your lung, but I didn't have a right to know why I'm having problems and how bad the 'white matter disease' is in my brain." A longtime nurse commented, "Patients need to know that they can request their radiology report for MRI or CT scans which will contain a text diagnosis with the area and location." Providers need to let their patients know this.

Overly Impressed

The lupus patient said the problem was compounded because her (new) primary neurologist was on the board of directors of a prestigious medical school, which impressed the other doctors she'd sought second opinions from. The connection with a med school also overly impressed the patient's parents, who didn't question the (mis)diagnosis. The lupus patient said, "It was like I didn't need to know, or that what they were going to tell me would be way above my education level, especially since I couldn't speak correctly at that time, so they're thinking, 'Obviously you're at a lower IQ level.'" She said, "By the time it's bad enough to be admitted to a hospital, they would just dismiss me." When you add a speech impediment caused by a neurological disorder, paternalism is this patient's norm. When I asked her what had finally made it so that people would listen to her, she shook her head and responded, "I don't think that they really did believe me, or that they ever would." This disbelief plagues her spirit whenever she knows she "should" go to the ER.

A Recent Trip to ER

This lupus patient described a recent Sunday when she'd decided to go to the pool after she'd been working in her garden. It was almost 10 o'clock, and she decided to hurry to the pool before it closed at 10. She was back to the house at about 10:20 p.m. and standing at the kitchen counter watching TV and thinking about getting something to eat. She said, "All sudden my eyelids fluttered, and my head dropped, and I face planted on the granite countertop. Then I fell backwards and bounced my head off the floor a time or two. I remember thinking to myself, 'Son of a bitch, that was loud!'" She said she got herself up and remembered she was standing and looking at the TV, adding, "and by golly, it happened again!" By about the third or fourth time, she had fifteen different marks on her face from the various impacts. She said, "You could literally count the different times I fell because of the marks on my face." She reflected, "I thought, 'Damn, I probably should call EMS.' And it was like 'Oh hell no!' because I'll have to explain to them what's been going on, and they'll look at me like I'm an idiot." She said then they'd just put her in a room by herself in the ER and release her four hours later, so she opted *not* to call EMS.

Two days later she decided she should probably get checked out because she had so many bumps all over the back of her head from hitting the floor. There was even a dent in the bottom of the oven door where she'd hit it one of the times when she'd fallen backward. She said, "My back was killing me, and I had huge knots on my head, so I decided to go to the ER. She had an MRI, and a neurologist told her, "'That cyst that you have is fine.'" She said she explained to this doctor, "I'd never had a cyst before, and I'd had an MRI a few months earlier because of a sinus infection. There wasn't one then." The neurologist said she had one now. The patient said she reiterated that she'd fallen several times and had hit her head. She explained, "It's like, 'Damn, my back's killing me and my head hurts, but the neurologist isn't listening to me.' When they released me later that day, and I got home, I saw that my entire back was completely black and blue from falling, and hitting, and bouncing." She emphasized, "And *nobody* looked at my back. *Nobody* looked at me or felt my head. It was like 'You're just making this up.' You could see and count the different places and bruises on my face from falling, plus the cut on my nose from hitting the dang center of the kitchen faucet." She said they didn't believe her various symptoms related to her illness. Instead, their response was "'Are you sure you just weren't dehydrated?' No! I wasn't damn dehydrated!" Summarizing this experience, she said:

> *I've always felt like this is how [medical professionals] look at you when you have something like my difficult-to-understand illness. If it's not a broken arm or something tangible that they can see, they don't give a hell about you because you don't fall into some protected or sympathy class for patient care like cancer. If they can't see it, or if it's not something that they can locate on a chart, something obvious like a lung that's littered with black disease, then whatever you've got, it's up to me, the patient, to prove that I have it.*

She said, "It's consistently been my experience, if it's not provable, the doctors and nurses aren't interested and the 'disease' doesn't exist." She added, "After that experience, I'll have to be really, really sick with something radical before I'll take myself back in and try to explain what's going on and ask for medical help." She concluded, "Going in seeking medical help, that process is more emotionally and spiritually distressing than suffering at home without any medication until it runs its course. For me, the 'cure' is actually worse than the process of the disease itself." She said it does her spiritual and emotional well-being too much pain and damage to go to the ER and *not* be listened to. She said she'd rather "suck it up and tough it out at home" than face this risk and vulnerability again at a hospital.

5 **Risk and Vulnerability**

Risk and vulnerability intersect with emotional, mental, and spiritual pain, beginning with a patient but also rippling outward to encompass their beloved ones. Physical pain might be the most common catalyst for a trip to an ER or hospital, but this physical pain contributes to emotional, mental, and/or spiritual angst, all of it undergirded or overshadowed by a deep and abiding sense of risk.

Risk

Risk can begin with a conversation about whether or not to go to the ER. A white female in her early sixties who'd been battling a stomach virus for six days said she decided she needed to go to the ER when she'd started having mini twinges, spasms, or convulsions in random areas throughout her body, sometimes in several different locations at the same time. She remembered it was 11:15 p.m. on a Monday when she said, "I felt like my entire body was trying to expel poison. I resigned myself to the reality that I needed to wake up my spouse to take me to the ER." After she nudged her husband awake, she said he responded by asking if she wanted to use the twenty-four-hour "Web MD" service their health insurance coverage included. She remembered responding, "I don't want to become one of those statistics when two old people discuss the other's waning health and basically watch their spouse die before their eyes. Plus, someone definitely needs to see me in person."

To go or not to go to the ER exemplifies fear-fueled anxiety which "discloses something threatening."[1] Anxiety and fear make the fearful thing real.[2] As Heidegger writes, "Fear is a fearing *in the face* of something threatening—of something which is detrimental," as in something very bad that will cause tangible harm.[3] Fear is fear because there's something to fear, a known or unknown harmful "thing" that's hovering in our future waiting to pounce. Fear and anxiety are beneficial because if we didn't have anxiety and we weren't afraid of the consequences of X, then that X wouldn't matter in the first place (and we wouldn't feel anxiety or fear). It's the fear and anxiety "which push people to be decisive about the choices they must make, selecting between the less horrible than [choices] in life."[4] The fear factor is very real, sending spirituality into overdrive. A Jewish American female in her early seventies remembered when she was quarantined in the ICU for two days with extreme influenza type A. She exclaimed, "It's freaking scary as hell to be in ICU." She was hospitalized while on a business trip near the US–Mexico border, far from home, so she was literally there all by herself. She said, "It was so scary. I was totally by myself. I didn't even have a phone once I got there."[5] Fear is a major contributor to a patient's spirituality during distress, requiring a caregiver's compassionate response and encouragement to engender courage.

Courage

Courage includes a physical, mental, emotional, and spiritual action to overcome the fearful unknown.[6] It requires a definitive choice to move from frozen inertia to a place of hopeful trust, which places "my life" into the care of unknown strangers at a hospital or urgent care facility. Courage guides patients-to-be from anxiety and fear, through inertia and frozenness between deciding, to that moment of choice that puts their care and well-being out of their control and into the charge or care of strangers who hopefully acknowledge, appreciate, and respect this responsibility and privilege. Courage to take action despite anxiety and fear moves forth from a connection to the inner self, to one's essence of being.[7]

Assessment and Admission

An ER patient recalled, "My only describable symptoms were the intermittent twinges independently twitching in different parts of my body, including my legs, arms, and torso." She added, "They kind of looked at me askance when I explained the twinges as if thinking, 'That's it? And you came to ER?'" She said she clarified, "I feel like my body is trying to expel a poison." After conducting a myriad of tests, her low sodium (109) was the only apparent issue, and she was admitted to the ICU until her sodium gradually came up to a safe level. What this patient later reflected on during stacked journaling (see Illustration 5.1), the medical record documented: "Due to a high probability of clinically significant, life-threatening deterioration . . . that could result in multi-organ failure the patient is admitted to ICU in stable condition as Inpatient 09." Describing her ICU experience, this patient texted a friend: "It's like a desperate feeling of sadness, helplessness, and vulnerability. You really don't want to go all the way to hopelessness, but there's definitely a sense of intense helplessness. Emotionally and spiritually you're gone."[8]

Anxiety

Anxiety is the self-description of a thirty-year-old Latina woman regarding her pregnancy, labor, and delivery of her second child. She explained, "I'm a very anxious person. I worry a lot, and my health is important to me, especially while I was pregnant." She added, "So, my entire pregnancy, I was worried about *everything*." Shortly before her scheduled appointment to be induced, her water broke around nine or ten in the evening. She said, "We were sitting on the couch when I felt something pop, and my water broke," saying the experience was "just like what you'd see in the movies." Even with the gush of water, she said, "I wasn't really convinced that my water had broken until after a couple of times of getting up and down and more water was coming out." She said they went to the ER "just in case, but the whole ride over I was convincing myself that this wasn't the time because we'd been to the emergency room twice before with false alarms." This time it was the real thing.

Reflecting on her labor and delivery, she said, "Towards the end of pushing, I felt so exhausted, I turned to my husband and said, 'I don't think I can do this anymore. I really think this baby's stuck.'" Her husband smiled and interjected, "She really did say that!" Resuming her story, she added, "It scared me." Her husband explained her confidence returned when a nurse brought in a mirror so she could see the baby's head. The mother, whose spirituality is informed in a healthcare context by safety, feelings, emotions, and family, said seeing something tangible gave her a goal that felt attainable. The mother remembered, "After they brought the mirror in, it took three or four more pushes, and then my daughter was born. I remember crying, and the feeling of love and happiness and being so grateful that I'm a mother of two now."

Vulnerability

Vulnerability is integral to the human condition.[9] There are ages, populations, conditions, and circumstances that are more vulnerable than others, but essentially all life is an experience in some level of vulnerability. It's what it

Illustration 5.1 *Inpatient 09* stacked journaling art-reflection of their admittance from ER to ICU. © Helen T. Boursier

means to be human, particularly when there's an unexpected glitch in health and wholeness.

Initial Cancer Diagnosis and Surgeries

A 22-year-old white male who was diagnosed with stage four cancer during the Covid-19 pandemic shared his whirlwind entry into being a cancer patient during what ultimately was determined to be melanoma from what initially had been a small circular brown spot on his face, resembling a pimple. The week before his dermatologist appointment to get it looked at in the UK, where he was a graduate student, the pandemic shut everything down, and his appointment was canceled. Four months later, while visiting his mother on the West Coast, she'd arranged in advance for him to see a dermatologist. He finally was able to have the spot looked at. This initial doctor wasn't concerned, but had a biopsy done "just in case" to determine whether or not it was cancerous.

The college student remembered, "About a week and a half later on a Friday, the doctor called very no nonsense and was like, 'Hey, so we got the biopsy back and its melanoma. We want to jump on this as soon as possible, so I took the liberty of scheduling your next appointments next week." The college student added, "So obviously, we weren't stoked with that, but we thought, 'Okay, let's jump on this." He said he called his dad, who'd worked for many years at a cancer research hospital. The young adult said, "The only time when I was worried about my safety, and like scared and upset, was during that hour or so when I couldn't reach my dad." When his father returned the call, his son remembered his dad saying, "'Okay, give me a sec.' He made some phone calls and about an hour later, the son had appointments at the research hospital where my dad had worked [until his recent retirement]." One airplane ticket later, he had multiple tests, with the initial surgery scheduled within a week.

Because it was melanoma, the doctors said it was necessary to take "much larger margins" around the spot on his face to ensure that all of the cancer was removed. He said, "So they took a big hunk out of my cheek. My mom said, which is actually kind of funny, 'You could fit a deviled egg in there.' which is true." The surgeon removed the melanoma, and the biopsies looked clear. After a "a gap of one day," while he had a large open hole on his face, he had facial reconstruction surgery where they folded his skin upwards to cover the hole left by the earlier surgery. The patient explained, "The idea is that they would stretch the skin so it would be pulled tight and then I would have sutures all the way around. Unfortunately, because I was really young, my skin didn't stretch that much." His skin began pulling away from the sutures. He remembered, "My skin would just not comply. They basically stuck some scissors into the cut and then cut those sutures out and the flap of skin just hung for a while. They just left it open." He added, "I was pretty heavily sedated, but I could still feel it, and it still hurt." He had a third surgery with a new skin graft a day or two later. He was cleared to go back to the UK in September to begin a master's degree in epidemiology.

When he returned to the States five months later for follow-up testing from his head and neck surgeries, these confirmed the spots in his lungs had grown, and there also was a six-millimeter metastasis in his brain, which put him at stage four cancer. He quickly added, "Which actually turned out to be a good thing" because his care shifted from head and neck specialists to a dedicated brain oncology team, which enrolled him in January 2021 in a clinical trial for a combination of immunotherapies given in low dosages. His six-millimeter metastasis was one of the qualifying criteria. Realizing that he'd have to put his academic plans on hold, he said the doctor asked, 'Do you understand what that means?'" He said he remembered being very cheerful to the point where the doctor asked again, "'Do you really understand what I'm telling you right now?'" The melanoma patient explained at this point his attitude was, "Either I'm gonna die, or I'm not. And if I die, there's not really much I can do about it, so I might as well just assume that I'm going to live, and then work out what I'm going to do." This quiet young man, an introvert who often keeps his feelings to himself, added, "So that was my attitude. That's how it proceeded." This young adult focused on life rather than death. By March or April, his metastasis was either stabilized or shrinking. After his final set of appointments, the patient remembered the brain specialist oncologist said that when he'd initially seen him, he thought "things were dire," and this MD "hadn't been certain about my future."

His Mother's Vulnerability

In a separate interview, his mother remembered the pre-diagnosis phase with more intensity to the risk and vulnerability. She said she'd called him often while he was away at college in the UK and encouraged him to see a doctor, saying, "But I couldn't get him to do anything." She explained he didn't see the small spot on his face as being an emergency, so she'd tell her son, "'It's damn well gonna be an emergency if it turns out to be cancer.'" She said she "was scared because he didn't do anything about it." When he came to visit her in July, she had a dermatology appointment scheduled for him the day after he arrived. She remembered, "They were kind of blase about it. They removed what was about the size of five dimes stacked up on top of each other of black tissue." She said, "We received the diagnosis on Wednesday while he was staying with me, then he flew halfway across the country and had his first appointments on Monday. Then he had his first of three surgeries a couple of days later." She added, "It turned out there were something like 120 mutations in the tumor which had been removed."

The intense vulnerability was exacerbated by living halfway across the country during a pandemic. She said, "It was stressful, *seriously stressful*? I get a diagnosis that my kid has nasty cancer, and a lethal one at that, and then I put him on a plane and he leaves me immediately for parts unknown. And then, because of the pandemic, I can't go and be with him through this." She said she'd had access through her son during the initial diagnosis while he was visiting, but she lost that access once he flew to another state for the treatments. She lamented, "So my youngest son was on his own, with his (slightly) older brother to help him. They were two young men in their twenties who were both trying to get through this as adults," adding, "and I admire both of them for doing that."

During his separate interview, this melanoma patient said he couldn't get a dermatologist appointment in the UK once Covid closed non-emergency healthcare services. He explained once he was being treated at a US hospital, still during the pandemic, "There was literally nothing that anybody in my family could do. I couldn't have visitors; people couldn't drop things off. I was really quite isolated." He promptly added, "I didn't eat, by the way. I was in the hospital for a week, from the time the second surgery to after my third surgery. The only thing I ate in those five or six days was a single bowl of chicken broth, and a Lindt chocolate truffle. That's it. That's it during that whole time. And that Lindt chocolate truffle was brought to me by a nurse or a PA on my doctor's care team." Recalling this four years later, he said, "I still have that chocolate." This young cancer patient, who'd stepped aside from the religious upbringing of his childhood, said his spirituality is informed by pain, personal agency, safety, physical, emotional, and psychological distress, loneliness, and autonomy.[10]

Patient Autonomy

Patient autonomy encompasses the entire care experience such that a patient feels they have independent empowerment in some aspects of their care.[11] Patients need to feel their input in the care process has value and that it's respected, rather than dismissed, ignored, or disregarded. In vulnerability, which honors patient agency even amidst the worst of healthcare contexts, it supports holistic patient well-being because their interior spirituality isn't being summarily dismissed while the exterior physicality is frantically being attended to.

Estranged by Distance, Covid-19, and HIPAA

Estranged by distance, the pandemic, and the Health Insurance Portability and Accountability Act of 1996 (HIPAA), the mother of the melanoma patient said the most challenging aspect was "navigating the HIPAA system."[12] She emphasized her child was still her child, but at ywenty-two he was considered an adult, so HIPAA prevented her from receiving updates on her son's health and well-being. She bemoaned, "Your child's still your child. You're still their parent. You look at your child, not as a kid, but as still your son, so therefore, I ought to be able to receive information about my son, but I couldn't." She added, "My son had three surgeries in one week. The first one failed, and they had to go back in again. When I was finally able to get a hold of my son on the phone, it was clear that he wasn't doing very well, and there wasn't anything I could do about it. Because of Covid, I'm trapped. Because of Covid, he couldn't get diagnosed [sooner]. Because of Covid he was delayed and got a diagnosis which may ultimately kill him. I couldn't control any of those factors, and as a parent, it's super stressful. You spend countless nights wondering if your kid's gonna make it or not."[13]

His mother said his physical pain had been exacerbated with spiritual and emotional pain because "his girlfriend broke up with him. She dumped him in the middle of the week." She said, "It was a very long week." explaining,

> *I'm not gonna say I was frantic, but it was close. You want information about your kid, you want to be there to do something for him, but you can't be there and you also can't receive any information on how he's doing. The few times that he called me he wasn't doing well. He told me about undoing the stitches, and I have pictures of where they unstitched it and left it just hanging open. So, my son's got this big skin flap open on his face, and on top of having these surgeries, it's all yucky looking and frightening. I don't know what's happening, and I don't have access to any information to know how he's doing.*

What she did know was that her son was alone and in pain, not just physically, but also spiritually and emotionally. This mom advised to be attentive to "what's going on with a patient beyond the primary or 'obvious' physical concern for a patient's treatment," including the emotional frailty fostered by loneliness and a sense of being abandoned, not because family and friends don't care, but because they couldn't/can't be there.

HIPAA Constrainment

The geographically distanced mother remembered during one of the few phone calls with her hospitalized son when he said, "'Oh, it's bleeding and spurting,' and then he texted me a picture of the blood spatters on his hospital gown. He was clearly alarmed by that." She said that with the third surgery coming up, she contacted the nursing station on the floor he'd recently been relocated to and let them know how alarmed she was by the limited information she'd been able to receive from her son. She said, "I informed the nurse I spoke with, 'You know he's got his third surgery in a week coming up. He's not eating. He didn't eat beforehand, and he didn't eat afterwards. He doesn't sound good. His girlfriend just broke up with them. Tomorrow he's gonna have to go on a fast for yet another surgery, and I'm concerned about his well-being.'" She told this nurse she realized there are HIPAA laws about her son, "but judging from what I hear from him myself, he doesn't sound good. You need to go check in on him.' They did, and they called me back. They probably asked him if it was okay to give information to me and he probably okayed it, but they called me back."[14] For clarity, she added, "I know he got good care while he was in there. It's just that I was heartbroken as a parent. You really want to do something, but you can't. That was one of the toughest weeks I think I've ever had in my life."

She said she appreciates that "everybody was hamstrung because it was during Covid," adding, "But it hadn't occurred to any of us, not to my son, and not to his parents, to advise him to authorize the release of information." She said it's a point for other parents to have a conversation with their adult children, particularly young adults who more likely aren't aware of, or thinking about, any need to release health information to their parents. HIPAA doesn't mean that a hospital can't give out *any* information. It means that the patient has to give informed consent beforehand to release the information to particular persons. However, if it hadn't occurred to the patient to give permission beforehand, or if they are in a condition that makes it physically impossible for them to give their permission, HIPAA protects their privacy while also inadvertently leaving loved ones to languish in unknowing anguish.[15]

Incoming patients, particularly young adults or first-timers to an emergency admittance, often don't realize the ramifications of signing off on their informed consent, often without reading it and equally often without even having had access to see the screen to view it, but mindlessly signing off these important rights on an electronic pad while an intake person says, "Sign here." The message from a distressed mother who desperately cared about her son's well-being is, "If you want anybody who's close to you to know about this, it's really important that you specify the names and phone numbers for anyone you want to give permission to be allowed to receive updates on your condition." An RN commented, "Of course, the best thing is to have a Medical Power of Attorney, but a patient so young probably never thinks that such a document would be necessary." Without the wherewithal to give permission in advance, it exacerbates vulnerability for the patient and for the beloved ones who are left in silence.

Physical (Parental) Presence Facilitates Information and Improved Care

In contrast to the distance and no information combination for this young melanoma patient's scary and lonely week in a hospital room, this mother was able to defuse the risk and vulnerability when she happened to be visiting from out-of-state when her older son chanced to have an accident at work that could have led to his finger, hand, or arm being amputated. Alarmed by the progressive unhealing in her middle son's hand after two visits to urgent care following what appeared to be a minor scrape on his knuckle while working with machinery, a few hours before her flight back home, she delayed it so she could be physically present to parent her young adult through this healthcare crisis. She said, "It was a good thing I was there because my son would've lost his hand if I hadn't decided to stay." Had she boarded the plane back to the West Coast, she said, she would've been in the exact same position of not knowing, not helping, and not being able to be present to help another son through a different critical medical crisis.

The Middle Son's Story

After what seemed like a mild scrape on the knuckle while checking machinery at work, a 29-year-old white male and father of two put a Band-Aid on the abrasion and then didn't think about it. His mother insisted its coloration and swelling weren't normal and that it needed to be looked at, so she drove him to urgent care (and paid for it), followed two days later with a second visit to another urgent care (and paid for it). In a separate interview, the scraped-hand urgent care patient who described himself as being "fairly happy-go-lucky and optimistic about my outlook of life," and whose spirituality is grounded in being "kind, polite, respectful, with strong feelings for morals and equality," said he's comfortable in hospital-type environments because "I spent a lot of time there as a kid with Crohn's Disease." Despite his normal inner and outer sense of calm, he said he felt "a little bit lost" and also that he "had this panic because it almost seemed like I was on a timer because of the nature of the infection." He said the first two urgent care locations he'd visited "didn't take on the same sense of urgency that I felt," which ultimately contributed to the infection escalating. He said, "It was incredibly painful, surprisingly painful actually for how small the cut was," which was later attributed to the infection.

His mother recalled, "The urgent care place referred my son to an ER, and the doctor there said, 'We can't touch this because it's over a tendon,' so they referred us to a surgeon's clinic where they asked, 'Why didn't you do something about this earlier?'" The mother exclaimed, "We did! We did!!" The son remembered, "The surgeon took one look at my hand and said something like, 'I can't believe they didn't send you to the hospital forty-eight hours ago. This is a very severe infection.'" The son added the surgeon said, "I'll be blunt with you, I might have to take your finger off depending on how bad it is.'" He added, "When you hear such traumatic and unexpected news, you almost feel your heart sink. This is very real and there's a very real feeling about the gravity of what's happening." The mother said the surgeon explained the infection was so severe that her son might actually lose his entire hand or even part of his arm. Although it was work-related, it required payment in advance. His mother paid the fees so her son's hand could be saved.

This young adult said his spirituality is informed by trust, respect, personal agency, being kind and considerate, and choice. He explained because he hadn't been aware that he'd be getting surgery that day, he'd eaten a big lunch. Consequently, they wouldn't be able to put him under. He had to be awake throughout the procedure. He said his adrenaline was pumping as he thought, "Wow! This is very real. It's all happening really quickly." They were able to remove the infection site, and they didn't have to remove his finger. The patient recalled,

> *At some point midway into the procedure, I think they forgot that I was awake, so they were just chatting. They were talking about a Christmas party that they were going to. While the surgeon was digging around my hand, a couple of times he said, "Oh, wow, look how bad this is!" or things like that. Every time he said something like that, I'd think, "Oh, my God, I'm gonna lose a finger!" It was all very nerve wracking.*

Intersections

It can be uncomfortable or awkward to be around people in vulnerable states because their vulnerability is a tangible affirmation that we also could become in such a vulnerable state, making us "ill at ease with vulnerability because it is a form of exposure to that with which we are unfamiliar or uncomfortable."[16] Their vulnerability points to our possibility to likewise be vulnerable, and it also places moral responsibility for how we interact with and care for them because of the very vulnerability that makes us uncomfortably aware of our own human frailty.[17] Their vulnerability requires our ethical response, which respects their anxieties, fears, and uncertainties that are often left unspecified and unsaid.[18] When a patient's vulnerability is viewed only in a passive state, it disempowers whatever empowerment a patient otherwise could and should have, if not directly through their voice and actions, then through the advocacy and presence of their beloveds when they necessarily must be the voice and witness when the patient cannot.[19] Vulnerability isn't a peripheral aspect of spirituality. It's central to the human condition, inside and outside of an ER or hospital setting.[20] Risk and vulnerability can be helped *or* harmed depending upon whether or not patients are treated with *dignity*.

6 Dignity

Dignity is a justice concern because it shapes how a patient receives care, which then helps or harms their spirituality. Without dignity, spirituality suffers. Without dignity, injustice tromps justice, and spirituality suffers. Dignity is rooted in justice through unconditional welcome and acceptance of what Emmanuel Levinas calls the "Other." Dignity exudes compassion. Compassion is the welcoming agent: in compassion, by compassion, for compassion, and with compassion[1] (see Chapter 10). Dignity translates into compassionate caregiving despite any isms or otherness, what French philosopher Jacques Derrida famously terms *différance*.[2] Unilateral sameness isn't possible; *différance* in the face of the other is the standard of excellence. Countering the argument for a "universal" definition of spirituality in healthcare (see Chapter 2), a nursing student said, "All people are different. Expecting everyone to follow the same pathway, pray to the same God, use the same religious or spiritual practices would be an injustice to the individual and to the world community as a whole. Only when we can find our individual pathway can we grow and find spirituality."[3] People are different. Period. We come from different backgrounds, cultural contexts, races, sexual orientations, genders, religious or spiritual practices, and more. To expect (or demand) people to think, feel, act, and be like us is arrogant, assumptive, disrespectful, and spiritually harmful. The onus is on the caregiver to be aware of how unkind thoughts, words, and/or actions harm the spiritual well-being of those they're caring for.

Testimonial and Hermeneutical Injustice in a Healthcare Context

Testimonial and hermeneutical injustice comprises what someone says (their testimony) with how it's understood or interpreted (hermeneutics). Patients suffer testimonial injustice when what they say, their testimony, isn't heard, believed, or acted upon, such as the lupus patient's experience (see Chapter 4).[4] What a patient says, such as about their level of pain or the cause of their health condition, will be believed (or not) based upon the credibility a caregiver gives when interpreting a patient's self-assessment. Patient credibility in the eyes of a caregiver could differ depending upon such variables as gender, race, sexual orientation, age, illness, medical history, etc.

Patient Examples

The lupus patient who's had her "constellation of symptoms" dismissed numerous times said, "Never look at someone while they're telling you their health background or symptoms with disbelief. Just because what they're describing is something that's not in the books or it's something you're unfamiliar with, trust that the patient knows how to tell their own story." She added, "If nothing else, get out your damn phone. You can ask questions about what's associated with the symptoms the patient is describing. Just because you've never heard of this before, or because it wasn't something you were taught in your books, doesn't mean that it can't happen." This patient with a rare chronic illness emphasized, "You're a part of it right now because you need to care for this person who is describing symptoms that you maybe haven't seen before." She said, "Don't dumb them down. Patients know their medical experience." Instead, give them the dignity and respect of accepting their self-description as reality.

Frequent Fliers

Stereotypes with the accompanying (internal) negativity include the derogatory *frequent flier* label. A Black male nurse manager at a large hospital in the Pacific Northwest said when he hears someone being called a frequent flier, "for people who supposedly are drug seeking," he tells all of the nurses he supervises, "Each person's pain is each person's pain. I teach my staff that each encounter is to be treated independently as *this* encounter." He explained when a nurse might say, "'in the past . . .' my response is to remind them to treat the moment, not the past." He added, "Let the past go." He said he also encourages his nurses to put themselves in the shoes of the patient. He said, "Consider if this was my father, or my mother, or my brother, how would I want them to be treated?" Mentally personalizing a patient adds empathy, which removes stigmas and adds dignity.

A white chaplain in her mid-fifties recalled a patient whom she'd gotten close with and who'd been labeled a frequent flier because "supposedly she was a drug seeker." The chaplain said, "I always cringe when people are labeled as a drug seeker or frequent flier. This patient had been there many times, and the nursing staff knew her, so they really didn't pay much attention to her. They felt like she was there for more drugs." The chaplain added, "The third time she was admitted, they found a major, *major* health issue that would most likely end her life sooner rather than later." The chaplain said when hospital caregivers place the negative label of frequent fliers or drug seekers, "It totally changes the way people can heal. It turns people into basically a number with a medical record, and that's it." When this happens, she added, "people like this young woman don't feel heard. She didn't feel seen." The chaplain explained, "It turned out this patient had sickle cell, which is an extremely painful disease," she reiterated, "*extremely painful disease*," adding, "This young woman was *not* drug seeking."

When caregivers *sub*humanize a patient by a label, it removes their humanness layer by layer until they're "no longer viewed as persons with feelings, hopes, and concerns."[5] It then becomes "justifiable" for them to receive a lower standard of care and compassion.[6] This chaplain described another sickle cell anemia patient who also was summarily dismissed as a frequent flier and drug seeker. She said this young woman had had this disease for most of her life. She knew the dosage of pain meds she needed and how long she'd likely need them, but the providers at the hospital "would not listen to her; they would not meet her need." The chaplain said the patient lamented, "'I'm in pain, but it doesn't matter. I just need to get out of this hospital.'" The chaplain said, "It's just so wrong, and it happens more often that you'd realize. Once people hear that label, it shuts everything else down. The empathy is gone." She added, "What's missing in your experience is the lack of the human in front of you." Dignity disappears amidst the labeling. A white female RN who has worked in numerous large hospitals in the southern Midwest during her long career said, "Medical people have a frustrating time with people who present themselves at the hospital with the same complaint because there's no easy fix for it, or maybe no one has been able to accurately diagnose what's going on. Still, medical providers are obligated to assess and treat symptoms rather than dismissing any patient," adding, "for purposes of liability if nothing else."

"Chocolate or Vanilla"

The lupus patient said her afflictions often manifested with various levels of mental cognizance and acuity. The illness impacts her brain so she has extreme difficulties speaking or writing. The testimonial injustice she receives when medical professionals don't believe what she says is likely influenced by her difficulty in communicating, so they make assumptions about her aptitude. She said, they might not say it out loud, but they're thinking, "She's goofy and stupid." The lupus patient said, "Granted, I've always been goofy and a little left of center, but that's normal for me," adding, "I'm really only ever given the choice between chocolate or vanilla." When medical professionals move from their own assumptions about a patient, it becomes testimonial and hermeneutical injustice, which negatively affects a patient's spirituality. Bias, preconceived assumptions, superiority positioning, and outright prejudice contribute to testimonial and hermeneutical injustice, which destroy a patient's spirituality because these disregard, disrespect, and dismiss their dignity.[7]

Power Differentials

Power differentials factor in with honoring (or not) patient dignity. Patristic dominance of males over females is the baseline differential that too often establishes male caregivers over the (weaker) positioned females, particularly with an already vulnerable patient.[8] There's also a power differential between caregivers and care receivers in general, with the power imbalance tipping toward caregivers rather than patients, who literally are at their mercy. A middle-aged white female who was on the surgery floor in a mid-sized suburban hospital described this power imbalance when a particular white middle-aged female nurse made the rounds to take patient vitals. This patient had just been sent to this floor from recovery and asked a simple question of the nurse about some aspect of her post-op care. The nurse immediately responded, "Silence! No one speaks when I take vitals. No one." The patient said she was so stunned at this nurse's rudeness that she did exactly as she was ordered: she kept silent. There are numerous ways/reasons/rationalizations to marginalize and de-dignify a patient, including gender.

Gender

American philosopher and gender studies scholar Judith Butler famously calls gender a "regulatory norm," which is foundational to all other categories of regulation.[9] Gender matters. Not naming inequalities related to gender—sexism—points to its normalcy. Gender justice aims to change the systemic gender inequity of society.[10] Sexism goes unnoticed and unchallenged because people begin experiencing sexism during childhood from their grandparents, parents, aunts and uncles, cousins, and siblings. How a male or female child is treated becomes normalized by virtually everyone around them, literally from birth on.[11] In the well-known statement in the classic feminist text *The Second Sex*, Simone de Beauvoir writes, "One is not born, but rather becomes, woman."[12] The normalization of sexism makes it harder to recognize how we're contributing to it through our attitudes, assumptions, words, and actions because our own views on this are part of our own essence of being.[13] It requires deliberate attention to recognize, notice, challenge, and change what's been ingrained in our understanding, outlook, and beinghood regarding gender.. If we can't or won't recognize and work to correct sexism, then how can we possibly work to challenge any breach in dignity due to any other isms? Women experience the most victimization because of their gender, but it also touches males when assumptions are made about who they "should" be and what they "should" say or do. Gender bias makes everything worse, including emotional and spiritual trauma.

Male Head of Household Makes the (Healthcare) Decisions

A notable intersection with spirituality in healthcare is who's allowed to make decisions, something that can become lopsided toward the elder male family member, who frequently becomes the default figure to make decisions on behalf of the females in their family.[14] For example, a middle-aged white female with a doctorate degree who'd recently been released from the hospital explained, that after several days of being unable to sleep while she was in the ICU, she was beginning to have hallucinations (see also Chapter 7). She remembered:

> *I started begging profusely for a sedative, anything to knock me out so I could sleep, but they kept ignoring me. I'd watched enough* **MASH** *and* **Marcus Welby MD** *to know that there were sedatives, and I wanted to be knocked out so the monsters would go away! Finally, the nurse said they'd check with the MD, who supposedly said my husband was the only one who could authorize a sedative for me. That did NOT make sense to me (then or now). So, then I turned all my energy toward my poor husband, saying, "You've got to be my advocate here. If they won't give it to me on my say so, then you've got to step up and be my voice. Please, please,* ***please****, you've got to do this for me!"*

Dignity 73

My poor husband. So unfair! He finally capitulated and said, "Okay, give my wife a sedative so she can sleep." Whew! I never did see what the big deal was; why they couldn't have given me melatonin or some other over-the-counter something, even a cup of herb tea would've helped to take the edge off. If there was a reason, they could've explained it to my husband and also to me. They never did.

Instead, they played the gender card and put pressure on the spouse to make a decision on behalf of his wife. She added, "Then amid all of this extra stress from the drama about me needing to get permission from my husband, I was supposed to make myself fall asleep." She described the scene as "extremely unsettling and spiritually stressful." Gender also interacts with other variables, most notably race.

Race

Race contributes to how patients are treated, which dramatically impacts their physical, mental, and spiritual well-being. Systemic racism in America is a documented given.[15] Race matters.[16] It has mattered in America's past, as it continues to in America's present, and will continue to be significant into the future because, as Audre Lorde aptly argues, "By ignoring the past, we are encouraged to repeat its mistakes."[17] Race crashes into the hierarchy of values of how someone positions themselves in comparison to someone else, including differentials between caregivers and care receivers.[18] The attitudes, assumptions, expectations, and biases caregivers consciously or unconsciously have about a patient's racial background could, but shouldn't interfere with the quality of care they give and what the patient receives.[19]

Racist Stereotypes in Action

A middle-aged Latina female patient who had higher than usual postoperative pain was being ignored (or dismissed) by her nurse. When a Latino physician attempted to counter the nurse's inattention and lack of compassion for the suffering patient, this nurse explained, "She took a course in nursing school and cross-cultural medicines and knew that Hispanic patients overexpress the pain that they're feeling."[20] The nurse's (misguided and racist) training blindsided them to the patient's suffering. bell hooks documents that racist stereotypes also abound of "the strong, superhuman Black woman are operative myths in the minds of many white women, allowing them to ignore the extent to which Black women are likely to be victimized in this society, and the role white women play in the maintenance and perpetuation of that victimization."[21] A nursing student posed a question in her weekly journal: "Do Black people, particularly Black women, still get looked at as inferior in our society today?" She responded:

> *When I was in my first round of clinicals, I was following a nurse who, at the beginning of the shift, told me that every patient should be treated the same because everyone deserves to be healed. Later in that shift, we had a patient who kept ringing her call light because she was in terrible pain from a surgery she'd had a few days ago. The first few times we went in there, my nurse told her she was not due for pain meds and she would bring them in when she could have them next. Later in the shift after the lady pressed her call light again, the nurse made a terrible comment. She looked at me and said, "Black women are so much more dramatic and have such a low pain tolerance." When I heard her say this, I was very shocked. I suggested we go get her medications and help her pain level so she could be comfortable.*[22]

The nursing student added, "No matter who someone is, they deserve to enter a healthcare facility with the right to not be judged, but to be heard and healed."[23] Another nursing student wrote in her weekly journal, "The healthcare system today seems backwards and broken to most, but for some it is even worse." Reflecting on Chaplain Allen's analysis in "Black Women's Pain," on the role of Black women in medical history, what this nursing student described as "basically being lab rats as they were mutilated and exploited in the name of science, and the belief that they couldn't feel pain (or at least had a higher threshold) was widely accepted," the BSN student added, "This belief is perpetuated today in the healthcare industry as pain is undertreated. As future nurses, we must fight against conscious and unconscious biases when treating patients. When we see this on our floors or being discussed by our peers, we must speak up and advocate for what is morally right and the best for the patient independent of race. We must overcome our fears and break the silence."[24]

When a patient is labeled a "strong Black woman" and doesn't get the attention, treatment, or care she needs, this racial bias against her causes her to suffer in body, mind, and spirit.[25]

A Black Woman Miscarries Her Fourth Child

A Black mother who was going to turn 40 when her fourth child was to be born was referred to an office that specialized in higher-risk pregnancies. There was a Black female doctor of obstetrics (OB) whom this pregnant mother wanted to be assigned to because of their cultural and racial connections. Unfortunately, this doctor was already overloaded, so she was assigned to a different (white) doctor, whom this Black female described as having the attitude, "'I've been there, I've saved all these lives.' It didn't feel like this provider was humble.'" She said this doctor's ego interfered with the quality of caregiving. Explaining she'd had a very low iron count, she remembered, "They asked me if I wanted an IV or if I wanted to take supplements. The IV would be quicker to get my iron back up to where it needed to be, so we said we would do the IV." A full month went by and nothing was scheduled. She had a miscarriage during the wait.

Not yet realizing this, the mother explained she and her husband brought their four children to the appointment to get the ultrasound, which would determine the baby's gender. The mother remembered:

> It was a really big deal, and the children were excited to learn whether they were going to have a little brother or a little sister. All of a sudden, the tech said, "I don't see a baby." At no point did she say anything about seeing the doctor or having the doctor verify. All she did was hand me some pills and say, "Here, these will help to abort what's remaining."

Her husband, a nurse supervisor at a large hospital in the Pacific Northwest, interjected, "It was an appalling breach of medical protocol." He explained, "Even if you have a broken arm, the tech is not supposed to say anything. It comes from the provider—the doctor. This ultrasound tech was diagnosing it, and she was not supposed to do so."

Recounting this experience from one year earlier, the devastated mother added, "At no point did she ever ask my husband to take the children from the room. She just blurted out that there was no baby. I didn't feel as if I was being treated as a person—especially being in a room with four small children." This mother said she didn't think her children would ever trust healthcare providers because of this experience. She said, "Our oldest child (a son) shut down completely, and our oldest daughter started balling. It went over the heads of the two little ones." How someone finds out about bad news is critically important and should never be casually done. Timing is everything. People need to be in a place and space where they are "ready to receive and grapple with the news; which may not be the time the consultant can most easily fit into [their] schedule."[26] It falls to the caregivers, not the care receivers, to find a place and time for sharing any bad news. Blurting it out spontaneously is unacceptable, unethical, unprofessional, and emotionally and spiritually harmful.

Recalling this painful experience, this mother added, "I've never had the best relationship with medical professionals because of being a Black woman. There's an inherent distrust. They were asking us to come back in for another visit, and I said, 'I don't want to see these people ever again in my life.' We were referred there because we were supposed to get better care, and instead, I had the worst type of care." When I asked if there was any relationship between her lack of care and her being a Black woman, she said, "I have thought about this point a lot. I would like to think not, but I cannot help but wonder because I am living in a state where there are very few Blacks (12.4%). I cannot help but wonder if I'd been a white woman (61.6%) would I have had that iron IV intervention and my baby would not have aborted."[27] This was her final pregnancy. To say that spirituality is about the meaning of life dismisses the inexplicable spiritual, mental, and physical harm done when racism is the basis for unkind and inept medical care. Until caregivers choose to become transformers of racist care, racism will continue to harm the physical, mental, and spiritual well-being of their nonwhite patients.

Ageism

Personhood often begins to suffer through ageism long before dementia settles in. Benedictine sister and theologian Joan Chittister writes about ageism in the *Gift of Years: Growing Older Gracefully*, explaining, "Negative stereotypes exaggerate isolated characteristics and ignore positive characteristics entirely. So older people are portrayed as slow, but not as wise or patient. We see them as ill, but not as quite in charge of their own lives." Chittister adds, "We are reminded constantly that they forget things, but not a single note is made of the fact that everyone else does as well." She proposes, "Worst of all, stereotypes absolutize characteristics, as if they were part and parcel of being Black or being a woman or being old—or of being young, for that matter." She said the tendency is to lump people together and categorize them, "instead of seeing them as individuals who are full of grace, full of the spirit of life." She terms it "a pathetic moment in the history of the human condition when the outside world tells us who and what we are—and we start to believe it ourselves."[28] Labeling leads to inappropriate, inadequate, and/or dismissive attention, which nets spiritual, emotional, and physical harm, which an RN in the Pacific Northwest noted, "is a considerable concern given that the elderly population comprises the majority of in-patient admissions in hospitals, rehabilitation facilities, and of course, long-term care."

Sexual Orientation

A transgender white male and his queer wife of Latina heritage explained their ongoing spiritual trauma that arises out of the husband's physical health concerns, which include stomach ailments and urinary tract infections that overlap with the hormone care he's received as part of his transgendering process. He said, at the beginning of his transgendering process, he thought the way he was received and treated was "all just coincidence." His hormone treatment and top surgery forever after changed how he was received and treated. His wife interjected, "After his first transitioning, it was always, *always* very awkward." Her trans spouse added, "Yeah, to have to come out to them each time." They live in a super-conservative midwestern state where they said they're consistently asked "inappropriate questions" related to the trans process. The queer wife said, "I can just see the anxiety on his face when it comes to the point in the visit where he feels like he has to come out." His example:

Patient: I'm trans.

Medical person: Okay, so you're transitioning to be a woman?

Patient: No. I have transitioned into a man, and I hope that you see as a man.

The trans male said sometimes the questions are relevant, such as when he's in for a urinary tract infection (UTI) because it involves anatomy, but other times the questions are irrelevant and inappropriate. For example, when he spoke with a person via telehealth who collected the information to relay to a doctor, the male trans said, "She got all kind of snarky and hostile." His wife explained the provider initially was "confused because he was having UTI-like symptoms and the provider said, 'Men don't usually get UTIs. Then my husband had to come out to her. Then the provider didn't understand what being transgender was. She didn't understand that you can change gender, but you still have anatomical female parts." His wife added, "This provider was just rude. We don't often call and complain about people, but you better believe I called and complained about this person."

He remembered another time when he thought he had more UTI issues so they went to see a urologist. He said, "When it got to the part where I was having to come out, the doctor said 'Okay, so you still have your lady parts.' Then this MD said, I needed to see a gynecologist, and I responded that I wouldn't even know what to tell them.'" The trans male finally got through to the provider and received the medical care that he needed, but the experience was spiritually demoralizing. The underdog of any dichotomy is expected to make the dominant view understand why and what it means to be different.[29]

This trans male, who said truth, truth-telling, and being truthful is the heart of his spirituality, specified, "I try so hard to live in truth, and to be completely truthful about things to the point that it's like ridiculous. It's so important to me to live in truth, and to be honest and open because to me, truth is spirituality." His truth shaped his decision to transgender, he explained, adding, "So when I go and somebody says, 'You still have your lady parts,' it's like, 'Fuck you!' It's humiliating." He reiterated, "It's humiliating. It makes me feel shameful. It makes me feel like I have this big secret, and I freaking hate feeling that way." He added, "I don't want my life to be one big coming out party, either. I just want to live my life." His wife said, "One positive thing that some clinics have started doing with the check-in paperwork is asking about your gender identity and if you're trans. That is so helpful."

Psychiatric

Mental or psychiatric instability claims another layer of dignity, which potentially radically harms spirituality through disrespect of a patient's full humanity. An RN with most of her clinical background in neurology reflected on her experience at a psychiatric hospital in a metropolis in the southern half of the United States. She'd already worked twenty years in nursing and wanted a part-time job "to make a little extra money, but also to try something different," so she took a "call working" position where she was part of a float pool. She signed up for a particular hospital and specified the days she'd be available. She said when she signed up to do this with a psychiatric hospital, she thought, "Psych, how hard can that be? I've taken care of people whose brains were bleeding." She said she quickly realized, "The people in charge were not even nurses, or doctors, or *anything*. They were 'mental health techs,' which were glorified college students who managed the activities of each little pod of patients based on gender and acuity." She added, "And because this was psychiatric, these mental health techs turned into little Gestapo police sergeants."

The RN described the scene when "a teenage girl who'd come in because she was cutting herself started to act out and was knocking things off the shelves. The mental health tech's way to react to that situation was to yell at her, grab her maybe with another person, and then take her down literally to the floor." She explained, "They did this in a way that was authoritative, rather than trying to calmly talk to her. The nurse's role was secondary. My job as a nurse in that hospital was to give the meds. These techs did everything else." They summoned the RN to come into the padded room with a syringe in their hand to give the patient something to sedate them. She said, "The nurse had seemingly no say in what was supposed to be a therapeutic environment for this teenager who'd tried to kill herself."

The nurse remembered: "There were times where I tried to intervene and just say, 'Let's just talk. Take some deep breaths. Let's talk a little bit about what's going on before we jump to sedating,'" she paused and then added, "But I was overruled in almost all of those situations." She explained, "This particular psychiatric hospital was a corporate-owned for-profit company, and they could save a ton of money because they would have one licensed person, *me*, and a bunch of college students. And then yes, these patients had therapy sessions. And there were physicians on call to deal with emergencies. They had a very cost-effective way of staffing, and this was their attitude. She said she completed a number of training sessions during the time she worked there, but they were related to self-protection, emphasizing, "We had no training on the means of therapeutic communication. None."

She said, "When a patient went out of control, the protocol of this hospital would be that they call code green, which was a behavior thing, and a team of people would come running. They'd have these code greens every single time I worked. It wasn't an unusual thing. Every time they would take this person down to the floor. Then they had a little room that had padding on it. They called the nurse, and a nurse would give the psych patient a shot, and down they'd go. Then they'd call this poor doctor who'd come in and try to talk with the patient. By this time this patient was out of it. And the doctor's job would be to make some notes, and then they'd shrug their shoulders like 'What the hell can I do?' And walk out of this room." She said this scenario "went on and on and on."

She said there also would be units of children and teenagers whom no one wanted to work with because of their behaviors. The nurse asked, "Did anyone listen to them? Hold their hand? Try to play a card game with them, or something? No." She said she remembered the many times when, if they approached the nurse's station, she'd be observing during "a couple of days in orientation with another nurse, and this nurse would tell that patient, 'You need to leave us alone. I'm training a new girl here.' I asked, Do you want to know what this patient wants? The nurse training me responded, 'Oh, that patient does this all the time. They just want a cigarette or something.'" The hostile environment began during admission.

Demeaning Psychiatric Patient Admissions Process

The nurse described when "one poor lady, probably in her fifties who'd tried to kill herself with an overdose. The hospital pumped her stomach and sent her to this psych hospital. The nurse said, "The patient comes and she's a mess. She's distraught. It's as if she's going to prison. They immediately went in and took away her shoelaces, and then they pretty much stripped her too." She said when this new psych patient was sent back with the RN for a physical exam, "there was no empathy. There was no kindness. There was nothing but harsh treatment. No one said, 'I know this has been tough for you.' Nothing. No compassion." She added, "Then the new patient was put into a room with a roommate in this very sterile, hostile environment." She added, "This woman is probably thinking, 'Death would've been better.'" She reiterated, "Yes, they do have therapy, but in the meantime, they live in *One Flew over the Cuckoo's Nest*. They're treated as prisoners. It would be, in my view, the worst possible place for a person with any mental issues." She concluded, "So the dehumanization of patients, the lack of respect for them, and that they become a diagnosis and a number" made this a very brief vocational experience. She noted, "Needless to say, that job didn't last very long. It horrified me. I felt sorry for the patients. I felt like the worst people in the psychiatric hospital were not the patients, even the ones who were profoundly psychotic. It was the staff who treated the patients so harshly."

Dignity requires *re*humanizing, which begins with a more compassionate, caring, personal presence between one living human being and another. It's a genuine beingness that disrupts assumptions and expands caregiver perspectives to enhance patient dignity as a proactive presence to lessen a patient's spiritual distress.[30]

7 Spiritual Distress

Spiritual distress was initially listed in 1978 in the classifications "developed by the North American Nursing Diagnosis Association (now NANDA International)."[1] This nursing taxonomy subsequently expanded to include related terms like "risk for spiritual distress," and "readiness for enhanced spiritual well-being," including the defining characteristics and suggested interventions and outcomes.[2] NANDA also specifies diagnoses for "spiritual pain, spiritual alienation, spiritual anxiety, spiritual guilt, spiritual anger, spiritual loss, and spiritual despair."[3] The various spiritual descriptions make a close connection with religiosity, such that spirituality becomes coalesced with religion. Spirituality and spiritual distress definitions vary dramatically between nursing/healthcare; chaplaincy/clergy; and patients.

From a Healthcare Perspective

As we've seen in Chapter 2, the nursing/healthcare literature prioritizes meaning in/of life as the heartbeat of spirituality, differing from how philosophical, theological, and religious experts understand it, and yet again from how patients describe their spirituality. An incorrect starting point nets an incorrect assessment, which leads to an inappropriate or unhelpful intervention to assist patients with a caregiver's *mis*interpretation of spiritual distress. Physiological care directly impacts spiritual and emotional well-being. Despite healthcare's consistent separation of the body, mind, and spirit, they're integrated: three-in-one.[4]

Spiritual Distress Nursing Diagnosis

A nursing diagnosis of spiritual distress defines it as "a state of suffering related to the impaired ability to integrate meaning and purpose in life through connections with self, others, the world, or a superior being."[5] The litany of defining characteristics includes:

> *Anger behaviors; crying; decreased expression of creativity; disinterested in nature; dyssomnia; excessive guilt; expresses alienation; expresses anger;*

expresses anger toward power greater than self; expresses concern about beliefs; expresses concern about the future; expresses concern about values system; expresses concerns about family; expresses loss of control; expresses loss of hope; expresses loss of serenity; expresses need for forgiveness; expresses regret; expresses suffering; fatigue; fear; impaired ability for introspection; inability to experience transcendence; maladaptive grieving; perceived loss of meaning in life; questions identity; questions meaning of life; questions meaning of suffering; questions own dignity; refuses to interact with others.[6]

After the lupus patient reviewed the *Nursing Diagnosis Handbook* articles on spiritual assessment and spiritual distress, she responded, "It seems they're allowed to make a lot of assumptions from a noncommunicating, distanced person who is there because they don't feel well." She added, "If they can make a diagnosis on spiritual distress, then they should be able to determine that you need another blanket when you're freezing or a pillow because the one you have is uncomfortable so you can't sleep." Some RNs might consider this "comfort care," without making the connection between physical *dis*comfort and increasing spiritual distress.

The suggested outcomes from nursing interventions to treat a spiritual distress diagnosis include "coping; dignified life closure; grief resolution; hope; spiritual health; and [reduced] stress level."[7] Notice the emphasis on meaning in the nursing outcomes when a patient will:

Express meaning and purpose in life
Express sense of hope in the future
Express sense of connectedness with self
Express sense of connectedness with family/friends
Express ability to forgive
Express acceptance of health status
Find meaning in relationships with others
Find meaning in relationships with Higher Power
Find meaning in personal and health care treatment choices.[8]

From a patient's perspective, the meaning of life isn't the root cause of their spiritual distress in a hospital or ER. Rather, it's more likely caused by the sterile setting, the uncomfortable and uncertain context, the numerous pokings, proddings, and disruptions, and the uncertainty that lingers throughout the experience as patients wonder, "How much worse does this get, and when can I go home?!"[9]

From a Chaplaincy/Clergy Perspective

Chaplaincy literature has some overlap with healthcare regarding "indications of spiritual distress."[10] A white female board-certified clinical hospital chaplain in her mid-sixties said nurses are the chaplain's "eyes and ears," and they're also "spiritual caregivers through their compassionate care." However, this chaplain emphasized, "My colleagues and I are the experts in spiritual care." The chaplain said she trained medical staff "in signs and symptoms of spiritual distress, so they could know when to refer to a chaplain." She said during her career as a chaplain, she's seen the professional role diminish across healthcare, usually related to money, particularly during the last decade. She said, "My concern is nurses have neither the time for nor training, in the provision of spiritual care." She said she's also concerned that "people in the executive suites may think having nurses offer spiritual care is financially savvy, but it blurs the boundaries and the patient as the patient is the one who ends up suffering."[11] A white, male, board-certified hospice chaplain serving in the southeastern United States said, "Spiritual screens can be conducted by RNs, but spiritual assessments are the realm of professional chaplains." A chaplain's broader role encompasses training in spiritual care amidst diversity to ensure all patients are treated with dignity and respect.[12]

A white female hospice chaplain who's worked in two large hospitals in the Midwest said, "When people experience hopelessness, they're definitely in spiritual distress, whether they know it or not. I see hopelessness when a patient believes they're not good enough to be accepted or when they're not in community or close relationships." She said she's been trying to figure out what makes one person hopeful and another one not, explaining she can go into one hospital room and be with someone who's hopeful and then to another room where they're the similar age and have similar diagnosis, "and one can be in distress, while the other is rolling with the punches."[13] She said she hasn't figured out why there's such a strong difference in their responses, but that her sense is it relates to her understanding of spirituality, which is that "it's formed around relationships and community, and how we all interact and come together and help each other."

Spiritual Distress Examples

This chaplain added that spiritual distress also can be caused by "invalidating a patient's beliefs and imposing my own belief onto them." She said, "It can be very harmful to really push a patient where they're not ready to be pushed. Patients let you know if they want to talk about whatever it is that's weighing on them." She said spiritual distress can manifest in different ways, adding, "People have so much baggage from their pasts."[14] She recalled a patient who was lamenting about a friend in the LGBTQ community," adding, "And of course, this friend wasn't receptive to her lecture . . . go figure." When I asked if this patient knew the chaplain's sexual orientation, the lesbian chaplain responded, "I'm not supposed to bring that in," adding, "It was very challenging to have a negative conversation about the LGBTQ community, but I knew my job was to listen."

She recalled another time when a patient was in renal failure and "came to the hospital with an expectation that she'd never go home because that she was at the end of life." This patient wasn't a person of faith, "but I'll tell you, holding space with her was probably one of the more spiritual things I've ever done." The chaplain explained this person's spiritual distress wasn't about her pending death but about her childhood trauma when she'd been rejected in a youth leadership role at a church because, at the time, she'd "battled anorexia," so she'd been told she wasn't allowed to serve in leadership. The chaplain said, the patient "wasn't valued because of that. And when I would sit with her, we would talk about value, and how someone values themselves, but she couldn't get past the fact that she wasn't enough, that she had to be perfect. Her spiritual distress was a response to what she'd experienced many years earlier as a teenager.

"Know Your Edges"

This hospice chaplain explained that a clinical pastoral education instructor frequently said, "'You've got to know what your edges are. You've got to know what things are going to push out and interfere with your ability to be fully present with a patient.'" This chaplain added, "You've got to know what your sensors are, what your edges are, and what makes you overly sensitive to a conversation that might unfold." Reflecting on the first time she walked into a patient's room as a chaplain, she explained, "It comes down to listening to what patients are saying. Using the example of her young adult daughter, who was in extreme pain, which would parallel passing a kidney stone, the chaplain said she realized her daughter "needed to be validated that it hurts like hell, that it's the worst pain she's ever been in. She needs to be validated because that's where her spirit is. She needs to have her spiritual distress, her spiritual trauma affirmed." The chaplain/mother explained, "It's my daughter's frustration with people not realizing how much pain she's in which was causing her spiritual distress." So, the chaplain/mother validated her and said, "'Oh, baby, I know this hurts. I can tell that this is the deepest pain that you've ever been in.'" She clarified, "And that's the role of spiritual care in a clinical setting. It's listening to the patient, listening to what they're experiencing, and not putting yourself into it. It's listening with compassion and kindness, and not interjecting or superimposing your views or beliefs in an inappropriate fashion."

The hospice chaplain added, "When nurses make a spiritual assessment, it becomes one more clinical thing that takes away from the needs of the human being before them. And instead, it overfunctions on how to analyze it, measure it, control it and make it quote 'clinical' and shove it into a box where spirituality doesn't belong."[15] She said she's observed medical staff "across the gamut," from those who have nothing to do with spiritual care, to those who "were trying to evangelize" patients. She said the latter emerges out of a "gross misunderstanding of what spirituality is," such as asking a patient if they want to pray, "so spiritual care becomes a response out of religiosity." The chaplain clarified, "But prayer to me, isn't spirituality. That's a religious connection through corporate prayer, which is not what spirituality is."

A white male in his mid-sixties who's the senior pastor of a bilingual Hispanic congregation in a large metropolitan city in the southern United States said, "Spirituality is the means by which we endeavor to connect the deepest core of our lives with the Holy which is discoverable in everything that exists." He explained, "We experience spiritual distress when we feel no such connection ... when we experience ourselves to be disconnected from this source of life and wholeness." He emphasized it's this disconnection that causes spiritual distress.

Crossing the Line

Reverend Sharon Risher, who served as a board-certified chaplain in two hospitals in Texas before shifting to advocacy for safer gun laws after her mother and cousin were killed in the "Emmanuel Nine" anti-Black mass hate shooting at Emanuel African Methodist Episcopal Church on June 17, 2015, said, "Because nurses are the first contact point for a patient, most chaplains visit a patient because of a referral from the nurses because the nurses know what a patient is going through. When a particular nurse is attuned to the patient, they can tell whether they need a pastoral care visit or not." Risher added, "Sometimes the nurse's referral is right on point, but then other times it's not. Sometimes the nurses don't make referrals and there's a need for one, and there's a patient who's struggling and no one's paying any attention." Risher said it's also a concern when "sometimes nurses take it upon themselves to give their own take on religion or spirituality and talk to the patient," which Risher said, "crosses the boundaries between pastoral care and nursing." She said she doesn't believe it's appropriate for a nurse to give a spiritual assessment. Risher emphasized, "That's not their job," adding it would be like a chaplain who came into a patient's room and checked their blood pressure or took their temperature. She emphasized, "That's stepping over the line," which is also evident in nursing academic literature, which gives the inappropriate advice, "Counseling a person in spiritual distress can constitute a growth experience for the nurse while also providing support for the patient."[16] Risher said she appreciates nurses have "such a connection" with their patients on a deep level, but it's important to respect patient-caregiver boundaries and not to let "a nurse's personal faith come out in their caring," what Risher acknowledged is more about a nurse's religious beliefs and religious care for a patient rather than spiritual care. She specified, "There's a difference."

Spiritual Distress from a Patient's Perspective

Spiritual distress arises from each patient's contributing factors to their spirituality and also from their lived context, including whatever baggage they lug around from their past, any loss of dignity during the medical treatment (see Chapter 6), and the unique circumstances around their healthcare experience. When the pastor noted above reflected on when he'd been a hospital patient himself, both when he broke his neck in Mexico and when he'd had a motorcycle accident in the United States, he said he didn't experience spiritual distress in either case because he "remained connected to the Holy." He added, "My distress came more during the rehab phase as I was frustrated by the length of time it took to recover. I was not patient. I kept wishing for faster progress." He explained, "It wasn't really an issue of medical care, more an issue of my own egoic impatience and lack of control over the rate of healing."

Pain and Medication Mismanagement

The stage four cancer patient battling melanoma highlighted an exception to his otherwise stellar medical care, which led to spiritual distress due to pain medication mismanagement. He was raised in a religious household, but he'd since disaffiliated, explaining, "I've never searched for meaning in religion or tried to answer any questions with religion." Instead, his autonomy and vitality inform his spirituality. He described a painful exception when he wasn't respected, which created a pain and medication mismanagement that snowballed into spiritual distress. He'd arrived at the hospital at 6:00 a.m. for his second of three surgeries. Because he wasn't supposed to eat prior to the surgery, the melanoma patient hadn't been able to take the pain meds for the surgery, which he'd had two days prior when a surgeon had removed a melanoma tumor from his face. He was in the waiting room for an extended time because the surgery before his took longer than expected. He explained:

*It was around 10:00 a.m., and I hadn't taken any pain meds in all that time, and there's this giant hole on my face from the previous surgery that's starting to hurt more and more. Finally, they take me into the surgery prep room and asked me to rate my pain on a scale of one to ten with, one being not bad and ten being you can't take it anymore. When I first got in there, I was four or five, and I said I felt I could use something for the pain. The nurse responded, "Okay, the **next** person is going to give that to you something."*

*Twenty or thirty minutes later, somebody else came into the room and asked the same thing. Now it's a six or a seven, so I said I could **really** use something. They said, "Well, somebody else is going to do that. The **next** person who comes in will probably give you that. Meanwhile, I'm thinking, "I'm really in pain here and no one is listening."*

Then, in the middle of this not getting pain medicine, another nurse asked, "Are you religious?" And I was "No, I'm not, but I appreciate you asking." Then this nurse said, "Okay, well, here's the thing. Jesus loves you," and then she gave me this lecture about how through the power of Jesus, I would be healed. Normally, that doesn't bother me, but in this case, I felt like, "Okay, you didn't listen to me, and you just kind of did whatever you wanted." And this whole time, I'm not feeling like people are listening to me. I'm not getting pain meds, and my face hurts. I'm a captive audience; I'm in bed, I can't exactly move. I like agency.

He said he understands, "in the nurse's own way," she was trying to make him feel better, but it wasn't. Rather, it was stressing him out because she'd ignored his request for pain meds, along with all of the earlier nurses. He said, "When she finally finished her Jesus lecture," I said, "Okay, *now* can I have something for the pain?" He said this nurse responded as all the previous ones had: "'The *next* person will give them,' and then she walked out." Altogether four or five different people who came in asking him how his pain was, and each time he'd asked for pain meds. The last medication he'd taken had been at 9:00 p.m. the previous evening.

The young cancer patient explained the worst part was when the surgeon arrived and asked, "'Well, why didn't you take any pain meds?'" When the patient responded that the instructions said not to eat or drink anything, the doctor argued back, "'It doesn't say that.' And I responded, 'Yes, it does.'" After more back-and-forth, the doctor said, "'Well, I'm the doctor, I should know.'" The patient said he thought to himself, "'Alright, buddy, you're the doctor. My bad for reading something that said not to eat or drink.' I didn't argue after that, but I was just thinking," Damn!" He'd been asking for pain meds for four or five hours. In addition to the escalating physical pain, he'd experienced spiritual and emotional distress because his agency wasn't respected, he wasn't heard, and he'd had to put up with proselytizing and a condescending surgeon. The young adult concluded saying, "It was rough."

"What Can I Do to Help You Today?"

Much of patient-explained spiritual distress in a hospital or urgent care setting has little to do with their meaning in life. Instead, it's created by the care and compassion that patients don't receive when they need it the most. I asked the lupus patient who'd been through so much, lost so much, and whose life had become totally discombobulated because of her illness: "Did anybody just come into your room and ask you, "'What can I do to be helpful for you today? What will make you feel better?'" She responded, "As a matter of fact, when I was seeing a therapist when the worst of all this was happening, and when I was telling her about it, the therapist asked, 'What can I really do to help you?' I looked at her and I said, 'You're the first person who's stopped to ask me what I need.' It just stopped me for a minute when she asked me because it caught me off guard.' And then the therapist responded, 'I am so sorry.'"

Hip Replacement Patient

A white female small business owner in her late sixties explained the spiritual distress she'd experienced when she'd had hip replacement surgery. She said she wasn't getting a lot of feedback from her doctor about what to expect, so she prepared herself by watching YouTube videos. She also collected and brought her medical records from two previous minor surgeries. She said the anesthesiologist looked at the reports briefly, then asked which anesthesia the patient preferred, who responded by asking, "What would you give your mom?" The anesthesiologist said he'd give her a spinal block, so the patient said she'd take that, adding,

> *I don't know how far into the surgery it was, but I actually woke up on my side and heard a hammer pounding, and I thought to myself, "God, I can't believe they're doing construction in the surgical room while I'm having my surgery. That's so weird." I didn't feel anything. I just heard it all. And then I realized I also heard muffled speaking from everybody who was in there for my surgery. I said, "Hello. I can hear you guys," thinking they needed to know I was awake because* **nobody told me I would be awake**.

She said she heard pounding and a drill coming out and then "a lot of muffled laughing." She didn't feel any pain, but she heard everything. She said, had the anesthesiologist told her she was going to be awake; she wouldn't have agreed to that type of anesthesia. She said it was "unnerving" to hear the procedures and also the laughter in the room.

"Everybody's Different."

When she was in the recovery room, the anesthesiologist told her, "'You're really lucky. You're not going to feel any pain until tomorrow around noon because of the anesthesia you got.'" When she asked if she'd feel any pain after it wore off, he responded, "We don't know,'" then he added what this patient said is "the most frequent thing she heard: "They all said, 'Everybody's different.' Nobody tells you what's going to happen because 'everybody's different.'" Because her blood pressure dropped extremely low following her surgery, she was kept overnight. She became agitated as she described her spiritually distressing overnight experience.

She said, "For starters, the drip machine buzzer would start ringing, and nobody would come. Then I would press my little buzzer. No one ever came." Finally, a nurse from down the hall came up and remarked about this patient's light being on for so long and asked how she could help. After this visiting nurse turned off the buzzing, the patient slept fitfully until about 3:30 a.m., when she started feeling discomfort in her hip. She rang her call button because she remembered she was supposed to have a pain pill at 1:30 a.m., two hours earlier. Thirty minutes later a nurse responded. After a back-and-forth debate about the timing of the pain meds, the nurse said she'd have to check with someone and that she'd be right back. She finally returned at 4:00 a.m. with the pain meds. The patient said, "You know, I was very gracious to the nurses because I know they have a hard job, but it was a very long and stressful night," adding, "It was a nightmare."

ICU Delirium

Delirium is one of the side effects of hospitalization, particularly for ICU patients, hence the diagnosis *ICU delirium*.[17] The exact contributing factors aren't specified in journal articles because, of course, "everybody's different." The strategies for preventing delirium include various medications which are *Twilight Zone* material, or what you'd read in a historic romance novel when the wife was kept locked up and/or doped up on opium.[18] The journal articles also don't discuss the contributing factors *from the patient's perspective*. ICU delirium is an extension of the systems, protocols, procedures, and environmental experience during their hospital stay, particularly while in the ICU (see Chapter 4). ICU delirium is *spiritual distress intensified*, especially for sleep-deprived patients.

Hallucinations and Visions in ICU

A white female in her early sixties who'd been admitted to ICU with extremely low sodium related to an extended bout of intestinal flu and who was later diagnosed with Addison's Disease described the setting for her ICU delirium, which netted exacerbated spiritual distress:

> *I'd had a minor physical setback the second evening I was in ICU, which caused my sodium to drop back down to when I'd initially been admitted. In addition, between getting poked with a needle for the labs every four hours around the clock, plus all the other ICU disruptions, I hadn't slept in three days, including the arrival night that I'd spent in ER. At 6:00 a.m. on the morning of my third day in ICU, a nurse asked for my husband's cell phone number, which they*

wrote on the white board along with the nurse's name. I texted my husband who worked about five minutes from the hospital:

Thursday   6:58 a.m.

ICU Patient: I'm worse than I've been. In multiple ways. FYI.

Spouse: Can you talk on the phone?

ICU Patient: No

Spouse: Should I come over?

ICU Patient: Yes

Spouse: Okay

ICU Patient: They told me to close my eyes. I won't see the phone. If I'm sleeping, please ask my nurse for an update. It's important.

Monsters in My Head

My husband arrived shortly after 7:00 a.m.. Around 11:00 a.m. I started having hallucinations each time I closed my eyes. Initially, it struck me as a bit bizarre and even a little bit funny. The first ones were little people floating in a circular, clockwise motion around my irises. I tried to figure out if I was supposed to know any of these people. They were mostly closeups of faces that were laughing, smiling, and talking with great familiarity.

I opened my eyes pretty quickly to ask what was going on with these visions. My nurse said it was normal to have hallucinations with low sodium and asked me to describe them, which I did. My poor husband heard what his whacked-out wife was describing. It got scarier, weirder, and more intense. Instead of the smiling, happy, faces, the images turned into twirling, three-dimensional, spinning, bird-like shapes similar to toys preschoolers put together. I opened my eyes and said, "I can't do this." The nurse said to my spouse, "Your wife hasn't slept in forty-eight hours. She just needs to close her eyes and sleep."

*The next time I tried to close my eyes, the sheet that was wadded up in front of my face turned into a Big White Monster that tried to eat my face! It scared the shit out of me—my eyes flew open. Again, they said I just needed to get some rest. At this point, I noticed that the "feet things," as I referred to them, were off. Since the ICU MD had just made morning rounds and had frowned at my **not** having them on, I suggested the nurse put them back on so I could be a team player. The nurse did.*

Spiritual Distress   93

Meanwhile, the monsters were still freaking me out every time I closed my eyes. I begged profusely for something to help me sleep (see also Chapter 6). The nurse suggested my husband go outside for a walk, saying, "It's a beautiful day, and maybe your wife will sleep when you're gone."

Two hours later, a nurse said that I'd gone to sleep on my own, without any sedative. I asked why by boot things were off of my feet, and she very vaguely said that I'd had a strange dream and had asked to have them taken off. I responded, "Oh, that's when the straps turned into monsters and were trying to eat my feet?!" She responded, "Yes, that's what you said." I remember thinking, "Yikes!" After I described my hallucinations to the ICU MD, he said, "Yours are a bit more intense than what they usually see," so he ordered a brain scan to see if something else was going on.

In addition to whatever physiological connection from the low sodium, the ICU delirium patient said what traumatized her spirit was "being turned into a specimen, being depersonalized, not being acknowledged as somebody with agency, and not being allowed to sleep for days." She added, "It took a long time to recover emotionally and spiritually from my four days in ICU." When she and her spouse debriefed about this experience after she was home from the hospital, they likened the hallucinations to the scene in the 1979 anti-Vietnam musical/comedy movie *Hair* when someone in Central Park passes out cubes of sugar with LSD and the lead player gets whacked out and has a series of crazy hallucinations.[19] She said, "Forever after, when we watch *Hair*, we'll think of my experience in the ICU." Physical care directly intersects with spirituality when it's understood as being *all of me* (not part of me).

8 **Intersections**
Spirituality as *All of Me*

A patient's perspective about what they want and need for spiritual well-being is the key to bridging the medical/scientific ↔ spiritual divide and creating intersections for holistic caregiving, which embodies caring for the patient in their fullness of being: body, mind, and spirit.[1] Embracing the whole-person approach to healthcare requires moving beyond the preconditioned scientific focus, which dismisses the physical body's intersections with the rest of the patient.[2] When spirituality is acknowledged as *all of me* (not part of me), it reshapes the meaning of spiritual care.[3]

Spiritual Care

Spiritual care is a fairly recent arrival to the caregiving scene in a clinical context, coming into usage only in the 1990s.[4] Spiritual care is the medicalized term of its nearest professional parallel, *pastoral care*, which has been a religious practice since the conception of any given world religion.[5] The shift to spiritual care in the United States occurred when the Christian church in America began to decline, with more people identifying as spiritual, not religious. So spiritual care became an attempt to offer compassionate care that attended to the full human being without having any particular religious focus. Separating spirituality from its mooring in a religion created a false impression that all (or most) people are religiously disaffiliated, which of course isn't accurate. In addition, even those who affirm they're a/religious have some cultural, familial, and/or otherwise inherited views, understandings, and beliefs that intersect with some sort of religious something (see Chapter 1).

The secular medical adaptation of spirituality and the requisite spiritual care emerged from an incomplete view of spirituality, creating a confused understanding of what spiritual care could and should be.[6] Because generic spiritual care has been clinicalized, it follows the requisite medical model, which added assessment and intervention for spiritual care, which once was included in pastoral care, and subsequently professionalized through chaplaincy.

Spiritual Assessment

Spiritual assessment is a clinicalized activity to determine what's bothering a patient deep within their inner selves.[7] Assessment leads to clinical actions, or interventions, which can assist a patient who's been diagnosed with spiritual distress.[8] Because the medicalized model begins with spirituality being a patient's meaning in/of life, the assessments are an extension of this limited perspective.[9] Clinical spiritual interventions include counseling, prayer, journaling, and meditation.[10] Suggested questions for nurses to reflectively ask themselves about their observations of patients during a spiritual assessment process to discern if a patient needs a referral to a chaplain include:

- What is sacred to this person?
- What connections are important to this person?
- What/Who is trustworthy in this person's life?
- Is this person's life marked by joy, fear, creativity, or caution?
- What about this experience is the most difficult for this person?
- With whom can this person share this experience?[11]

Though some assessment variations ask patients questions, these questions aren't asked of the patient, but rather they're based upon a nurse's clinical observations.[12] Notice these questions don't address how a patient's physical care has helped or hindered their spiritual and/or emotional well-being.

Patient Perspectives on Spiritual Distress Assessment

Patient perspectives about what contributes to their spiritual distress differ significantly from a medicalized assessment. A middle-aged white female who's religiously affiliated said when she was getting asked spiritual assessment questions, she said, "I thought to myself, 'This is none of the nurse's business.' If I wanted to share this, it'd be with somebody who's trained, qualified, and someone I already know and trust." The patient added, "I'm certainly not going to share my innermost feelings with a nurse who rotates in-and-out every twelve hours." Paraphrasing several patients from the previous chapters, their physical, emotional, and spiritual well-being intersecting with spiritual distress concerns would ask:

- Colonoscopy patient: Don't you realize how condescending it is to speak about me while I'm right here? It's frustrating and irritating that instead of speaking *with me*, you are speaking *around me*.
- ICU room 11: Why do the hospital procedures make it impossible to get any sleep in ICU? Don't you realize this is what contributes to hallucinations, spiritual distress, and ICU delirium?
- Lupus patient: Why doesn't a doctor have the humility and professionalism to do a courtesy consultation with my previous doctor, who'd offered to help with my transition to a new team of caregivers? Why didn't my new MD read my medical history? Why did they waste time and money starting over from scratch?
- Transgender male: Why don't they realize that my collective experience with top surgery has forever harmed my spiritual well-being because of everything that went wrong? I don't feel safe doing the bottom surgery. I wanted to fully transition, but now I don't think I can do that. Can't they see that this has literally negatively affected my entire life?
- Queer spouse of transgender male: Don't you realize how the physical care harmed his spiritual well being? It impacted his and our thoughts about any possible future for him to have bottom surgery? I don't think I could watch him go through the emotional and physical suffering again. How could we trust any doctor again, particularly since it'd be in a much more sensitive area?
- Hispanic male senior citizen Covid-19 patient: Could the doctors stop bumping into each other in my room and make a firm diagnosis so I can start to get well? I thought I was going to die those first two days when they weren't making any decisions about how to treat me.
- Black mother in maternity: Why can't they figure out how spiritually and emotionally stressed out they're making me by not letting my baby sleep in my bed? The baby keeps screaming for me. I'm not sleeping. I'm desperate to get out of the hospital so I can get some sleep and have my new baby beside me.
- Stage four melanoma patient: Why don't the nurses realize how much pain I'm in? Why did four or five nurses blow off my request for pain

meds? Why did that last one push Jesus on me when I'm a religiously disaffiliated stage four cancer patient whose spirituality is centered on my agency and autonomy?
- Black female in her early seventies who had hip replacement surgery: Why can't the nurse just help me go to the bathroom? I don't know if I can stretch my bladder any more than I already have been.

These patient-centered concerns might seem like they're physical issues, but they illustrate how physical care *intersects with* emotional and spiritual well-being.

Chaplaincy Perspective

Womanist Chaplain Risher said this physical ↔ spiritual disjuncture "is what pastoral care has been dealing with forever and ever. How do you see the person as a whole person, regardless of whatever illness or whatever else they're going through?" This chaplain and ordained minister added, "Hospitals tend to put pastoral or spiritual care on the back burner, not realizing that a person's spiritual or religious care is very important in their recovery." Instead of worrying about the meaning of life amidst their physical distress, these patients were concerned with why caregivers didn't make the connection between how their physical care directly impacted their spiritual and emotional health. When caregivers miss the connections between physical care and spiritual and emotional well-being, they don't see and don't respond to alleviating how these physical aspects are harming spiritual and/or emotional angst. Instead, they offer stereotypical "spiritual interventions" like prayer.[13]

Chaplain Allen said her womanist perspective defines spiritual care as "speaking to a whole human being." She said, "So many people are coming into a hospital already feeling diminished, whether it's in their health status, or their humanity, or they're disabled, or they're in some other darkness. I think many people are coming in feeling vulnerable and other, period." Calling hospitals "liminal spaces," transitional spaces that operate at the boundaries, edges, thresholds, or in-between places, Allen believes, "All medical attention should be in the light of spiritual care" (see also Chapter 11). She explained, "When I think of spiritual care, I think of something that is pure, something that is holistic, and something that is kind, compassionate, and honest. So, when I think of medical care, when I think of health care, I'm thinking of something that should be good, and honest, and pure, and patient-centered."

Spirituality's Intersections with Direct Patient Care

Spirituality's intersections with direct patient care aren't always self-evident to caregivers or even to care receivers, largely because of the misunderstandings about what spirituality is and what spiritual care involves. So much of spirituality intersects with physical caregiving through how this hinders or helps a patient's inner sense of peace and centeredness *from the patient's perspective*.

Care through Being There

Patients want to experience care and concern from the medical staff through *being there*. Care expresses itself tangibly through presence in the process of how medical procedures are completed.[14] An experienced white female RN said, "You could have an excellent person technically. You could have a robot come in, who would check your IV, and maybe change that bag out, and take your blood pressure, and then they whisked out of the room with no interaction. *Or* you could have a person who would chit chat with you while they did these same tasks, and make you feel like a human being." The nurse elaborated, "The nurse could talk about whatever the patient wanted to talk about, and also answer questions because the patient always has a lot of questions. Maybe they're too afraid to ask their doctor, or the doctor was only there for two minutes, or they're asleep and the doctor comes." She said these simple actions of engaging kindly and compassionately with a patient reach "deeply into spirituality because it makes that person feel like they have a spiritual side and that there are good people in the world. The kind interactions also restore their faith in humanity." She said, "On the other hand, if a nurse is doing the bare basics and taking care of a patient in just as sparse a sense as possible, they could basically be a robot." What Heidegger would term the "everydayness" of a healthcare professional is how they live into their existence and calling by how they show themselves to and with their patients. Heidegger summarizes, "Everydayness is a way *to be*—to which, of course, that which is publicly manifest belongs."[15] So be a robot in their everydayness caregiving, or to be a kind and compassionate person who interacts with each patient as a human being.

Listening to the Patient

Listening is the most basic form of being fully present with a patient, particularly with patients who don't have many or any visitors. Patients want and need caregivers to listen to, *and hear* their concerns. Listening is a spiritual practice that also doubles as spiritual care. When friends and family can't or aren't available to be present, it falls to the healthcare professionals to provide the necessary compassionate and listening presence, not as an extra or separate task, but while doing the physical care. Listening isn't a separate activity. It's part of caregiving, which becomes a form of spiritual care. Not listening, not being heard, contributes to spiritual distress and unpleasant medical memories which linger.

Painful Memories Linger

A white female in the Midwest shared her experience when she was forty and her "thyroid storm" went undiagnosed when she had three children, including a baby who was less than a year old. She remembered,

> *I knew something was wrong with me. I was crazy emotional. I was off the charts like psycho, and my whole body felt off. I knew something was wrong, and yet, the doctor was saying, "You're fine, you're fine, you're fine," I knew I wasn't fine. And then I was bedridden. When somebody from the church came by to check on me, I was in bed. My husband was at work, and my nine-year-old was taking care of the baby."*

She said her oldest child was working as a lifeguard that summer and was working when a friend from church came in to check on her. She said, "When I staggered out of the upstairs bathroom, this person called my husband at work and said, 'I'm not leaving here until you come home. You need to take your wife to the hospital,'" which her husband did. She was in an isolation unit because she'd been given radioactive iodine and couldn't have visitors. She said, "I was miserable. I was really, really alone." She said if she'd been listened to sooner, she wouldn't have had such a distressing and long-lasting traumatic experience, not only physically, but emotionally and spiritually. She asked, "How can we get healthcare professionals to listen to us sooner rather than later?"

A repeating leitmotif of former patients is their lament that caregivers, including doctors and nurses, didn't listen to them. Sometimes they didn't even make an attempt to hear what the patient was experiencing and describing. Instead, they looked over, looked around, or looked down to the chart they were fiddling with. Listening is spiritual care, and spiritual care requires listening.[16] Patients know their bodies; they know when something is off-centered; they know when things just aren't right. Caregivers need to listen, to really listen, to what patients are saying.

Trusting the Medical Team to Deliver Exceptional Medical Care

Spiritual care is also upheld when patients receive exceptional medical care because they feel safe and they trust the providers to give the quality of medical care that's needed. A Jewish American female in her early seventies described an experience she'd had when her appendix burst and the subsequent medical care, which informed and uplifted her spiritual well-being during this time of extreme threat to her life. Her spouse took her to the ER at a prominent teaching hospital in the Northeast. She said, "I sat there forever in the ER, and my appendix blew up by the time they got me in to diagnose me four or five hours later." She was diagnosed with appendicitis within five minutes, but the damage had been done by the long delay. She had emergency surgery at four o'clock in the morning. She said, "I was probably sicker than when I'd had cancer. I was so sick because all these toxins were thrown into my whole body when my appendix burst." She had multiple flare-ups related to these toxins, which brought her back to the hospital several times.

During one of these repeat visits, she said she almost died due to internal bleeding. She added, "But no one ever tells you the whole story because they think you don't know your ass from a hole in the ground." She explained she knew much more than she was credited with because she'd grown up with a father who'd started the first poison control center in the United States.[17] The night she almost died, she said she remembered telling herself, "You just have trust in your higher self, and surrender to the medical team because you can't be in charge right now. You have to surrender and hope that whatever's going to happen is going to happen." She said it was the "exceptional care" of the nurse on the night shift that kept her alive through the night. She continued, "The next morning, when of course the surgical team showed up as always at the crack of dawn," she said she thanked them for their excellent care, saying, "'I'm talking to you this morning because you guys made good decisions. I trusted you last night and just totally let go of everything. I trusted my higher self and your higher knowing to keep me here on this planet. I can't thank you enough for all your attention and your caring. You made good decisions for me." She also thanked the night nurse. She said, "You could've heard a pin drop." Adding, "When they finally regained their composure, they worked on the problem of my internal bleeding." Feeling physical safety through trusting that they're receiving the necessary care is a critical component of patient spirituality and holistic caregiving.

Not All Phlebotomists Are Created Equal

Not all phlebotomists (or all nurses, doctors, and/or chaplains) are the same. A middle-aged patient who'd had labs drawn every four hours for five days said, "Very few have the true gift to insert the needle with zero to nominal pain. They call it a 'pinch' but it's really a *stab*." This patient described the multiple bruises she'd had on both of her arms from the numerous misses by the various phlebotomists and nurses who'd drawn blood. The inevitable, "This will pinch" frequently became a miss and another bruise. This patient remembered one gifted phlebotomist who never missed, adding, "If I happened to have my head turned the other way, I couldn't feel the needle going in, including when she poked me on top of my hands, which you'd think would be super sensitive." A middle-aged white female RN in the Pacific Northwest said, "Some patients do have tricky veins to find or they're very dehydrated, so it can be difficult even for an experienced nurse." The important point to note is that excellence in physical caregiving becomes spiritual care when the technical execution of inserting a needle isn't painful, contributing to a patient's internal peace, in contrast to technical ineptitude, which contributes to emotional and spiritual distress.

Patient-Centered Physical Care Is Spiritual Care

After being in the hospital for one week to get her blood pressure under control, a Black mother who was pregnant with her third child went home for two weeks, with a return date scheduled to induce labor. (See also Chapter 4.) She said that throughout this third pregnancy, she'd forthrightly expressed to her obstetrician that she *did not* want a C-section because of the risk factors in general, particularly the higher risk factors for Black women and Black babies. Trained as a social worker, this expectant mother explained, "I had done some reading and taken classes during this third pregnancy, and I knew that the mortality rates for Black mothers and Black babies are much higher than for white mothers and white babies. I did not want to have anything to do with having a C-section and increasing the mortality rate for myself or for my child." She said the advanced reading prepared her for what to expect, but she said it also "caused me to be really on guard about whose care I was in." Because her husband is a nurse, she said it gave her a lot more confidence about how the medical staff would be caring for her, knowing she had an educated advocate who also knew the medical language and what was going on.

When she returned for the planned inducement, she said it became apparent when the dilation didn't progress over the night of her initial labor, and that an emergency C-section needed to be done because of the mother's high blood pressure and the increased stress on the baby. This Black mother reflected, "I wasn't going in expecting a C-section. My whole world just rocked, but I knew that my blood pressure was so high that they thought I was going to stroke out. There really wasn't a choice to make. I had to have an emergency C-section." The mother said after the birth, "They raised the baby up high so I could see her (above the tented area) and they placed her on me soon after. They let us take pictures so we could send them via Messenger to the family." Because this was during Covid, no one could be with her except her husband, and even then, he was only allowed part of the time. The mother and father both expressed how compassionate and understanding the staff was, including respecting the mother's wishes to not have a C-section but helping her to understand how important it was and also how necessary for the baby's safety and well-being. The pregnant mother and father-to-be became part of the solution because they'd been brought into the conversation about what would be best for their unborn child.

Caring for (and about) Patients

A Hispanic male in his mid-seventies who was a Covid-19 patient after the pandemic had waned said what makes the difference between a good and a poor caregiver is "a good one spends time with you, looks you in the eye, and pays attention to who you are." He added, "They're also attentive in coming into the room more frequently to check in and see how you're doing." He said it's all "the little things they do that show they care about who you are and that you're not just another patient taking up a bed on their floor." He explained, of all the various caregivers he experienced, "the one thing that I've been very impressed with is their physical therapists, and also occupational therapists. They all seemed concerned, and they also educated patients very clearly." He added, one was so personally concerned about something that wasn't quite right "she got on the phone with the doctors. Wow! Now this is a physical therapist," commenting, "She didn't have to do that." Instead of just working through a checklist, this physical therapist was personally concerned about the patient.

Physical Miscare Harms Mental and Spiritual Well-being

An ICU patient said her mental and spiritual distress began as physical discomfort during the shift change from the day to the overnight RN. She said she'd pressed the call button during the shift change time frame and was told someone would be there "soon." Since she'd passed the point of physical crisis and was waiting for her sodium to (slowly) rise, she was a "critical care patient," but no longer required the same urgent attention she'd needed earlier. She said her overnight RN was "unresponsive and clearly not available." The ICU patient said initially she simply wanted the upright position on the bed to be lowered (which was out of patient reach), but as time passed, the extended time in the uncomfortable sitting position made her feet fall asleep because they'd been pushed against the metal frame at the end of the bed. The ICU patient was worn out physically, but she also was angry emotionally and frustrated spiritually, explaining "After several hours of trying to sleep sitting up, I felt quite beat up." At one point, the patient also needed to go to the restroom. What had been mild physical discomfort escalated to all-out distress: physical, emotional, and spiritual, so much so that she became tired and wired.

Tired and Wired

In a digital journal to herself during her third night in the hospital and her second night in ICU, she wrote:

> *Digital Journal to Myself 6:33 AM*
> *Can't sleep. I tried. I keep sneezing every time I drift off. I pushed the button at 6 AM. No response. All I can do is blow my nose and wait. This nurse is a lovely person, but also the least proficient one of all. Tonight is the only time I've felt stranded. It's a very helpless feeling. I hear my nurse out there laughing, but still no response to my call button. My phone is plugged in out of reach, so I can't call my spouse. I feel extremely vulnerable; not from my new illness, but from the lack of adequate physical care.*

Digital Journal to Myself 7:09 AM: My RN finally came in to check on some equipment.

> Patient: "I rang the call button at 6:00 AM."
>
> RN: "No you didn't. I'm sitting right outside."
>
> Patient: "I know. I heard you laughing."
>
> The RN challenged back.
>
> Patient: "Maybe the call button doesn't always work. I know that I pushed it. Maybe it doesn't always work."
>
> RN: "You're being rude."
>
> Patient: "I don't want to fight about it. I'm hungry and I want to order breakfast ... "

This super-bad-night of *non*sleep contributed to a critically ill patient being stressed out: physically, emotionally, and spiritually because this argumentative and inattentive caregiver didn't recognize the intersectionality of physical care with spirituality. Spirituality isn't part of me; it's *all of me*.

Spirituality as All of Me

Spirituality is all-encompassing, particularly amidst the vulnerability in a healthcare context. After spending a semester learning about the intersectionality of spirituality in a healthcare context, the closing class discussion invites nursing and social work students to discuss the contributing factors to their spirituality and then to circle the top ten contributing factors they imagined would help or harm a patient's spirituality while they're in a hospital or urgent care facility (see Illustration 2.2). A white female nursing student in her early thirties specified:

Myself: Self-respect, freedom, peace, relationships, morals, fears, assumptions, pessimism, dignity, self-understanding, personal agency, happiness, community, friends, anxieties, safety, respect, ethics, nature, personal maturity, healing, compassion.Patient: fear, pain, respect, sexual orientation, substance abuse, equality/inequality, religious beliefs/values/practices, autonomy, sex/gender, safety, disabilities.[18] This nursing student said, while there are many factors that contribute to a patient's holistic spiritual well-being, she explained, "I chose these words because they encompass a patient's possible emotions during a healthcare visit and also their view of themselves in that context." The newly pinned and graduated nurse added, "Healthcare visits can be stressful, multi-faceted, and sometimes even dehumanizing. Keeping the concept that all patients are human beings with human feelings and have their own personal autonomy and goals at the forefront helps to keep healthcare workers accountable for treating them with dignity and respect."[19]

A white female nursing student in her early thirties said, when she considered what would contribute to a patient's holistic health, "the words that caught my attention were those of harm more than help. It's always possible to become stronger in one's spirituality, but when you're in the hospital, it's usually for a negative reason and I think that shakes a person's spirituality." She explained, "Factors such as pain, distress, anxiety, decreased abilities, discomfort, expectations, and dignity contribute to a patient's spirituality." She added, "However, positive factors include personal spiritual practices and religion, personal values, and health. I believe each of these has an impact on spirituality."[20] Another newly graduated nursing student summarized how spirituality as *all of me* intersects with a patient's healing and wholeness:

- Compassion: Compassionate care from healthcare providers fosters a sense of connection and understanding, which can significantly impact a patient's spiritual well-being.
- Music: As a board-certified music therapist, I truly believe music as therapy provides comfort, evokes emotions, increases communication, and provides a safe space for individuals to express themselves.
- Healthiness: Physical health is closely linked to spiritual well-being. When patients receive proper healthcare and support for their physical ailments, it contributes to their overall sense of well-being, including spiritual well-being.
- Meaning of life: Discussions about the purpose and meaning of life, often deeply rooted in religious values, can provide patients with a sense of purpose, hope, and broader perspective, contributing to spiritual well-being.
- Religious values: For many individuals, religious values are integral to their spiritual well-being. Healthcare providers acknowledging and respecting these values can offer spiritual support aligned with the patient's beliefs, fostering a sense of spiritual comfort.
- Acceptance: Feeling acceptance for who someone is, including their beliefs, background, health condition, and values, contributes significantly to a patient's spiritual well-being. Acceptance creates an environment where patients feel understood and respected.
- Stress: Techniques such as mindfulness, meditation, and prayer can help patients manage their stress level and find inner peace, positively impacting their spiritual health.
- Physical comfort: Creating a comfortable environment for patients, whether through pain management or a soothing ambiance, contributes to their overall health and aids in their spiritual well-being.
- Inclusion and safety: Being free from discrimination or exclusion is crucial for fostering a sense of spiritual well-being.
- Equity: Ensuring fair and equitable access to healthcare services without discrimination based on someone's beliefs, backgrounds, and socio-economic status is essential.[21]

Another nursing student in their mid-twenties said, "Kindness, expressed through compassionate and empathetic care, creates a supportive environment which addresses the patient's emotional and spiritual health." She said it's also important to acknowledge the healing process, explaining, "This is not solely physical. It involves both emotional and spiritual dimensions. Integrating these elements into patient care not only aids in the recovery from illness but also nurtures a patient's overall spiritual health."[22] Another new nurse specified, "Patients should have a supportive community, whether it be family or friends. Caregivers need to help patients maintain their dignity, which is also highly important for their spiritual well-being," adding, "Some things that could harm your patient's spiritual well-being would be injustices, food insecurity, housing insecurity, trauma, loneliness, and discomfort." A Korean American male in his early thirties and newly graduated nursing student highlighted:

> **Pros for a patient:** physical comfort, self-respect, political, dignity, health, transcendence; beliefs and values; delight; freedom; ethics; hopes; morals; peace; joy; Higher Power; family; a spouse or partner; friends; respect; compassion; being kind and considerate; safety; justice; nature; dignity; spiritual practices; and healing.
>
> **Cons against a patient:** physical discomfort; physical, emotional, psychological, or spiritual distress; physical, emotional, psychological, or spiritual pain; chronic illness; being unhealthy; anger; fear; verbal, physical, emotional, or psychological abuse; stress; death of a loved one such as a spouse or parent; adversity; anxieties; their geographic location; disabilities; rape; substance abuse; pessimism; insecurity; and inequality.[23]

Patient autonomy and choice are nearly always selected by future nurses as being critically important for a patient's spirituality. They also consistently identify physical comfort or discomfort, distress of any kind (physical, emotional, psychological, or spiritual), healing, and being kind and considerate.

A newly pinned white female nurse in her mid-twenties said patient spirituality also includes the people who are providing care. She explained, "It's also important to maintain "an overall sense of compassion, no matter the patient's financial or social status because everyone has a right to receive proper health care services."[24] Another nursing graduate said it's important to acknowledge, "since most patients don't plan to end up in the hospital, outside factors such as stress, anxiety, and physical discomfort around their illness or injury can negatively impact their views on spirituality. There's fear of the unknown and frustration with pain and discomfort."[25] Spirituality is never *part* of a patient. Rather, it intersects with literally every aspect of their physical care. Spiritual care with patients is influenced by a caregiver's own death anxiety and their reflective practice, which examines personal mortality as an aspect of spiritual maturity.[26]

9 (Reducing) Death Anxiety

"Life is *precious* because life is *precarious*, bounded between the finite physical limitations of birth and death ... Death is what makes life precious."[1] Because we can't and don't live forever on this earth, we're limited to the time between our physical birth and our physical death, a timeframe that philosophers and theologians refer to as *human finitude* because of the finiteness of human life, contributing to what I've termed a *spirituality of finitude*.[2] It's a spirituality that embraces the reality of death, not in a doomsday or morbid sense. Rather, by accepting death as being normal for all human beings, we can embrace the preciousness of the here and now with gratitude and joy. Acknowledging the inevitability of death also lessens the sting of death because it becomes an *un*feared given of life. From the point of our birth, we're moving toward our (future) death. If caregivers can't acknowledge, accept, and prepare for their own death, their discomfort and death anxiety will spill over to the patients they're caring for because anxiety is contagious.[3]

Human Finitude

Finitude is a derivative of the word finite. It's used in philosophy and theology to address the reality that we're all going to die. Death is a part of life. Time itself may go on into infinity, but each person's life is finite, conscribed within their particular parameters of how long they'll live on this earth. Life is finite. Life has a physical beginning and a physical end.[4]

Death

Death is the reality of human existence, what Heidegger called our "*ownmost* possibility."[5] The closer we get to the possibility of death, the more we realize our finitude, our shortness of living. It's also this ever-present possibility for death that highlights the things left undone, the possibilities we haven't quite gotten to. Death is a negatively perceived finite end to the positively embraced life of living. Even for the most religiously faithful, death still represents an ending to this life on earth with the people whom we know, love, and want to be physically near. Death is the Great Divide, the Grim

Reaper, the Ultimate Equalizer. But death also is an invitation for so much more. Instead of fearing death, let death be what shapes how you live life. In other words, live while you're still alive.

Hiddenness of Death

Another (related) problem is that death hides itself so the general population doesn't have to see it or deal with it until a prettied-up corpse is neatly boxed up in a coffin at a funeral home. Death is hidden away.[6] Hospitals are associated with birth and healing, but hospitals also are associated with death. Sick people, particularly older adults, will put off going to the ER because they "don't want to go to the hospital and die." Somewhere in the mid-nineteenth century, there was a gradual decline in any public witness to death. Friends, family, and neighbors were no longer included; death was for the dying and the dying *alone*. This separation changed how the general public viewed the end of life. It also changed how medical science viewed death.[7] By removing death from society, shutting it behind closed doors in hospitals and other institutions, it removes having to think about or "deal with" dying and death.

Prolonging life through the various and sundry scientific and medical advancements seeks to delay death, what Gadamer calls "a fading away of the experience of the self. This process culminates in the gradual disappearance of the experience of death,"[8] which separates death from the reality of human life. We know it's out there somewhere, but it's been carefully hidden away and anesthetized so it no longer seems like it's really going to happen to us. Logically we acknowledge death is a part of life, but emotionally and spiritually we move into denial. With all of the artificial ways to scientifically and medically extend life, death becomes distanced or removed from everyday life.[9] Dying and death are done behind closed medical doors.

Death Anxiety

Patients experience death anxiety in differing levels of intensity. A Jewish American woman in her mid-seventies said when her appendix burst and she was in critical condition, she was at peace with dying, but that she was concerned for her husband who "wasn't ready yet" for her to die. A white female ICU patient in her early sixties said she was prepared for the possibility of death. She explained she'd had a "very full and active life," but her death anxiety was that she didn't want to die in the city or state where she was languishing in ICU. She said she'd recently had a conversation with someone a decade older who'd planned to move, but then they'd been diagnosed with colon cancer, which delayed their relocation nearly two years. The ICU patient explained she and her husband were in the process of listing their home for sale and that they'd plan to move back to the West Coast. She said, at one point while she was in ICU, she'd texted her husband, "Get me out of HERE!" She clarified, "I meant the city and state where we were currently living; not ICU." (See Illustration 9.1.)

The stage four cancer patient in his early twenties who's religiously disaffiliated and whose spirituality is centered on his personal autonomy and agency told his mother if he didn't survive that he'd feel like his life had been worthwhile because of what the cancer research hospital learned through the experimental treatments he'd been receiving. The wife of an elderly lung transplant patient said that continuing with education in the midst of trying to heal "is what keeps you going." The anxiety is there, but the focus shifts elsewhere. A sense of a future keeps you going, as Hans-Georg Gadamer argues, "We can be said to have a future for as long as we are not aware that we have no future. The repression of death reflects the will of life."[10] It also reflects anxiety about dying and death.

Dying Well

Reflecting on a passage in Nouwen's book, *Our Greatest Gift*, when this Catholic priest discusses the death of a dear friend, a nursing student wrote:

> Nouwen ponders the question, "Where and how do you want to die?"[11] I have probably pondered this question more often than the average person has. In my work in a memory care unit in a nursing home, I help several people die every year. I consider their deaths a "good death." Most of those I care for are in their 90s, have lived a long life, and have the opportunity to die surrounded by family. This is exactly how I hope to die someday. For me, the worst death would be unexpected, like if I were to die today in a motor vehicle accident, completely unprepared. I am not ready to die today, there's much that I've not done, or said, so much left unfinished. I think to myself from time to time, I should always live in a way that if I were to die, I could be satisfied with the life I've lived. But then I become so busy, that I tell myself "When this is over..." "I will do that later..." "When I am not so busy... then I will... pray more, visit my dad, call my sisters, and spend more time with my husband and children."[12]

Illustration 9.1 *Get Me Out of Here* pastel painting of Morro Bay, California, reflects a patient's urgency to be released from ICU and prepare to relocate (back to) the West Coast. The artwork was her post-release spiritual selfcare. © Helen T. Boursier

Dying well shifts the focus from the fact *that* we're all going to die to embracing the reality of death as the culmination of life, thereby giving ourselves permission to cherish life in this moment. Instead of fearing our future death. Dying well means to live intentionally in the present with gratitude, appreciation, and respect for life. Instead of fearing death, dying well embraces living *life*.

Befriending Death

A defense mechanism is to avoid thinking or talking about our own mortality, but such denial can interfere with caregiving, particularly around people who are critically and terminally ill. Their vulnerability sparks our vulnerability, which can become a tangible, visceral anxiety about our own death, which then overflows and interferes with our caregiving. Withdrawal, denial, and/or ignoring death doesn't and won't make death disappear. Instead, caregivers need to spend reflective time considering their own death anxiety, including what triggers it and how to become comfortable with the reality of their mortality, beginning by naming death as death.[13] Naming death allows dying to be another normal aspect of what it means to be alive. Dying isn't an illness. In contrast to being death-phobic, Nouwen offers befriending death as the solution to fear or phobia about the inevitable finale of each human's life.[14] Instead of focusing on "my life," befriending death looks to the interconnectedness of all human beings: past, present, and future. It means the "worthiness" of life isn't dependent solely upon "my" life alone, but on the greater connections with the world. Nouwen believes, "In our dying, we become parents of generations to come,"[15] through our connection with the entire human race. Befriending death leads to *caring well*.

Caring Well

Nouwen explains, "Befriending our own death and helping others to befriend theirs are inseparable. In the realm of the Spirit of God, living and caring are one."[16] It's an interconnectedness that embraces diversity of all variations to care for all those who cross our paths. Nouwen specifies, "To care for the dying is to keep saying, 'You are the beloved daughter of God, you are the beloved son of God,'"[17] regardless of the myriads of socio-economic-religious-racial-sexual orientation-whatever differences humans use to mark off otherness and exclude. Befriending one's own death is the bridge from our death anxiety to graciously caring for others with loving acceptance. It's Buber's well-known "I-Thou" that's free from the isms and judgments. Caring well is a deliberate choice, just as it's also an intentional decision to die well.[18] It's a choice to move from being a robot-correct-machine providing technically perfect patient care to someone who completes the same actions with excellence, but with their heart and compassion clearly evident through their words, actions, and attitude.

Reflecting on Nouwen's insight, "Believing that our lives come to fulfillment in dependence requires a tremendous leap of faith . . . explains why it so important to care for the dying,"[19] a nursing student wrote about being present with patients who are dying:

I consider it a great privilege to care for someone who is dying. I have a sense of awe; I think to myself, "Who the hell am I to be here at this person's death? I am not a family member or close friend. I've not known them their whole life. I've no business attending their deaths." But I'm needed. The family often doesn't know how to care for the dying person, and the dying person cannot care for themselves. I'm very good at caring for dying people. I understand the dying process, I know what needs to be done. I know how to sit in silence with someone who is dying and with their family. I know how to teach others how to care for a dying person.

It's extremely important for the aide and the nurse to remember, and respect the fact, that we take care of people in the most vulnerable of circumstances. We care for them when they are disabled, sick, and in crisis. We see them naked, help them bathe, and go to the bathroom. We help them die. We must be very conscious of how vulnerable they are to us, and we must have a very high level of respect for this fact. Too often, it can become so routine that we forget to be sensitive to the fact, for example, that nakedness makes a person feel very vulnerable. We see naked people all day long, so we forget to be sensitive.[20]

The nursing student said, by living in solidarity with those she cares for, she remains mindful, "Someday, I will be in their shoes."[21]

To Tell or Not to Tell

Being personally prepared to die well leads to *caring well*, which includes how to share the news with a patient and their family that their condition has become terminal. Caring well doesn't mean hiding the truth from a patient with the misguided idea it's somehow more compassionate for the patient.[22] Elisabeth Kübler-Ross explains in *On Death and Dying*, "The question should not be 'Should we tell ... ?' but rather 'How do I share this with my patient?'"[23] Nouwen's concept of caring well helps to facilitate dying well by being fully present in solidarity with the patient. Instead, as Paul Ramsey proposes in *The Patient as Person*, when medical professionals can no longer solve the health problem and death becomes the marker for their "failure" at conquering a disease, the patient becomes the recipient of their doctor's inattention as the MD avoids being around a case that has "failed." Ramsey observes, "Desertion [of doctors] is more choking than death, and more feared." Ramsey explains the biggest problem for a dying patient "is how not to die alone."[24] Caring well includes the full cycle, from birth through death, without dodging the dying by avoiding being present.

From the Family's Perspective

With her son's stage four cancer in view, his mother said she realized, "They could have come and told me that my son had incurable cancer and that he was gonna die in a few months. I could have gotten that news—thankfully I didn't. She added, "But when you have to impart bad news to somebody, deliver it in a compassionate way, and then be there for people to help and comfort the family and also to give them a chance to grieve." She added, "I think being present is important. As uncomfortable as it is, if you have to deliver somebody really horrible news, be compassionate in whatever capacity that's allowable in the situation." She said she'd also hope nurses would be more proactive about "letting people know that if they want news to get to their relatives, to make sure that the patient knows what to sign so their family can know how they're doing." She explained, "It doesn't hurt to remind people of the importance of keeping their families in the loop, especially when we're in a pandemic situation, which adds another layer of unpleasantness." She remarked the pandemic might seem like a distant and extreme past tense scenario, but there would be other instances, including distance, which prevent family members from being present. She said the isolation is particularly harsh "when it's a terminal situation or something like cancer because everybody's antsy and on edge because cancer scares the bejesus out of everybody." She added that the need for connection through communication "clearly applies much more broadly, particularly with something like heart disease or a stroke that's potentially incapacitating or lethal." Caregivers have to confront their own feelings about their personal mortality before they can be fully present with patients who are confronted with their own (un)expected mortality.

Embracing Life Respects the Reality of Death

A *spirituality of finitude* is a spirituality that embraces life because of the inevitable (future) death.[25] That life is differentiated from death might seem too obvious, but it's the intersections with life because of death that dispel fear of death. It's by rediscovering, refocusing, and recentering on the whole human being, between physical birth and physical death, which offer the possibility for "personal identity and wholeness of self to emerge."[26] When the emergence of the whole self, body, mind, spirit/soul, is framed in the reality of finitude, the shortness of human life makes each moment much more precious. Things that didn't matter, now do. What once mattered becomes superfluous and unimportant.

Clergy and Chaplain Reflections on Dying and Death

Reflecting on her pastoral work with various congregations, a middle-aged white female ordained clergy said, "The end-of-life moments and the discussions around them have been some of the most meaningful of my ministry. What I've heard over the years was not so much a looking forward to whatever is next, for many of the folks didn't believe in an actual heaven, but an exploration into the value of life." She explained they'd asked questions like, "'Does my life matter? How will it go on? What continues after we die?'" The pastor added, "The hope was found in the mystery that life and love supersede physical limitations and continue. Certainly, some were looking forward to heaven, but in my experience, the questions more often centered on the intrinsic meaning of life and each of us as part of a process much greater than any one life."[27] A board-certified middle-aged white male hospital chaplain with twenty-four years of experience said, "People who suffer due to illness, body, mind, and spirit oftentimes desire for meaningful connection, and the majority of these connections have less to do with a higher vertical power of transcendence, and more to do with re-connecting with those around them. This is their paradise, their spiritual healthcare."[28] It's by accepting the reality of their finitude, their impending death, that they're able to continue to lean into and embrace whatever precious life they have remaining.

Preparing for Death

In response to Nouwen's questions: "Are we preparing ourselves for our death, or are we ignoring death by keeping busy? Are we helping each other to die, or do we simply assume we are going to always be here for each other? Will our death give new life, new hope, and new faith to our friends, or will it be no more than another cause for sadness?"[29] an Indigenous male student in his twenties, whose mother was in the final stage of her life with chronic obstructive pulmonary disease (COPD) wrote: "My family is definitely ignoring death by keeping busy. COPD is something that cannot be cured, with every hospital visit she moves into a new phase of life." The patient's son explained the slow decline of his mother and the various close calls she'd had that'd brought her to the ER. After each visit to the hospital, her abilities lessened, and her world at home became more and more limited. He said, "After another hospital visit, she could no longer make it the distance to her bathroom down the hall, so my dad bought a new house, a single-story house so she wouldn't have to climb any stairs, and one where the bathroom was right outside her door, as close as it can be without us just moving her bed into the bathroom." Writing from his mother's bedside in a hospital, he wrote she'd declined further. She was unable to walk even the short distance to the bathroom, so they'd brought a commode into her bedroom. Her son explained, "She now only has to take one step from her bed to the commode. Yet this still causes her to rest twenty minutes to catch her breath." Her son added,

> *My family, especially my dad, thinks that as long as we keep buying the best equipment, and keep taking her into the hospital, that it'll help. She's at a point in COPD where most people consider hospice, which could give her meds so that these twenty minutes of trying to catch her breath, this "air hunger" as the doctor calls it, would be reduced significantly, and overall can improve her quality of life. My family however thinks that the word "hospice" and "quitting" are one in the same.*

The busy-ness and denial aren't helpful for the family, and they're not helpful for the patient. Somewhere during his mother's declining journey, her son said he came to accept her failing health and impending death. Because she recognizes that he's accepted her present condition and future death, it's this son whom she wants to spend time with. He doesn't want his mother to die any less than the rest of his family, but he's accepted it, and she takes comfort in his calming and caring presence.

Befriending death leads to what Nouwen terms *a good death*, which "is a death in solidarity with others."[30] For Nouwen, it's this celebration of interconnection with all of humanity that makes it possible to have a good death. He explains, "Instead of separating us from others, death can unite us with others; instead of being sorrowful, it can give rise to new joy; instead of simply ending life, it can begin something new."[31] He believes it's a choice between clinging onto this life as if that's all there is, "as if death were absurd and we had better not talk about it, or we can choose to claim our divine childhood and trust that death is the painful but blessed passage that will bring us face-to-face with our God."[32] It's all about perspective, whether "this is it," or whether, as has been the case documented in *Death Stories of Hindu, Tibetan, Buddhist, and Zen Masters*, "death is not death but liberation."[33] Similarly, "in the Zen tradition, to die is nothing special,"[34] or in Tibet, where "death is regarded as a mere point on a continuum marking the transition from one form of consciousness to another."[35] It's ultimately about preparing for death by owning up to the fact that we're all going to die. How we prepare for this reality becomes the grace and graciousness we exude as we're sitting in solidarity on a deathwatch with a patient or a beloved one who's making the transition from life to death.

Dying Well by "Entering a Second Childhood"

Reflecting on a passage in Nouwen's book, *Our Greatest Gift*, a nursing student wrote she was surprised but agreed with Nouwen when he said, "becoming a child—entering a second childhood—is essential to dying a good death" and that "life is lived from dependence to dependence."[36] The nursing student observed:

> *One thing I frequently notice about patients that really bothers me, is that they apologize for needing help and taking up too much time. There was a woman today who called frequently for the bathroom, and apologized every time. I tried to reassure her every time that it was no bother, and please, call as often as you need to. In referring back to Nouwen, it's hard for us to be dependent on others. I do not wish for patients to apologize for needing help, but I can relate that I might do the same thing. Because I take care of people who are sick, elderly, and disabled, I try to frequently remind myself that I too, could be in their shoes someday. I'm no better than anyone I care for. I often hear fellow nurses and aides talk about how they never want to end up like their patients, and they never want to live in a nursing home. I tell myself; it's okay if I someday end up in a nursing home. I try to have a sense of solidarity with my patients. I too, could one day be diagnosed with multiple sclerosis, have a stroke that leaves me with hemiplegia, or a tragic accident that leaves me disabled. I too, could be just like them, I try to remind myself.*

The student added that their spouse's grandfather "seemed to understand the circle of life and the need to become childlike in death. He did not become angry as he was dying of cancer and became completely dependent on family to care for him." The nursing student recalled, "When he was incontinent, and had to rely on my mother-in-law (his daughter) to clean him up and bathe him, he turned to her and said, 'I'm helping you to build character.' I think he's a role model of someone who's embraced his death."[37] Preparing for the reality of death is a deliberate journey that moves forth from, and also engenders, spiritual maturity.

Spiritual Maturity

Spiritual maturity is a lifelong journey, a quest that integrates personal maturity with spirituality.[38] It respects and prioritizes the greater good, individually and collectively, over personal (selfish) aims and desires. A retired hospital chaplain said, "A characteristic of spiritual maturity is equanimity due to the intimacy and trust in a greater reality and purpose other than my own."[39] Personal maturity isn't easily achieved, partly because of the crowd mentality and the views of a collective group. It takes guts and gumption to separate from peer pressure, not only during our formative years but lifelong. Spiritual maturity requires the courage to think for yourself about moral, ethical, and justice concerns with selflessness and compassion. It shifts the view off-center, from the self to the other. In order to find what Rohr terms, the "True Self,"[40] we have to let go of the preconceived, inherited, and often biased perspectives that have undergirded our assumptions, expectations, and worldview. Spiritual maturity lets go of self and looks for how to be present in solidarity with those around us. Instead of being me-centered, spiritual maturity welcomes differences with openness, hospitality, and compassion.

Spiritual Maturity in a Healthcare Context

During a final class discussion on spiritual maturity, responding to a peer, a nursing student differentiated between openness and tolerance, saying, "You discuss spiritual maturity as being foundational for understanding, openness, and tolerance. I wholeheartedly agree that spiritual maturity does include a lot of understanding and openness, but I would argue for a different word than tolerance." The student clarified,

> *When I think of tolerance, I think of **allowing** someone else to take up the space that they do in this world. You're allowing someone else to live their life and choose their spiritual pathway, when in reality, they don't have to ask permission. I think the idea of tolerance contributes almost to the ideals of oppression in which one group has to seek approval from another group, when in reality, we're all equal beings.[41]*

Instead of "allowing" or granting permission, this nursing student said spiritual maturity requires unilateral acceptance and openness to the differentness of another. It's not about gaining approval; it's about complete and total acceptance. Similarly, another student said, "Spiritual maturity is actively working to respect individuals from all backgrounds and walks of life. It's embracing everyone's uniqueness and taking the time to develop an understanding of where they come from."[42]

A female Muslim nursing student in her mid-thirties said, "Spiritual maturity encapsulates a progressive and enhanced understanding of spirituality, which encompasses the individual's advancement, moral cognizance, and perception of their interrelatedness of the self with their fellow human beings and the universe." She added, "Spiritual maturity constitutes a journey that includes introspection, compassion, morally upright conduct, conversion from discord, and involvement in communal activities."[43] Spiritual maturity isn't only *my* journey of growth. It also includes developing a better understanding of what spirituality means for other people. Spiritual maturity reshapes perspective to foster (attitude) reorientation.

10 (Attitude) Reorientation

Caring for a patient's physical well-being overlaps with their spiritual and emotional comfort. It's an attitude reorientation that understands it's never part of me; it's always *all of me*. Compassionate and spiritually attuned nurses, doctors, social workers, medics, and others recognize that each of their interactions with patients contributes to holistic caregiving through the intersectionality of a patient's body, mind, and spirit.

(Spiritual) Care Intersections with Physical Care

The spiritual care disconnects explained in the earlier chapters illustrate how the attitudes and actions of caregivers rendering physical care (inadvertently) have harmed patients' spiritual and emotional well-being. Patient-centered caregiving that's spiritually savvy recognizes the intersectionality of physical care with emotional and spiritual well-being. Describing the best caregivers and why, an ICU patient specified:

- The phlebotomist I had for my last two days in the hospital who had no misses, no mistakes, no unnecessary infliction of pain.
- The ICU floor manager who was like the *hostess with the mostess* with kindness and compassion overflowing.
- My final RN in the ICU because he was prompt, efficient, thorough and didn't get rattled or put off by my questions.
- The supervising MD in the ICU who was kind and patient. He never ever talked over me. He listened and had genuine concern for my distress.
- The kitchen person who delivered my meals to the surgical floor. She treated me as if I were a dearly beloved family member. I experienced nonjudgmental acceptance.

Unilateral Acceptance with Nonjudgementalism

A nursing student said, "It's a temptation for nurses to judge patients for their infirmity, describing it as a 'politics of consequence for their own sin,' so they're not treated equally." The nursing student said this judgmentalism is particularly prevalent and problematic "when we see people come in with drug and alcohol problems, or even when we see a diabetic who doesn't take good care of their health, or the heart failure patient doesn't take their medications." Making observations from their clinicals, this nursing student added, "It's tempting for us as nurses to be indifferent towards these patients and to not treat them with the dignity and respect that they deserve." Referring to concentration camp survivor and Nobel Peace Prize winner, Elie Wiesel's lecture on indifference, this student said, "When we're indifferent towards patients, it takes away our own humanity."[1] The student also highlighted the American Nurses Association Code of Ethics, which states a nurse is required to practice with compassion and respect for the inherent dignity and worth, and unique attributes of every person.[2] The student emphasized, "We are called to care for our patients and not judge them or be indifferent towards them."[3]

Cultural (and Spiritual) Humility

When studying cultural competence in comparison to cultural humility, my nursing and social work students consistently place themselves at the point of being "pre" culturally competent. They realize they aren't as culturally competent as they want or need to be, but they also acknowledge that they're "working on it." Cultural humility is more difficult because humility in general seems to be the opposite of the inbred human condition. Pride is the norm. Humility is counter-intuitive, particularly after a hard-earned journey to become an RN, MD, chaplain, or ordained clergy. Cultural humility challenges this pride of self, pride of place.

The Basics of Cultural Humility

Cultural humility fosters equity, equality, and respect. It's an attitude reorientation that requires lifelong learning and critical self-reflection about attitudes, bias, assumptions, heritage, point of view, and what's shaped that perspective about literally anything and everything. It includes a self-examination of any baggage from the past that informs a particular viewpoint in the present.[4] It's about being honest about who we are, what we believe, and why we believe it. Interpretation "is inescapable . . . even the most mindless couch potato does not live by instinct alone."[5] Each one of us becomes a collective *We* of the various ideas of those who've gone before us. *I* can never be a solo Self for *I* actually am the *We* of the diverse perspectives that have shaped my *I*.[6] Cultural humility requires lifelong learning and self-reflection, particularly about biased assumptions and power imbalances, to reshape how we interpret anything and everything. Like a pair of glasses, cultural humility is the lens we must view life through.

Healthcare institutions also have an important role to play in cultural humility by modeling what this means at all levels, from the top down and from the bottom up.[7] Cultural humility acknowledges equality and equity at all levels because of the interrelationship of being human. Whereas cultural competence moves forth from a sense of pride based on "my" knowledge about people who are different from me, cultural humility is powered by an openness to *not* knowing everything and also not needing to be number one. Cultural humility is built upon relationships, which are shaped through silence by listening.

Listening

Listening requires silence, attentiveness to the speaker, and being open to hear what someone else is saying. Listening also includes stepping aside from the power/powerless dynamic inherent in the caregiver-care recipient relationship to *really* listen. Empathic listening doesn't (mentally) compare what someone's saying to what I think I know. It also isn't "multitasking" and doing whatever practical caregiving tasks while also saying you're listening (when you're probably not). Listening requires being fully present with a patient, with eye contact and rapt attention to what they're saying. It also requires physical silence (not talking; not interrupting) and an internal spiritual attending to the spoken words and visual body and facial movements to discern what a patient is saying through their body, mind, and spirit.[8]

Deep Listening

There's listening, and then there's *deep listening*. In *Peace Is Every Step: The Path of Mindfulness in Everyday Life* Vietnamese Buddhist Thich Nhat Hanh offers an important reminder of the difficulty of being centered in the present moment. Instead of being fully present, our minds are rewinding to the past or fast-forwarding to the future. We're never fully present here, in this moment. Without this sense of centeredness and presence at the moment, it's too easy not to listen, and certainly not to hear, what a patient's saying verbally and nonverbally.[9] Hanh proposes, "Listening is an art we must cultivate."[10] The Zen master explains:

> *The practice of deep listening consists of keeping compassion alive in your heart the whole time you are listening. You do not listen in order to judge, criticize, or evaluate. You listen for one reason alone: to offer the other person a chance to express him- or herself. That person is going to say things that irritate you. He or she might express disapproval of you, heap blame on you, say things that are false. You have to be ready to listen to anything. You have to say to yourself, "I'm listening to this person not to criticize or judge him. I'm listening to give him a chance to express himself, to provide him with some relief—that's all.*[11]

Being fully present in the moment makes deep listening possible, which the Sikh-American activist and author Valarie Kaur describes in *See No Stranger* as "an act of surrender." She explains, "We risk being changed by what we hear. When I really want to hear another person's story, I try to leave my preconceptions at the door and draw close to their telling. I am always partially listening to the thoughts in my own head when others are speaking, so I consciously quiet my thoughts and begin to listen with my senses."[12] Listening includes hearing and seeing the feelings the words are expressing.[13] Deep listening leads to what Hahn terms *compassionate listening*,[14] also known as *active listening* in a healthcare context, which means exactly what it sounds like: being actively present to listen (and hear) what the patient is trying to communicate. Active listening includes curiosity, which asks questions until a caregiver fully understands a patient's concerns, not only a surface complaint or request but the bigger picture of what's at stake. Asking questions and carefully listening to a patient's responses helps them to become agents and active participants in their care. Instead of being passive recipients, patients become agents of their own healing and wholeness. Attitude reorientation through cultural humility listens, hears, and accepts all of who a patient is.

Acceptance

A Black, male, Muslim nursing student who worked in a large metropolitan hospital in the upper Midwest where patients came from diverse cultural backgrounds said, "I've observed many caregivers tend to not understand, so they make stereotypes and false narratives, all because they don't understand another's way of life."[15] Instead of pigeon-holing someone into category X, acceptance is the heart and soul of cultural humility, a humility that extends to encompass a patient's self-understanding and description of their condition. Acceptance respects their level of pain and suffering as a patient feels it, experiences it, or describes it. As the Black male nurse supervisor emphasized earlier, "Their pain is their pain." Their pain doesn't get to be mediated through a litany of caregiver assumptions, presuppositions, and biases about a patient (see Chapter 6).[16] Stepping aside from any position of power and authority, whether it's the Nurse Rachet of *One Flew Over the Cuckoo's Nest*, an ICU nurse who proclaimed, "I'm responsible for you now," or an RN who barks, "Silence! No one speaks while I'm doing labs," cultural humility respects the whole patient.

Respect

Respect is intimately related to spirituality because respect is at the core of what every patient said intersects with their spiritual well-being (or not).[17] Spirituality and spiritual well-being are embodied in every aspect of a person's being human. When someone's humanity isn't respected, it puts a visceral dig into their spirituality, their essence of being. How the whole patient is treated can be helpful or harmful. Because of the interconnectedness of body-mind-spirit, harm to one aspect harms the others, just as support or assistance to one also uplifts the others.[18]

Patient Perspectives

The queer wife of Latina heritage who's married to a white transgender male, both in their mid-thirties, described when they "finally found a really amazing nurse practitioner who was just super supportive and understanding," including when her spouse was going through the hormone treatments at the beginning of his trans process. His wife said they were "desperately trying to find a new doctor who would manage his hormone treatment, and this nurse practitioner took extra time to talk to us on the phone to help us try to find a doctor who could care for the hormone treatment." There wasn't any judgment or disrespect for this couple's then-lesbian marriage or the trans process that one had chosen. The nurse practitioner helped them connect with an OBGYN doctor who treats a lot of trans patients. The trans male said this OBGYN doctor was "so amazing, understanding, and respectful of me, and it's been consistent every time I go in." His wife added, the doctor "takes their time, answers our questions, and makes both of us feel like we're both part of the care team together. The doctor really listens and gives verbal understanding, affirmation, and validation." The couple emphasized that there's also no sense of them being treated as "just a number." Instead of feeling rushed like the doctor was hurrying on to their next patient, they said they felt listened to, heard, and respected. In striking contrast to the bad experiences during his top surgery, the trans male said, "I left this doctor's office feeling like, 'Wow! It's really such a good feeling to be respected,'" adding, "It makes you appreciate good doctors a whole lot more, that's for sure."

Reiterating a common lament of the patients in this research project, a thirty-year-old white male who almost had a finger, hand, or arm amputated due to a nasty infection that went underdiagnosed for several days said his "parting shot" for future caregivers is to realize, "We're not numbers. I know patients might seem that way sometimes because you see a thousand people a day, but in the most recent experiences I've had with medical in general during the past couple of years, I've felt like a number." He added, "Even though the surgeon who worked on my hand was brilliant, for example, I still felt like I was just another case." He emphasized, "It's really important to make everybody feel like their being there matters, because it matters to them. It could be a joyous experience, like when my wife gave birth to a beautiful little baby, or it could be something scary, like losing a finger, but every one of these patients is a patient who has worries and fears." He closed, saying, "It's important to show a little bit of humility and also a little bit of humanity."

Revisiting Autonomy and Agency

Anyone who's ever been admitted to the hospital through the ER for anything other than something "obvious" like a broken bone has experienced their loss of autonomy and agency, as one test after another is done during a *medical scavenger hunt* to figure out what and where the broken parts are. Personal agency and autonomy as a human being disappear amidst the amazing miracle of medical science. The human being's spiritual, emotional, and mental health tend to be ignored during their physical care, inadvertently harming their holistic well-being. This patient could then be swept away to surgery or ICU without any voice or vote. They might receive a cursory explanation using medical language about the pending procedure (already) a fait accompli, while this urgent care patient is a numb bystander and object of care. Kübler-Ross observes a critically ill patient "is often treated like a person with no right to an opinion. It is often someone else who makes the decision if and when and where a patient should be hospitalized. It would take so little to remember that the sick person too has feelings, has wishes and opinions, and has—most important of all—the right to be heard."[19] Instead of working to save a seemingly inanimate object of care, exceptional medical attention reorients and acknowledges the integrated humanity of each patient. Doing so will engender empathy to further enhance caregiving.

Empathy, Compassion, and Caring

Empathy is often used interchangeably with sympathy, but these emotive feelings, which shape response through action, have nuanced differences. Martin Luther King, Jr. distinguishes between pity and sympathy, with the former a kind of "paternalism that no self-respecting person can accept." Sympathy is "the personal concern that demands the giving of one's soul."[20] Reflecting on these nuances, a nursing student wrote:

> *King's discussion reminded me strongly of teachings of Dr. Brené Brown, only Dr. Brown defines pity as sympathy, and sympathy as empathy. In this view, sympathy is feeling sorry for someone, and empathy is feeling sorry with someone. Dr. Brown describes crawling down into a hole to be with someone, becoming vulnerable, and feeling their feelings with them. This is a beautiful way to describe true compassion and a point of view that leads us to be truly altruistic and non-judgmental of each other. Imagine, when considering our neighbor, if we truly took the time to try to see things from their point of view, experience what they experience, and feel what they feel. Dr. Brown builds on*

the concepts taught by Dr. King and helps elucidate what it means and looks like to have empathy for another person.[21]

In order to be empathetic, a few things must happen. First, it requires seeing the other person as a human being, not as "the other." When we see someone as the other (the other race, other religion, other nationality, other group, etc.) and not as a fellow human, we cannot have empathy. It requires vulnerability and disregard for oneself.[22]

This nursing student concluded, "This kind of sympathy/empathy cannot be legislated or required by law." Instead, it must originate and move forth willingly from the hearts of human beings who want to care and to care empathetically. Empathy inspires compassion.

Compassion Informs Caring

Compassion is enacted empathy.[23] In the *Value of Compassion*, Nancy Rue differentiates compassion from sympathy, explaining, "Sympathy is a close cousin. But *compassion is not sympathy*."[24] Sympathy includes a deeper concern than pity, including prompting a tangible action. Sympathy is the start of having compassion, but compassion moves forth from a feeling to doing something tangible. Compassion requires action.[25] Compassion not only wants to do something to help but *needs to* as an expression of genuine care and concern. The founder of modern nursing, Florence Nightingale (1820–1910), is known for her work during the Crimean War (1853–6), when she organized a hospital unit to care for wounded soldiers. Her compassion led her to make rounds with the wounded soldiers at night, which gave her the fond title of "the Lady with the Lamp." Compassion goes beyond the call of duty and does a little extra, whatever that something more might be.

For example, the young man who was diagnosed with stage four cancer at age twenty-two remembered three particularly touching acts of caring, totally unrelated to his physical medical care, which uplifted his spirit during the week he underwent three major surgeries during the Covid-19 lockdown. Different caregivers on his team (1) brought him a Lindt chocolate truffle; (2) gave him a pair of shark socks, which he was allowed to wear (uncharacteristically) during his next surgery; and (3) stayed after their shift to play a video game with him, which the patient had brought to the hospital for entertainment but had been too sick and despondent to use. The caregiver came to his room at the end of their shift and played Nintendo with him for an hour. The cancer patient reflected, "That was really touching. It wasn't so much because we were playing Zelda, but because I realized that the nurse took their own time and stayed after with me." Each of these might seem innocuous, but each simple action by a caregiver was profoundly meaningful and spiritually uplifting for a solo patient who desperately needed some TLC.

Buddhist spiritual guru Thich Nhat Hanh suggests, instead of focusing on the negative with the oft-asked "What's wrong?" shift to a positive outlook by asking "What's not wrong?"[26] He's not writing for a healthcare context, but his suggestion highlights the importance of including positive, hopeful, and productive aspects of healing in a caregiving conversation. On a similar note, a chaplain said their first question when they walk into a patient's room is simply, "What can I do to help make your day better?" Or, similarly, "What can I do to help you today?"

Compassionate Care in Maternity

A Hispanic woman in her early thirties who recently gave birth to her second child said she wanted medical professionals who "can be normal human beings and show compassion and understanding in a situation." She said it didn't matter whether it was a difficult or happy situation, but she wanted caregivers to show their compassion through "little thing like saying, 'You've got this, Mom, you can do it.'" Expressing empathy through compassion with encouraging words humanizes patients *and* caregivers. Her husband, who was present for the birth of his first child, said:

> I don't want to come across as if any part of this was a negative experience, but one thing that made me a little bit uncomfortable was they spent, and rightfully so, all of their attention on my wife. But it was new for me too. It was scary for me too. (See Illustration 10.1.) I know my job as a husband was to sit next to my wife and comfort her, but if somebody had leaned over when it was all happening and say, "Don't worry, Dad, this is normal," I think that would've helped me.

Describing the anxiety he'd experienced during the wee hours of the morning when his wife exhausted slept while his eyes remained glued to the baby's heart monitor, the first-time expectant father said:

Illustration 10.1 *New Father: "It's All New to Me Too"* graphite pencil portrait of a new father holding his newborn daughter. © Helen T. Boursier

I don't know the technical name for the heartbeat belt that she wore around her stomach, but the baby would move out of that. My wife and her mom were trying to rest, but I couldn't sleep. I remember looking at this thing going up and down, measuring her contractions, and I remember hearing the heartbeat fade, then I'd look at the machine and see the heartbeat disappear. It was terrifying every single time that happened, and if any one of those nurses had come in there and said "That's normal, the baby's just moving around. This happens all the time, with every pregnancy." If somebody had just told me that, it would've done me a world of good.

Their daughter was born at 3:31 a.m., healthy and whole to her exhausted and relieved parents, particularly the new father whose spirituality had been shaken during his not-knowing. Caring needs to include family members who are struggling with the health issue even as they're present in solidarity with their beloveds.[27]

The "Absolute Best Experience"

Reflecting back on her four experiences being pregnant, with the fourth ending in a miscarriage, a Black mother in her early forties said her "absolute best experience" was birthing her second child in a different hospital and city but in the same state in the Pacific Northwest, where Blacks also are the minority and where she'd earlier had a less than optimal birthing experience with her first child. She said it was her best experience, despite being far from her extended family, because "They listened to me. If I wanted to try a different position, they helped me get to that position. Also, my son was able to be in the hospital with me." She explained that the family had recently moved to this area, "and there was absolutely no one I could trust to leave my firstborn child with. I needed my husband to be with me during labor, so he couldn't be home with their toddler." The hospital allowed the husband/father and son to be a supporting presence during her labor and delivery. The mother remembered, "They were awesome. They brought in extra snacks and drinks for my husband and son, and they were very supportive of us all being there together." (See Illustration 10.2.)

The mother remembered, "My son was so young that he doesn't remember anything about the labor or the birthing, other than what he sees in the pictures we show him." He doesn't remember the details, but it's a mom moment that I will always cherish." She said her spirituality is uplifted "from having family around me, which makes me feel safe and centered." Comparing her second birthing to her first, she said with the first birthing, all of her family were in the delivery room. She said, "I felt relaxed. It's nice to have a choice of who is in the room with you." With the first birth, her choice was that everyone in her family who could come did. With her second birthing, they lived too far from home for anyone to be there, and with the third, the pandemic prevented anyone from being present except her spouse. She emphasized, "It's nice to just have a choice." With her extended family located halfway across the country, she said the bedside manner of the nurses helped her not to feel so alone for the second birth. Compassionate care factors high on this mother's list of important traits for caregivers. She said, "I like being with people who see nursing as a ministry—it's not just a job—it's their calling, much like a minister has a calling."

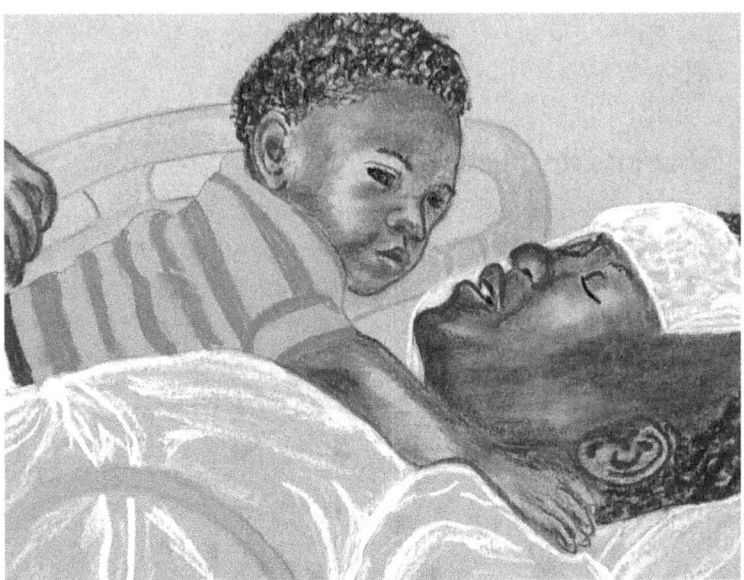

Illustration 10.2 *Labor of Love* pastel portrait on Toned Tan of a toddler resting on his mother as she labors to deliver her second child. Artwork © Helen T. Boursier based on a digital image by the mother's birth photographer JaNae Boyter; shared by permission.

Her husband, a nurse manager, interjected, saying, "The single most important trait for a nurse is to have empathy, followed by not taking something personal when you get yelled at or a patient gets mad at you." He reiterated, "Don't take it personal. The patient has had their freedoms taken away. They're in a traumatized situation. This is not their normal. What's happening, what they're experiencing, is beyond their control and beyond their sense of reality." The nurse manager said, as a result, a patient isn't "going to respond 'normal' because their being in a hospital is not normal." The nurse/father advised, "Imagine yourself in their position, in that bed, going through that treatment. Nurses absolutely must have empathy and compassion and see this profession as a calling. If they don't, then they probably shouldn't be nurses in the first place." He summarized, "Compassion, empathy, and calling are what it means to be a nurse." Compassion overflows into and informs caring.

Caring Comes First

A Black octogenarian who has been hospitalized several times and has experienced a variety of nursing care over his lifetime said, "Knowledge is secondary to caring." He said, of course, caregivers need to know something about what they're doing, but *how* they care matters so much more. He said genuine care and compassion are obvious to a patient when they move from a caregiver's inner spirit of who they are. He said when it's a mask they put on to "just show up" to do the job, it's evident to patients. He said, "I can spot a phony." As nursing literature documents, "Much of nursing has to do with hiding from the patient. *Professionalism* becomes a mask."[28] Patients like this octogenarian observe, "If they're not caring from the heart, it's immediately obvious." He said it's the simple things they do, "like checking on you; not leaving you stranded." He said it also means looking directly at patients and calling them by name. He said, "I'm not just an old Black man who had a hip replacement surgery. I have a name. Call me by my name." He said even though there's usually a whiteboard where they write a patient's name, "most of them don't even look at it." He said, "It makes a big difference, *a big difference*" when caregivers address patients by their name. Patients don't want automated robots who are "task bunnies," as an RN described it. They want caregivers who actually *care*.[29] Attitude reorientation involves emptying one's caregiving self and being fully open in compassionate service with another.

Kenosis

The morning after his only child died at age forty-five from eating disorders and alcohol abuse, her father reflected on the care he'd received along with his daughter during her final weeks and days while she was in hospice in a mid-sized suburban hospital in the southern Midwest. When I asked him how or if he'd experienced spiritual care from the nurses, and if so, what that looked like, he responded, "*Kenosis* is the first word that comes to mind." This Greek Christian theological term means to empty yourself in order to be receptive to God's divine will.[30] This retired Christian clergy said he experienced this from his daughter's caregivers each time they entered her room and listened without having an agenda of their own. He said, "It's obvious that they were concerned." He said what differentiated a genuinely caring nurse from one not so caring was they allowed their heart to be present in their caring. He said he experienced their inner person, their inner beauty, as they emptied themselves of agenda and cared for his daughter. Patients want and expect exceptional medical treatment, but they don't want the rest of them to get dismissed during the medical shuffle. Patients want, need, and deserve to have caregivers who are fully present with them, which transforms the secular sterility of a hospital setting into a sacred space.

11 Sacred Space

In Rudolf Otto's well-known book, *The Idea of the Holy*, he writes about an incomprehensible mystery that arises from someone's experience with the holy. As with spirituality, this sense of the sacred is uniquely experienced, but the commonality is something that's indescribable for its awesomeness, its mystery, its majesty, and the calming peace it brings within a raging storm. It's this sense of the holy that has the potential to move within a secular space of healing, not in a religious sense, though that's certainly possible for the religiously affiliated, but through the nonanxious presence of caring people whose calm through the storm engenders hope in the present for the future. This essence of the sacred is a combination of a patient's spirituality and centeredness, the calm competence of their caregivers, and literally every action and interaction patients experience during the dailiness of healing. A sense of the sacred clings to the space, including, and perhaps especially, during dying and death. Yes, there's ambiguity. Yes, there's uncertainty and even fear, but a feeling of the sacred consecrates each patient's room as a holy place of and for healing.[1]

A white male chaplain in his late sixties who works in a mid-sized urban trauma hospital said, "I've seen, more often than not, a patient proclaims, that the life changes they've had to make due to a chronic or terminal illness which made their suffering worthwhile related to forgiveness, reconciliation, and the ability to speak truth to family members heretofore not possible." The chaplain added, "Instead, they proclaimed their suffering to be worth it and thus found meaning in it." It becomes their holy ground.

Liminal Space in the Present with the Future in View

Chaplains and clergy like to talk about *liminal space*, which marks a transitional time or place when things are changing.[2] In a caregiving context, this liminal sacred place and space includes the caregivers, family, friends, and even strangers who interact with a patient in some context.[3] Womanist chaplain Allen said that chaplains often work in a liminal space, especially when they're "operating at the margins of the margins with patients who are marginalized." It's the calling of a chaplain, in particular, to *walk together with patients in this liminal sacred space.*

Accepting this calling and respecting the sacred space of each patient, a middle-aged white female hospice chaplain said she honors this by how she enters each patient's room. She said she acknowledges that this is their bedroom. She specified, "It's their place and they have control over whether they want me in or not." She honors this sanctity of their space and place.

Responding to Nouwen's point, "One of our worst fears about dying is that we might die without anyone at our side. We want someone to hold our hand, someone to touch us and speak gently to us, someone to pray with us,"[4] a newly graduated nurse said:

> *As a nurse, I choose to be that person, especially if my patient isn't surrounded by loved ones. I choose to love that human as if they're my sister or my brother. Even though I do not know their life, I choose to hold onto them, remember the feeling of their skin and the curve of their face, speak gently to them, and be in solidarity with them for their death. I will wait until their last breath and a little longer. I will take care of their bodies and console their family and friends. I will then cherish my drive home, walk through the threshold of my home, and I will breathe in the air of my life. I will cherish the now to ensure I too can have power in my death and know the fruitfulness of my life-bearing. I will choose to live today to greet death as a friend whenever it decides to come.*[5]

Another new nurse explained how this presence was enacted when she stood at the bedside of a three-year-old who was dying. The nurse described,

> *I was preoccupied with so many tasks that I finally reminded myself to take a moment and just be present. This is so hard to do, especially in the healthcare field. You try to not get too attached to patients. You try to keep your work life and home life separate. It feels like the only possible way to cope with some of the things you see daily. But this is hard to do, and I often struggle with it. I stopped at the bedside in between cares, and I just stroked this child's head.*[6]

The nurse explained their mindfulness of Nouwen's writing about the importance of care being "the loving attention given to another person—not because that person needs it to stay alive or some insurance company is paying for it, not because care provides jobs, not because the law forbids our hastening death, and not because that person is a child of God, just as we are."[7] In the brief moments of stroking the dying child's head, the nurse reflected, "It reminded me in that second that I don't do this for a paycheck, or because I have to. I do it because of the love I have for these sick children. And if I can make a small impact on their lives through love and support, then it is all worth it."[8] This new nurse honors the calling to walk on holy ground in the sacred space of their patients.

Patient Perspectives

Struggling for Peace during a Brain Scan

An ICU patient recalled their claustrophobic near panic attack when they had a brain CT scan, explaining, "The most freaked out I was throughout the ER/ICU experience was the few minutes my big fat head was inside this tiny space with a bright light shining on me. I have super light-sensitive vision, and they hadn't provided any protective eyewear, which sent my spirit into a panic." The patient explained, "I knew I needed to find a way to be centered: FAST." Remembering the contemplative music of the contemplative Taizé services they'd attended, the patient said in their "state of frozen fear, I couldn't remember any of the words except from a song we sang on Maundy Thursday about the Lord remembering me when he comes into his kingdom." The patient explained, "It's a song about dying, death, and resurrection, which did *not* seem helpful when I was scared out of my mind." The patient said they leaned on the prayer of faith that a friend had texted earlier that day from the Holy Lands, where they were on a spiritual pilgrimage. The patient said, "For the duration of the brain scan, I sang in my head, 'Oh Lord hear [name of friend's] prayer for my peace . . . " over, and over, and over again. I survived the ordeal with my spirit intact."[9] Somehow that tiny space became sacred.

Compassionate Caregiver

An ICU patient described "a wonderful employee who worked the day shift at the ICU as the 'floor manager,' or whatever her title was. She was the most kind, gracious, and helpful person I interacted with in any capacity. She reminded me of a 'candy striper' from earlier years. This very professional non-medical caregiver said her job was to make things easier for the nurses, but what she really did was make life much more bearable for the patients." The patient said this caregiver ordered and brought the meals and did oddball errands like refill a cup with ice or fill a thermos cup with hot water. The patient remembered,

> *She also always had a wonderful smile and a bubbly, vivacious personality. Though the ICU floor was full, and she clearly had plenty to do herself, she never rushed, patronized, or made me feel like any request was too mundane or a waste of her precious time. She was fully present, if only for a moment or two. When she was in my room, she was there, present, for me. I wondered if this was her innate personality, her longtime experience, her own centeredness and spiritual maturity, or her appreciation and respect for the calling to work in direct patient care. I also considered if it might be her age or personal maturity since she's a grandmother several times over.*

This ICU patient said they also wondered if this caregiver's countenance and mannerisms could be teachable or transferable to others.

Sacred Space in Maternity

A Black female who was almost thirty when her first child was born, almost thirty-seven when her third child was born, and who'd had a miscarriage of her fourth child shortly before she turned forty said, "My scariest pregnancy was my third child. I had depression, anxiety, and dangerously high blood pressure. It was also during Covid, and I had to spend an entire week in the hospital by myself while they tried to get my high blood pressure under control." Her husband had to be home with the kids. She said what got her through this distressing time alone in the hospital was a connection she'd made through a friend who sold curative oils, who knew someone who was a nurse at this hospital. The mother recalled, "She was wonderful. She brought in a diffuser and was praying over me and the baby. We had a strong connection through a mutual friend, but we only met as strangers, yet she stepped in and took amazing care of me. It turned out that she has a special needs child that she adopted, which we also do, so we were directly connected through that common bond." They've remained friends thereafter. The patient added, "What made her an exemplary nurse was her willingness to go the extra mile. She was an amazing nurse who stepped in to be a mother to me when I most needed mine, but couldn't have her there because of Covid."

Sacred Space with Her Dying Adult Daughter

When her only child was diagnosed with stage four metastatic breast cancer, her mother and a two-time breast cancer survivor herself, said she dropped everything and flew from the East Coast to the West Coast to be with her daughter during this new battle with cancer. Her daughter had beaten an earlier round of breast cancer, including having a double mastectomy, but the cancer had returned and spread to other areas in her body. Describing her daughter, known as Maxx by the beloveds in her life, the mother wrote, "She was my exceptional angel who I was blessed to give birth to, bring up and have as my best friend. She changed my life in every way. She is always in my heart ♥ I believe she was an enlightened soul, and we were blessed to nurture each other for just shy of 54 years." A Jewish American who described her spirituality as "believing in a higher knowing, which for me, I believe in the God within me, and that is my directional device," said it's this sense of knowing that prompted her "to jump on a plane and go to California in about two seconds" after learning her daughter's cancer had returned. She said it's this "higher knowing" that kept her spiritually centered for the remainder of her daughter's life.

The doctor originally had given her daughter three to six months, but Maxx *lived* more than four years. *Lived* is the key word because Maxx didn't simply tolerate or suffer through. She lived each day to the fullest, spending most of them with her mother. Her mother remembered:

> *Every day, we did something fun. That was how Maxx handled her cancer. We redecorated her whole apartment. We called it "the girl pad." As a mom, in a way, you don't get to be with your adult children so much, and I got this wonderful opportunity to be with her. We were best friends. We never knew what we were gonna do or what we were up against. That was the excitement.*[10] (See Illustration 11.1.)

"We're here until we're not," is the mantra her mother said she regularly cited to her daughter. The mother said that leaving behind her vocational calling, her home, and (temporarily) her spouse while she walked together with her daughter during her cancer was her "higher calling." She said she learned the importance of "living in the moment," a lesson she learned with Maxx, which she says is "even more important now than ever."[11]

Illustration 11.1 *Lee and Maxx* Posterized digital image "selfie" of mother and daughter. © Lee F. Estridge; shared by permission.

Her mother reflected, when her daughter finally went into hospice, she told her mother, "'I need to be free.'" Maxx's dearest friends and family came to be beside her during her final days. Her mother said, "We performed rituals and created a loving place to give her as good a death as you can have. We never left her alone once we started hospice. We protected her."[12] There was deep mourning and loss, which continues today, but the mother said she also realizes she wouldn't feel such loss if she also hadn't experienced so much love and joy from her daughter. Her mother said, "I brought Maxx into this world, and unfortunately as a mom, it's the worst thing letting her go. I feel that was part of my mission. And we did it with grace and peace."[13] The sacred space Maxx and her mother created during the daughter's experience with cancer continues to be a blessing in all those who knew and loved her. Cancer "beat her" in one sense, but through the sacredness of the many encounters during Maxx's journey, she and her beloveds also experienced a sense of walking on holy ground.

Goodbye Mommy: A Young Daughter Says Goodbye to Her Deceased Mother

The father who sat vigil at his dying daughter's bedside said, "It'll say 7:10 p.m. on her death certificate, but I was there, and it was 7:01." It wasn't that she'd stopped breathing. He said her spirit, her essence of being, was no more. He knew the hospital allowed time for the family to come in and say their farewells before the body was taken away so he went to where his five-year-old granddaughter was staying a few miles away, and asked if she wanted to come and say goodbye to her mother. The youngest of the recently deceased's four children, she'd already visited her mother several times in the hospital during her dying. She said she wanted to say goodbye. The father/grandfather, who shares custody of this five-year-old, explained his granddaughter was familiar with the concept of death because of the farm animals plus the family pets they cared for at his home located in a small town on the outskirts of a Midwestern city. When a family pet died, they buried it in the back corner of the yard, and it wasn't uncommon for his granddaughter to stretch her arms wide and rest on top of the small mound where the pet had been buried. He said when he'd ask what his granddaughter was doing, she replied that she was listening to her beloved pet. When they entered the hospital room where her mother's corpse was shrouded in the bedsheets, he said his granddaughter flung herself on her mother with her arms wide open, just as she'd done numerous times before with her beloved pet. (See Illustration 11.2.)

A retired Christian minister, he said he'd regularly talked about faith and spirituality with his young granddaughter, as he'd done with the three older ones. He said, "We're believers that God is bigger than death. And in fact, so big that God used death to create the plan of victory." He wanted his granddaughter to have the opportunity to say goodbye to her mother but also to feel the peace of her mother's passing so that this young child wouldn't grow up with a fear of death. Instead of using euphemisms, this grandfather wanted his granddaughter to experience the peace that passes all understanding, a peace she could experience viscerally in the sacred space of her mother's hospital room. What some might see as a difficult choice, the father/grandfather easily opted to invite his granddaughter to say goodbye to her mother.

Illustration 11.2 *Goodbye Mommy* pastel portrait of a five-year-old daughter saying goodbye to her mother. Artwork © Helen T. Boursier based on a photograph by the father/grandfather Mark McNeese; shared by permission.

The father/grandfather said when they arrived back at the hospital and stepped out of the elevator, the view before them was a sign pointing to the birthing center to the left. His daughter's room was to the right. He said he hadn't been quite sure how he'd explain death to his granddaughter until that moment when he told her, "Dying is like being born into another phase." Describing this experience the morning after his daughter's death, he said, "I'm used to my granddaughter being happy, gleeful. She wasn't happy, but she also wasn't sad. She was intuitively appropriate for the job of saying goodbye to her mother." He said, "So many grownups use that language of death as 'being asleep.'" He said he attributed his granddaughter's calm sense of understanding to her young lifetime of hearing the stories of faith, reading her the sacred scriptures, and singing hymns. He appreciates that there's much she didn't understand and that he'll continue to answer questions as they arise, but he also knew she experienced the sacred space as she said her last farewells to her mother. Her grandfather helped his young granddaughter come to terms with her mother's death through hope in the religious sense, but hope also functions to offer the possibility of something better, whatever that something may be.

Hope

Hope is an existential, spiritual, emotional, relational, rational, and physical disposition toward something in the future. It's often anticipated as "better than" a present experience, moment, or physical reality. Sometimes it's hope for something that's totally beyond a person's control, but other times hope shapes attitude reorientation in the midst of what otherwise could seem, feel, and be hopeless.[14] Hope helps to reframe hopelessness, to dispel its insidious negativity, and to reorient to something else that might be. Whatever the illness or treatment, whether short-term or someone who's in hospice or palliative care, womanist chaplain Allen explained, "the presence of a chaplain, the mere presence of a chaplain, if they know the chaplain to be someone who is employed by the hospital, gives them a sense of hope." She added, "Hope comes because the patient senses someone who's 'on their side.'" Chaplain Allen said the value of a chaplain is better understood and received in a hospice setting than in hospitals, where there isn't always understanding or respect for spirituality's intersections with direct patient care.

A hospice chaplain who'd previously worked in two metropolitan hospitals explained a chaplain's preparation includes "digging into your own vulnerabilities so when you sit with somebody who's in their most vulnerable place you can be a listening presence without bringing in any of their own baggage." The hospice chaplain said it's also helpful to "be curious," to gently discover what a patient is thinking and feeling, which helps discover or uncover their hopes. Hope helps to make something feel tolerable, even worthwhile, reorienting from something else that otherwise would be long-suffering, unbearable, and hopeless.

Hopelessness

Hopelessness has similarities with hope in that both orientations include existential, spiritual, emotional, relational, rational, and physical disposition toward something in the future. Hopelessness sees, feels, and experiences zero hope in the same situation where another person might find some sliver of hope, not necessarily in everything being "all better," but in finding something beneficial amidst the struggle, even if it's something they'll never directly experience, such as the husband who transferred his hope to his wife living a rich, full life after his death.[15] It's interesting that, while hope is sometimes viewed as being a crutch or a mechanism to help get through a rough time, hopelessness actually can be much more irrational because hopeless people can't think or feel or see beyond their despair in the present.[16] While hope looks for and expects to see some sort of bright side to the gloom, hopelessness begets a despairing inability to envision any other option.[17] While hope might seem elusive and possibly illogical, it sustains the human spirit, which sustains the physical body, by fostering some form of agency.

The Agency of Hope

The agency of hope is the practical, tangible, actual "thing" that someone can think, be, or do to make the present reality more bearable, including caregivers, patients, and their beloved family members.[18] Agency is visceral, tangible, and real because it gives a sense of control. Instead of someone being a passive recipient of whatever their hopefulness informs, the agency of hope reorients them to having some sense of control. Whether it's religiously disaffiliated or religiously grounded, hope is at the heart of human emotion, desire, feelings, beliefs, and actions to make this hope real. Hope is particularly relevant and necessary in a hospital or urgent care context because hope has always been born in the midst of lament.[19] It's when someone is at their worst, lowest, poorest, most afraid, or whatever low point in life that hope rises up through lament to offer a promising something new. Hope sustains; it becomes the reason for living. Hope fuels hopefulness and makes it possible to endure the next chemo treatment, to tough it up and have the courage to be inside a claustrophobically distressing space for a brain scan, and to suffer through whatever other torturous medical anything with the hope of getting better soon.

Hoping for a (Better) Future

Danish Christian philosopher Søren Kierkegaard has contributed to hope and hopefulness in context with this understanding of what it means to be human. Kierkegaard "describes persons as possessors of actuality, freedom, and possibility. All three are part of the self, and a good relationship among all three is necessary for authentic existence."[20] His understanding encompasses three factors:

> **Actuality** *refers primarily to the past; it includes our context, our physiological predisposition, and choices we have made.*[21]
> **Freedom** *is what we have in the present. It is a finite freedom, exercised within the limits of our situation and abilities, our givens and past choices. Because of our actualities, we cannot become whatever we want to be—not even "if we only try hard enough." We make choices, and act, from the range of options available to us.*[22]
> **Possibility** *addresses the future. It is what we can become as we use our freedom. In this respect, our possibilities are not predetermined. We can imagine and—within the givens of life—we can become something new.*[23]

Given the actual circumstances of what happened to each of us in the past that brought us to the future, each person has the freedom to make choices that will shape the possibility for the future. Clearly, those choices are limited, not only by who and what we are from our past but also by the various options presented as choices in our present. Nevertheless, the combination of these three factors offers hope and hopefulness in the present for a new future.

It's not a dumbing or a numbing down, but the intricate reality of the spirituality of being fully human, living in these three dimensions of time: past, present, and future. In the midst of the extreme suffering that he witnessed and experienced in a Nazi concentration camp, Frankl argues the important point is "to stop asking about the meaning of life, and instead to think of ourselves as those who are being questioned by life—daily and hourly. Life ultimately means taking the responsibility to find the right answer to its problems and to fulfill the tasks which it constantly sets for each individual."[24] Sacred space arises in the liminal spaces when, instead of throwing in the towel of despair, it's about living each day like Maxx, until we don't. Sacred space arises when we live while we are *still* alive. In each of those moments and sacred places and spaces, caregivers and care receivers experience the blessedness of profound presence.

12 Caring Presence

Early in my preparation for vocational ordained ministry, the oversight committee didn't think I had it "in me" to be still and fully present with people who were experiencing any type of distress. They saw me as a "type A" overachiever and compared me to the Energizer Bunny that was always on the go *doing* rather than *being*. It slowed up my ordination process while they figured out what they could have me do to prove that I'd be a compassionate, caring pastor who was able to be fully present with parishioners during their times of trauma and distress. With their collective approval, I spent several months as a volunteer chaplain at a mid-sized religiously affiliated hospital in the Midwest and also at its nearby long-term care facility for seniors. Ironically, this aspect of vocational ordained ministry proved to be the easiest, the most natural, and the most enjoyable.[1] I discovered I easily embraced being a ministry of non-anxious presence, who's the calm within a storm that accompanies patients in solidarity and compassion, which is also referred to as a caring or healing presence in chaplaincy and nursing.[2] Through a caregiver's willingness to be still and be fully present, they're able to become a portal for spiritual care.

Spiritual Care

Spiritual care is misunderstood when spirituality begins from an incorrect starting point. When spirituality is defined primarily as being a person's meaning in/of life, rather than their all-encompassing essence of being, spiritual care then overly focuses on helping someone to "work through" their meaning in/of life worries. However, when spirituality is understood as *all of me*, it significantly changes spiritual care from working to solve someone's internal struggles to being fully present in whatever capacity or context that may require. Spiritual care is about accompaniment.[3] It's about *being*, not doing. It prioritizes embracing a presence of beingness while doing a task, not by brusquely rushing through it but by being attentive to the patient through the doing to personify being a caring presence. Patient-centered spiritual care moves forth from patient-centered spirituality.[4] Spiritual care isn't something that's facilitated as one more task in an already overloaded schedule. It's about *being together with* someone in solidarity, empathy, compassion, kindness, and a listening ear. Spiritual care is a loving heart being fully present with someone for the sake of the someone and not the self. It's not something that's "done" as an extra task or activity in addition to [fill in the blank]. It's not "more" to do. Rather, it's the intentionality within the already doing that surrenders primacy of self, primacy of action, to a compassionate and fully present *being together with*.[5]

I've included a unit on being a ministry of presence, or *caring presence*, for nursing and social work students for a decade. The students often remark that it's a foreign concept and also that they're "too busy" to do one more "thing" amidst their already overly full list of tasks as they scurry from one client or patient to the next. I've asked students to observe their interactions with patients or clients and to notice the opportunities to reorient their energy from busy-ness to *being-ness*. It's an automatic reflex for caregiving professionals to run-run-run, because there's always so much to *do*. It's much more difficult to pause briefly *during the doing* to be with each patient, each client, fully and wholly for them. It's about *being together with* instead of being *busy*.[6]

During this unit on being a caring presence, students engage Nouwen's *Our Greatest Gift* as their conversation partner for five reflections, one for each of five different days, to reflect on their interactions with patients or clients and observe when/if/how they engage in *being* rather than *doing*. Because spiritual care includes a reflective practice of the caregiver observing their interactions and responses, literally observing how they're being fully present (or not), I invite students to observe what it means to be fully present and how that impacts their caregiving relationships and activities. Through the exercise of intentionality, their experiential learning becomes praxis through caring presence.[7] Students also learn the importance of caregivers being more than task bunnies. They learn they're urgently needed to be a fully attentive, caring presence.

A Caring Presence

Being a caring presence is difficult to do because it's counter-cultural to the fast-paced life, particularly in an urban context where overloading, over-committing, and multitasking have become the norm. Being present doesn't come naturally. It's a learned skill that requires practice and intentionality, not only through our caregiving but also with the dearly beloved in our inner circle of family, friends, and colleagues. It ultimately comes down to our willingness to be present with the people we're in community/connection with.[8] Caring presence is almost a form of mindfulness because it's about being mindfully and completely present in this moment, with this patient, client, friend, or family member, letting go of any agenda and settling into the beautiful moment of now.[9] It isn't about the doing; it's about being together in solidarity with. Spiritually trained specialists like chaplains and clergy are vocationally called to be this caring presence, but it's also something that's available, possible, and desperately wanted by patients for all caregivers.[10] Patients don't want to be just another patient/number/hip replacement/ or whatever. They want their presence to matter, and the only way they're going to know, feel, and believe this is for caregivers to offer them their fully attentive, caring presence.

Caring Presence in a Clinical Context

A nursing student reflected on their experience in being intentionally present with a child who'd been born "normal" but who'd suffered a brain injury at age four that left them disabled and unable to care for themselves. Instead of looking at doing "total cares" for this patient as being one more task to complete, the student chose to be fully present, including noticing the patient's facial expressions and nonverbal utterances. The intentionality reminded this student of the privilege it was to care for someone else, particularly that someone else entrusted their child to this student's care. The student reflected, "It's amazing what a smile or small gesture can do for someone's day," sharing what Nouwen calls "the inner life," which is "always for others."[11] Slowing down to be fully present gifted the nursing student with the inner life of a patient, something that wouldn't have happened had the bathtime care been done in a perfunctory rush. When all caregivers at all levels lean into being a caring presence, their quality of care becomes a *healing presence*.

Healing Presence

It might seem like it's easy to be a healing presence through being a caring presence, but it actually is all-encompassing. It requires energy and focus to set aside all the things that are busy distractions to literally be fully present. It's a proactive internal activity that shows up as a calm and focused external being.[12] The primary resource is the desire to want to be present. If it's something a caregiver has "got to do," then being mindfully present becomes one more task to add to the list. When caring moves forth from *get to* instead of *got to*, then caring presence becomes a companion to the prescribed tasks, not making them more work, but enhancing the blessing of the *doing through being*.

Caring Together With

I learned early in my pastoral care ministry of presence with parishioners, instead of *caring for*, to shift the language to *caring together with* which emphasizes the mutuality in being a caring presence.[13] It's by giving ourselves permission to be ourselves in the presence of others, *during the caregiving*, that it becomes a caring presence instead of a task-driven function. It means being you, who you are in your fullest. Instead of hiding behind a sterile, emotionless mask, it's giving yourself permission to allow a peek of your emotional innards to escape so that you are caring as a human being and not a robotic machine. A caring presence is a compassionately oriented art of what it means to be fully human: as caregivers and also as care receivers. The masks come off, and we give ourselves permission to be our own essence of being, in all of its diversity and richness. The being doesn't dismiss or negate the doing. Rather, the being infuses the doing with kindness, compassion, empathy, and a caring presence.

A nursing student connected Nouwen's point that all human beings are dependent upon one another to the vulnerability of patients who literally are totally dependent upon medical care, observing how easily it would be to "get into the habit of rushing from one thing to the next." Instead, this student chose to take "the time to listen to their concerns and validate them, follow through on the things that I say I'll do, and ask questions to understand where they're coming from." By spending these few moments of active presence during caregiving, the nursing student observed, "It's amazing how taking the time to build rapport with patients can change the tone of the entire shift. I notice how differently patients respond and how thankful they are when you give them your full attention."[14] The point of spiritual care isn't to *do things* in a sacred or holy fashion. Rather, it means all actions and interactions move forth as a caring presence, expecting, noticing, and honoring the essence of being of each patient through compassionate caregiving, which offers a comforting presence.

Comforting Presence

Being a *comforting presence* facilitates spiritual care through the mutuality of beingness, for the patient and also for their beloved ones who are sitting in vigil offering their own comforting presence. Steve Nolan suggests comforting presence can be done actively through conversation and "friendship building," but it also includes being present in solidarity and silence.[15] How, and when, a patient chooses to share their deepest thoughts, feelings, and concerns generally depends on whether or not they feel safe, which means there must be a sense of trust, which is most likely earned through friendship building, which then engenders feeling safe to share.[16]

Reflecting on Nouwen's point, "to care is to stand by a dying person and to be a living reminder that the person is indeed the beloved child of God,"[17] an Indigenous student shared his experience of being a comforting presence with his mother during her waning battle with COPD. He said the first two weeks of his mother being in the hospital, she was in the ICU in a near-comatose state. He explained:

> Her CO_2 was so high it was forcing her to sleep, only waking up for a few seconds at a time. Every time she waved her hands in the air, signaling for someone to come help, she was unable to speak for unknown reasons, she could only use body language to communicate. The first few times of her waking up and waving for help, I'd rush to her side along with the Certified Nursing Assistant (CNA) in the room. As soon as my mother saw me, she lifted her hand towards me. I would ask questions like, "Are you in pain?" to try and gauge what she wanted. Every time she nodded "no" with probably the most fearful look I've ever seen in her eyes. Eventually, I noticed the way she was lifting her hands, and I asked, "Do you want me to hold your hand?" She immediately nodded, "Yes." So, I held her hand. Before I even finished cupping my hand to hers, every look of fear had gone. She had rested her head down, and went back to sleep with my hand in hers.

This Indigenous son in his mid-twenties said this continued for two weeks, adding, "I didn't need to ask what she wanted. She would wake up with that same look of fear, I'd grab her hand, and she would go back to sleep peacefully." He observed, "The few times I wasn't able to make it in time to hold her hand before the CO_2 forced her back to sleep, the look on her face while sleeping was significantly more uncomfortable than the times when I did hold her hand before she went back to sleep."[18] Compassionate caring prioritizes showing up and being there, which reduces patient angst and takes the edge off their fear, pain, loneliness, and uncertainty.[19] (See Illustration 12.1.)

One of nine siblings, this Indigenous student said, "I've been preparing for my mom's eventual passing for a while now. I believe that's why my mom wants me specifically to be the one holding her hand. I have no fear in my eyes, no sadness, no tears, just love." He thoughtfully observed, "I am not the oldest nor the youngest, but in a crowd of everyone, she reaches for me specifically in those moments when she's on the line between passing and getting better, when it's a 50/50 chance on whether when she closes her eyes, if they will ever open again." He added, "It's abundantly clear to my family that she wants me there in those moments, so it's been decided that when she's at her worst, it is I who will be spending the days and nights with her until she recovers." He explained it's in these moments when his mother is at her physical worst, he realizes he's the only one in the family who can see the look of fear in her eyes and continue to be the comforting presence she needs.[20] His comforting, caring presence disarms her fear.[21]

Presence Doesn't Include "Fixing"

A chaplain in her mid-fifties said one of the biggest challenges she faced in transitioning from her social work background to becoming a board-certified chaplain working in hospice has been not to try to "fix things" for patients. She said, "I'm not going to go in there and do a song and dance and make them happy, and I tend to lean that direction." She explained, "I have to rein that in and be present, be still, and hold those complicated places they're grappling with." She said it's been difficult for her to not want to cheer somebody up but to instead reflect what somebody's feeling, what they're sharing, and then to acknowledge that without putting herself into the story or getting in the way. During her residency training for chaplaincy, she said she was constantly reminded, "Stay in your lane; stay in your lane," which keeps the focus on being fully present and not trying to "fix things." The chaplain said, "I'm a people pleaser, and I'm a problem solver. I want to help you. I want to be the social worker, and the spiritual caregiver, and the friend, and the

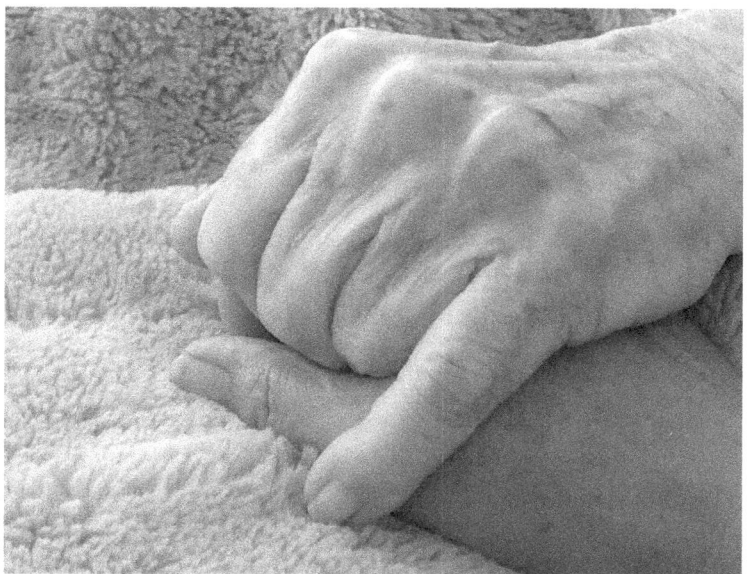

Illustration 12.1 *Holding Hands* digital image of a 96-year-old mother holding on to her son's hand. © Helen T. Boursier

cheerleader. But that's not my job," she said, adding, "Part of chaplaincy is to help people recognize their vulnerability in that circumstance, and help them process it and get to a place of equilibrium." Part of healing includes acceptance, which is an important aspect of a caring presence to listen to how a patient is handling or processing an unpleasant diagnosis.[22]

Practical Presence

Much of spiritual care arises through being a caring, healing, comforting, listening presence, but there's also *practical presence*, which circles back to the doing. Practical presence is important, as long as it doesn't become another Energizer Bunny *overdoing it*. Some actions might seem supercilious and completely unrelated to what's "spiritual" or what "spiritual care" is, but they can become profoundly important for the physical, emotional, and spiritual well-being. For example:

- Responding (promptly) to a call button, or at least acknowledging that someone will be there as soon as possible.

- Plugging a cell phone into a charger that's located just out of reach from a patient whose mobility is limited.
- Giving prompt assistance to help a patient to the restroom.
- Making a phone call to a family member on the patient's behalf (by permission) when the patient is unable to do so themselves.
- Keeping the whiteboard updated with the names of relevant caregivers on the current shift.
- Asking, "How can I make your day better for you?"
- Providing physical care with sensitivity and allowing for interaction during that care.

An experienced RN said, "Even repositioning a patient in bed doesn't have to be a task that's without communication. Include them in the task by asking what feels most comfortable, have a short but friendly chat, and look them in the eye before leaving the room and give some reassurance, even if it's just a hand-squeeze." None of these actions will be included in a typical conversation about spiritual care in a healthcare context, but these are the issues of angst that start off small enough but that become serious stressors when they're ignored. The little stuff festers, partly because it would be "so simple" to correct, so when it's not attended to, it magnifies exponentially.

Ultimately, a caring presence means full and complete presence of the caregiver with the care receiver. Ram Dass, an American spirituality teacher who's called the "guru of modern yoga," highlights the importance of the inner and outer self being intricately included in what it means to be fully present. Dass reminds, "You finally understand the message you communicate with another human being has nothing to do with what you say. It has nothing to do with the look on the musculature of your face. It's much deeper than that. Much deeper! It's the vibrations that emanate from you."[23] By being fully present, including really listening to each patient, "little things" would already have been taken care of. They would've been discussed or noticed and resolved.

Practical Caring Presence with the Dying

Dignity is the heartbeat of a compassionate, caring presence with the dying and also with their families, who gather around during the slow and even tedious moments of witnessing a beloved make their journey toward death, literally one breath at a time. It's a commitment to being present like no other. Being a caring presence with the dying and their family matters above all else; yet it's also a transition that makes many people uncomfortable, particularly those who have death anxiety and who've not prepared themselves for death (see Chapter 9). Honoring dying time is as simple and yet as challenging as what William and Nancy Martin describe in *The Caregiver's Tao Te Ching: Compassionate Caring for Your Loved Ones and Yourself*, "All we need to do is sink into the gift of 'just this.'"[24] They added, "We can stand as true companions to the ones we care for when we honor their experience. We listen when they tell us that it is time to stop struggling and rest. In this way we allow their days to be filled with tenderness, sadness, and gratitude rather than the efforts of battle and war."[25] *Being present* with the dying is a being that always takes the lead from the one making their final journey.

No Assumptions

Caregiver anxiety needs to remain in a locked box, out of sight, out of mind, and out of discussion. There's no place in a dying person's space for anything else to worry about, and they certainly don't want to hear or sense any anxiety exuded by their caregivers. It's also a season of *no assumptions*.[26] As the Jewish mother who walked alongside her daughter when she received the terminal cancer diagnosis, "We're here until we're not." Despite how difficult this challenge would be, the mother and daughter were committed to their mutuality of presence. In all of this pending intensity, they were in it together.

A Father's Morning After Reflection on His Daughter's Death

The father who sat vigil when his daughter and only child died at age forty-five, a retired minister, said his spirituality is shaped and informed by his belief in the resurrection of Jesus and the promise of eternal life. He said because he's centered in his spirituality, he focuses on the good instead of "fixating on the negative." He said, "It doesn't remove the sadness and pending loss, but it helps to make it bearable."[27] He said he'd come to terms with his own sadness and loss because he knew his daughter would be in "forever peace." He explained, with her many trips to hospitals and rehabs through the years, he'd prepared himself that this might one day become her death. Because he'd done the difficult work of preparing his spirit for her death, he was able to sit at her bedside hour after hour and day after day, often completely alone without any other family member. In contrast, he explained, his daughter's mother "just would not go to the hospital, and she did not," adding, "The last few days at the hospital have been the loneliest of my life" because the patient's mother and his daughter's three older children didn't come visit. He said, "They were about five miles away, and they wouldn't come to see her."[28] Into this absence of family, others are invited to step into the gap and provide a practical, caring presence.

Practical Caring Presence for (Family) Caregivers

People who are sitting in vigil with the dying need a *practical caring presence*. This father who'd waited in vigil, virtually alone, at his daughter's hospital bedside, said he came to depend on the caring presence of another retired pastor who'd offered a practical caring presence through hospitality by delivering homemade meals for breakfast, lunch, and supper. He remembered hot coffee with an egg sandwich in the morning, and fried chicken with iced tea in the afternoon, with homemade desserts for an afternoon snack. He said, in the middle of his grief and pending loss, he'd think to himself, "It must be about time for [this person] to drop by with a meal." Much of the food went uneaten, but the presence of caring during his daughter's ultimate and final battle lessened the pending sting of death. This presence becomes an affirmation that their beloved matters, that they're important enough for someone to take time out of their day to support and witness this transition. The ones doing the lengthy vigil aren't forgotten or alone.

During the death watch in this mid-sized suburban hospital, the nursing staff regularly checked on the dying patient. Her father said the nurses were very intentional about asking about his daughter and also about how he was doing. They asked if there was anything that was needed for her comfort. Whoever came into the room, whether it was to offer him coffee or tea, showed a "great deal of kindness." They lingered to be present during the vigil, and they consistently asked him, "What can I do for you? How can I make your time here easier?" He said they were very understanding and compassionate with the grief process. They also were patient and understanding during the dying. When a nurse stopped by, they often simply opened the door, walked in a few feet, and quietly said, "Just checking to see if you need anything. Is there anything I can do for you?" almost as if they were acting as a hostess or a maître d' who was floating around and checking. As the time of death drew nearer, the patient wasn't their primary point of concern. It shifted to the lonely father in the room who was awaiting his daughter's death. Presence becomes an invaluable gift for the recipients of compassionate care, but also for the ones who prioritize the suffering other as being more important than anything else they could possibly be doing. *Being* matters more. Spiritual care isn't limited to being. Sometimes solidarity through presence necessarily requires advocacy for patient-centered agency.

13 Advocacy for (Patient) Agency

Spirituality becomes enacted in public through advocacy for (patient) agency.[1] When justice, equity, compassion, dignity, agency, respect, and inequity are in question, spirituality rises up to challenge and change, through advocacy and action, anything that's unfair, unkind, and unjust.

BYOA: Bring Your Own Advocate

Everyone over age sixty who participated in this conversation about spirituality in a healthcare context stressed the importance of patients bringing their own advocate as a survival skill for patient well-being. Without an on-site advocate, too many things could slip through the cracks, contributing to emotional, spiritual, and physical distress. For example, a Black male octogenarian said his wife would never leave him alone in a hospital, specifying, "My wife was there with me all the time." If she couldn't be there, he said a family member would be "right there making sure they didn't mess with me." An elderly minority Black male who gets around using a walker said he's grateful for his wife's diligence in making sure he has a family member with him at all times whenever he's in the hospital. However, even if someone wasn't there to advocate for him, this quietly reserved elder said he wouldn't let anyone push him around because, "I've got a combat spirit" from his years of military service as a young adult.

A white female in her upper sixties who'd had hip replacement remarked, "There needs to be somebody there for the patient at all times." Her daughter had come with her for the surgery, but she'd left soon after her mother was moved from recovery to a hospital room, leaving her alone to fend for herself. She explained she's "four months out" from the surgery and that everything was physically healing on schedule, but internally, her experience was very different. She said, "I feel like I have a little PTSD after all of this," referring to the trauma during the surgery and the night shift nurse who didn't respond to her call button or administer the pain relief meds on schedule (see Chapter 7). She said, "I just wasn't prepared for how it was going to be after the surgery, nor was I prepared for being awake during the surgery," adding, "I must've been asleep when I signed off on that section." She said she felt like the human factor was missing, clarifying, "You're going to be in pain, and you want to be taken care of." She said, "The human factor just doesn't exist anymore in healthcare, and that's why I think patients need an advocate of some sort," suggesting someone who "goes around to patients' rooms and checks on them and says, 'Hey, how's everything going? Are you okay?' Someone who just helps you out, so you don't feel like you're alone in there." This senior added, "I know nurses probably are short-staffed, and they don't have time to pat you on the back and ask, 'Is there anything you need?' But those little words would mean a lot to a patient who's undergone surgery and who's scared."

A Black female in her early seventies who has nearly forty years of experience as an RN said, "I'm afraid to be alone in a hospital room as a patient," adding, "Literally, as my family will tell everyone, if I go into a hospital, somebody's got to be with me 24/7. I need somebody in the room when I cannot care for myself, when I cannot make the decisions on my own, and when I cannot say I need to be turned over because I've been laying in the same position for six hours." She emphasized, "I need somebody there to say what needs saying on my behalf."

The younger research participants didn't specify advocacy, but a parent often did so on their behalf. The spouse whose late husband died from leukemia shared when her middle daughter was in her twenties and required knee surgery. The mother explained, "She was upset about it when she called to tell me about needing to have this procedure done." The mother said she was committed to going on a mission trip to Costa Rica during the time frame her daughter's knee surgery could be scheduled, and the mother said she told her daughter she'd fly in from out-of-state and go with her adult daughter if she'd schedule the surgery *after* the mission trip. Then she gave the daughter the dates that she'd be out of the country. After she returned from the mission trip and called her daughter to ask when the surgery was scheduled, her daughter said she'd already had the surgery.

   Mother   *What*?! Who did you have go with you?
   Daughter: Well, I just took a cab.
   Mother: *What*?! Who was there with you?
   Daughter: Well, nobody.

Explaining her daughter was twelve or thirteen when her dad was sick, the mother said, "I went through the roof. I asked her, 'Did you learn nothing from your dad's illness?! Did I teach you nothing?!'" Animated as she shared this memory, the mother added, "I was livid. I said I didn't care that I wasn't the one to be with her, but that she needed *somebody* there with her when she went under anesthesia." When the mother asked how she'd gotten home after the surgery, the daughter said she'd taken an Uber. The mother said she told her daughter, "You *always* need an advocate with you when you're under anesthesia. *Always*." She remembered, "I just, I went off! I told her, 'Don't ever do that again.'" Having someone physically present from start to finish is critically important for any urgent care *or* scheduled hospital stay.

When There's No Familial Advocacy

A white female in her early sixties who was in the ICU for dangerously low sodium and later diagnosed with Addison's disease said her spouse briefly visited her three times a day around his work schedule while she was in the ICU, including first thing in the morning on his way to work, during his lunch break, and then again after work around supper time. She said,

> Ultimately, I was alone twenty-two out of twenty-four hours, which is a lot of **feeling** alone and being on your own in a scary and uncertain situation. Your mind just can't quite flip into a positive upbeat mode when you're alone for so long. It also means that you don't have anyone there to advocate for you, leaving anything related to advocacy up to the patient.

She explained when they later debriefed about her hospital experience, including her candidly saying how lonely and alone she'd felt, he asked if he should've been there more. The patient responded, "Absolutely, yes."

Recognizing Covenant Relationships

A queer woman of Latina heritage and an ordained minister who works as a community organizer who's married to a trans male said, "A big issue for queer people is family and having recognition of your being the partner." She said a queer couple, whether officially married or not, consider themselves "family," but the medical complex doesn't. She said there were many times when she or her partner was at a medical appointment, urgent care or scheduled, and the "other" wouldn't be allowed in because they weren't legally married, so they didn't "count as the spouse." Without any recognized "family" present, patients don't have the comforting presence of knowing their loved one is beside them. Acknowledging covenant relationships, instead of shutting out half of them when one is having medical care, would be an easy and nonconfrontational step forward for compassionate patient care that's open and affirming, not only for the LGBTQIA community but also for others like seniors whose spouse predeceased them and their related-by-blood family can't or won't be present.

Provider Advocacy on Behalf of Patients

Audre Lorde's *The Cancer Journals* is assigned reading in my Introduction to Spirituality course during the unit on cultural diversity, which also addresses racism in a healthcare context. Students consistently point out Lorde's emphasis on finding and using your voice to challenge and change any injustice, particularly Lorde's point, "My silences had not protected me. Your silence will not protect you."[2] Reflecting on Lorde's emphasis to find your voice and use it, a white female nursing student from the upper Midwest reflected, "From a young age, many of us are taught to be seen and not heard. We're told it's disrespectful to talk back, and we're supposed to let the adults do the talking. Before we realize it, we've become the adults, and we don't have anything to say as we've spent our lives listening." When her generation is now being called upon to lead and speak out against injustices, she asked, "How do we find our voice? Is it better to sit back and wait for others to do the talking for us? As future nurses, can we address discrimination seen in the healthcare system?"[3] The student explained:

> *I was always taught that it was disrespectful to speak back to adults, and along the way I lost my voice. I would force my thoughts and feelings down as I got scolded for x, y, or z. Much too fast, I became an adult who was unable to communicate my feelings or share my thoughts for fear of controversy. Fear is the thief of many great things in our lives. We've all experienced holding ourselves back due to fear of repercussions, ridicule, judgment, shame, etc., the list goes on and on. Lorde explains how we can break the silence and use our voices to close the gap between our differences.*[4]

Being an advocate doesn't necessarily mean being angry, contentious, or nit-picky. It *does* mean using your voice to draw attention to the appropriate persons about your concerns, of course doing so in a respectful and courteous fashion.

Teaching Patients and Their Families to Advocate for Themselves

A seasoned nurse reflected, "You get a lot of theory during school. You do use your training in anatomy, physiology, pharmacology, and all the science, which makes a big difference in being someone who's not just a task bunny. I can explain to a patient how their heart works or what's going on with their stroke." She said she also lets visiting families know what changes to look for in the patient and says, "Come get me" if there are notable changes. The nurse explained:

> *Many times, there'd be family in the room or a spouse. Especially with someone who's had a stroke, if they started to bleed, the change can be subtle at first. Well, who knows that patient better than the family? I'd ask, "They're a little off from how they were earlier, what do you think?" If anyone would notice the subtle changes, it would be the family.*

The nurse reflected on the "excellent neuro training" she'd received during nursing school, which made her "particularly adept at assessing someone who'd had a stroke." The nurse said, "I could be pretty confident with my own diagnosis. However, if there were subtle changes, if their speech was a little different, they just didn't seem quite right, if they seem more agitated, the family could tell me, 'Oh, you know, my husband's never like this.'" Then the nurse would phone the doctor for follow-up action.

She recalled a clinical she'd had more than thirty years earlier when she'd been "under the supervision of a good neuro instructor on a medical surgical floor," where she was taking care of someone who'd been there for a surgical procedure. She remembered, "Everybody was focused on the procedure this patient had had, the stitches, and how the incision was healing." Imitating the doctor and nurses, she said, "'Does the site look okay, blah, blah, blah, blah, blah.' One day I came in, wearing my little student uniform, and the patient's daughter came out, and she said, 'There's something wrong with Mom. She doesn't seem to be responding that well, and I noticed that she can't use her left hand.'"

The now seasoned RN remembered, "I grabbed my instructor and went to see the patient." After conducting a full assessment, she said they'd determined, "This lady had a classic stroke." One side of her body was completely affected, and nobody had noticed. The nurse remembered saying, "'Hey, she's had a stroke!' She said they were proud they'd diagnosed it, "but the sad part was here this poor lady had had a full stroke while she was in a major acute care metropolitan hospital, and it had gone unnoticed." She explained, "Strokes are silent, but if you go in there, you take their blood pressure and ask, 'How're you doing?' If you notice they didn't eat much of their food because they can't see half their plate or use the affected arm, you're going to notice this person has had a stroke." Instead, this patient's stroke had gone unnoticed for "probably a day or so. There had been several shifts ahead of this. It was only because the daughter caught me in the hall to come in and see her mother that something was done," emphasizing, "This was *after* the doctors made their rounds. Not a word, nothing. But, again, even with physicians, they're looking at *their* thing, at the incision site. They're not looking at the neurological signs." She said she's not dismissing or disrespecting doctors because they have their own myriad of tasks to complete, seeing all their patients, reading labs, and writing orders. She said the point is how important it is to bring the families in on being attentive and watchful so they can advocate for their loved one. She added, "That experience kept me up at night. I was like, 'Holy cow. Is this it?'"

Self-Education as Advocacy

Self-education becomes self-advocacy for patients and their families, particularly those who have a chronic illness that will (inevitably) bring them back to the ER or a scheduled hospital stay again (and again).[5] The young adult with stage four melanoma said, soon after he was diagnosed, he decided to do a lot of reading. He recalled, "I had so many questions. I wanted to get to the bottom of what was going on. What were the primary mutations? What did these mutations mean?" He said part of his reading was based on wanting to know what was going on with him, but it was also inspired by his own curiosity. He said, "Obviously, I didn't want this to be happening to me, but I also saw it as an opportunity for me to learn, simply from a curiosity standpoint." He used his curiosity to inspire his reading, which led to a myriad of questions, which he said the providers graciously answered. His self-agency through education helped him to understand the tedious healing journey before him, using his agency to choose his response. His spirituality, shaped by his autonomy and agency, inspired, informed, and affirmed how he responded not only to the devastating diagnosis but also to his tedious treatments during the healing process. Agency of response became his *spirituality of perseverance*.

Finding Your Voice

A middle-aged white female chaplain who'd recently completed the required residency and was in the process of becoming board certified said, "The chaplain's job, as part of the interdisciplinary care team, is to advocate on behalf of the patient." Referring to a patient who'd had sickle cell anemia and was being labeled as a med seeker (see Chapter 6), she said a Black chaplain who didn't have sickle cell but, as part of the Black community, made it a point to be aware of it from when they'd previously been a social worker. The patient was highly educated about her disease, but the providers "wouldn't take her seriously." The new chaplain said her seasoned colleague "stood up to the providers and said, 'No, she's not a drug seeker. This is a real disease, and she needs to be taken seriously. She needs to be heard. She's in pain and needs pain meds.'" The new chaplain said she witnessed this near the conclusion of her residency training. She said, "Seeing this chaplain's passion about this and how upset she got, really triggered my empathy for the circumstances of what was going on."

The new chaplain said when she was completing her chaplaincy residency, she'd had a "really significant" experience observing an interdisciplinary team discussing the doctor's proposed care for a homeless woman. A chaplain who was head of the ethics committee stepped in to make decisions on behalf of this patient. There to observe the procedures, the chaplaincy intern explained the providers were discussing a procedure they wanted to do on a female patient, a procedure this patient vehemently objected to. The new chaplain remembered, "She had some kind of uterine mass, and the doctors wanted to go in and remove it. This homeless woman had already been diagnosed with terminal cancer, and she was adamant that she did *not* want anybody checking her in that area of her body." The new chaplain reflected, "The conversation moved around to different people who were putting their two cents in, saying they needed to 'go in to figure out what this is.' When it got to the chaplain, who was representing the patient, the chaplain said, 'I'm not okay with this. We don't know why she doesn't want somebody to invade her space, her body. She deserves full autonomy.'" The then intern remembered the chair of the ethics committee saying, "'We do not need to traumatize this woman,'" adding, "And they didn't do the procedure."

The new chaplain said she remembered thinking, "'Yes! That was cool.'" She said she learned, "It's important to speak up for patients who maybe can't do it for themselves and tell the doctors, 'It's not gonna happen.'" She added, "They didn't know if this woman had been violated or what kind of abuse she may have experienced, especially in her homelessness condition. You don't know what she's been through on the streets." In addition, the intern, now chaplain, said the patient was "so adamant in speaking for herself, it clearly meant a lot to her to not have the procedure. We're not going to violate her body that way. It's not okay." The new chaplain said she didn't think it was a case of the doctors not listening to the patient, but more so that they were "just doctors being doctors," which she described as "a mindset of investigating, digging around, and trying to fix something." She said they're thinking, "'We're doctors, and this is what we're here to do,' but what the doctor can do isn't always the most important thing for what that person values." She continued, "What did this patient value? It sure wasn't being treated vaginally." New to the chaplaincy calling, she said, "I'm still trying to find my voice and recognize when I need to use it, and what's mine to do."[6]

Presence Obligates Advocacy

The one who witnesses any ethical, moral, or patient disjuncture, including from the patient's perspective, has the responsibility to call it out, moving a caregiver-turned-advocate towards what Heidegger calls their "ownmost possibilities, as a summons to its ownmost *potentiality*-for-Being-its-Self."[7] Moral agency informs and empowers patient advocacy through resistance to whatever systemic brokenness is interfering with a patient's healing experience, which could be as simple as their call button being ignored or as blatant as deliberately not responding because of labeling a patient as a frequent flier or drug seeker.

Divine Rage

Advocacy is a form of resistance that moves forth from what the Sikh activist Valarie Kaur terms *divine rage*, which she clarifies isn't a form of vengeance but compassionate actions that are "precise and purposeful" and intended "to reorder the world."[8] Divine rage informs moral agency to take action for the betterment of each patient amidst the particular circumstances they're struggling with, which impede their personal agency and holistic healing. Advocacy begins with finding your voice and point of entry, including looking for ways to enter in from the periphery. A caregiver's agency is empowered and enhanced through the calling to, and doing of, patient advocacy, while patients benefit holistically as their own personal agency is respected.

Defiant Spirituality

It's necessary and possible for providers and patients to embrace what Traci West calls *defiant spirituality*, which becomes the guts and gumption to see this "thing" through to completion, whether it's a patient who's dealing with a dreaded diagnosis or a caregiver who needs to find the courage to advocate for a patient when it's urgently required and necessary. West proposes, "Defiant spirituality gives birth to hope."[9] It's hopeful because there's a potential for change, for something becoming better in the near (or distant) future. Defiant spirituality begs the question, "What is mine to do?" Defiant spirituality becomes the catalyst to move from being stuck or frozen to a place of action to make changes for the better. Defiant spirituality distracts from being fearful.[10] Who you really are is evident through what you're willing to do for someone else during difficult circumstances, especially when peers, supervisors, and whatever Powers-That-Be disagree. Who a person is, their nettle, is most evident, as MLK, Jr. notes, during "times of challenge and controversy," adding, "The true neighbor will risk [their] position, [their] prestige, and even [their] life for the welfare of others."[11] Spirituality is the motor that propels personal agency to act for advocacy, particularly in situations and circumstances when someone can't do so for themselves. Overcoming fear, finding the courage to act, and moving forth from stuck-on-center is a lifelong spiritual calling that becomes, through time and practice, a pathway for spiritual maturity that embraces *holy boldness*.

Holy Boldness

A Black female retired U.S. Army nurse who has a master's degree in hospital administration and who owned a long-term care business for over 35 years, which includes assisted living and adult day activity, explained the difference between her years as an RN and her new vocational calling as an ordained minister. She said now when she does hospital visitations, she does so with what she terms *holy boldness*. Calling herself "unapologetically spiritual," she said, "Holy boldness looks pleasant. It smiles and it's giving." She clarified, "The love you give should be tangible so people can feel it. Sometimes it's when you sit at the bedside of someone who's nonverbal and you sit in silence being a ministry of presence. That's *holy boldness*. I can sit beside them and not say a word, and you know that the Spirit of the Lord is near." She added, holy boldness means "all I have to be is humble, loving, caring, and prayerful. God does the rest. You can be humble and have holy boldness." Her holy boldness encompasses patient advocacy.

Holy Boldness Example

A mother and grandmother, she used her holy boldness and experience as an RN to call medical professionals to accountability when they allowed an important aspect of a diagnosis to slip through the cracks and go undocumented. She said, "The diagnosis and the ability to read it and understand it does *not* include the right to take control." She added, "Again, that word, control, and medical providers don't have the right to do that." She remembered when she advocated for a family when their medical records withheld the details of their child's care. She said, "You do the patient harm by withholding information about their care. You harm them, but unfortunately, they don't know it or realize it until it's too late." During a staffing meeting with healthcare providers, including nurses, physical therapists, doctors, and social workers present, who were discussing the release of a Black child who'd been severely burned the advocate explained, "This infant was four months old with third-degree burns who'd been getting heart medicine and also lung medicine. Everyone was discussing the burns. No one mentioned that a four-month-old child was being treated for congestive heart failure." She said she asked the mother who was present, "How was this diagnosis made?' And somebody in that room said, 'You don't need to worry about that.' I lost my Holy Ghost. Thank God, who is the real Holy Ghost, held me down, as I said:

*How **dare** you say that to this young woman? How dare you say that to any human being? First off, she's in a state of crisis. Her child is burned over eighty percent of the body on a four-month-old with third-degree burns, and you're giving medicine for congestive heart failure, which is normally a disease for the elderly. And you tell her she does not **need** to know? On what planet are you residing?*

The nurse/pastor/advocate said this mother didn't live in the city where this hospital was located, and while they were grateful that the child was at this hospital and receiving "the very best cutting-edge care," the advocate told the gathered group, "However, *you* now are in violation. When she goes home and she walks into any emergency room and is asked for her medical history, she won't be able to give it to them. It won't be because this mother is a poor historian. It will be because you told her she didn't need to know, and that's wrong." She said there was a proliferation of apologies and that all the information was presented and given to mother in writing. She reflected, "Now we're ten years later, the child is living in another city, but her mother has the health history of what the child went through, and why she'd been treated for congestive heart failure, which predisposes you to heart issues. Her ten-year-old has been predisposed, but at least now mom knows."

The advocate said she'd had a follow-up conversation with the staff, including the social worker and nurse, about their withholding important medical information from the child's mother. She said their response was, "They didn't want to overwhelm people who aren't medical, and don't know anything, so they didn't want to give them too much information." Reiterating her earlier point to them, she said she told them:

But you're wrong. When you withhold information, you're withholding care in their future. You could be taking their lives, the lives of their children. You don't have that right to withhold information. You're harming them in the future. Ten years down the road when something happens, you won't be there, but that mother will.

She said their response was to say that they were rethinking their policies. She followed up, saying the responsibility for advocacy is whoever's there. The onus for advocacy falls to the person in the room. Ultimately, it comes down to *choice*, the choice to participate in advocacy for patient agency or not.

Choice

Choice is an extension of human agency, which is what makes freedom of choice so important in a person's spirituality, including whether or not someone has the freedom and agency to choose or if a choice is made *for* them. The culmination of Frankl's argument centers around what he terms, "the last of the human freedoms—to choose one's attitude in any given set of circumstances, to choose one's own way."[12] The meaning of life, as Frankl sees it, revolves around how we respond when bad stuff happens. For patient advocacy, it's not if we respond to whatever (unnecessary) bad things a patient is experiencing, but how (or if) we will respond on their behalf. It comes down to the last of a caregiver's freedom: how we respond to injustice and inequity in our midst. In other words, advocacy for patient agency is each caregiver's choice.

With spirituality as *all of me*, choices focus on what the patient is experiencing and their understanding of how their physical care is helping or hindering their spiritual and emotional well-being.[13] By being attuned to the myriads of intersecting and interconnecting contributing factors of spirituality as the essence of being, patient-centered spirituality through holistic caregiving can become a reality.

14 (Spiritual) Call to Action

Practical theology begins in a particular context, in this case, direct patient care and the patient's self-understanding of how this experience helps or hinders their overall essence of being, their spirituality. After working through all the theories, readings, testimonies, and documentation, practical theology then circles back to the context to consider the call to action.[1] What is ours to do? More specifically, what is *mine* to do? How am I to become a more compassionate and spiritually sensitive caregiver based upon all that I've learned, read, and reviewed, including all of the testimonies I've read and reflected on?

Self-Assessment: Spirituality as ~~Part~~ *All of Me*

Spiritually sensitive patient care begins with a self-assessment of the contributing factors to my spirituality as ~~part~~ *all of me*. Review Illustration 2.1 and highlight the aspects, pro or con, that contribute to spirituality for your normal, healthy self. Then review the list a second time and circle or underline the top ten factors that would help or harm your spirituality when it's your turn to be a patient in a vulnerable health setting. Then reflect on how all-encompassing spirituality is, particularly how these contributing factors help or hinder patients. Holistic caregiving that's attuned to patient-centered spirituality moves forth with spiritual humility.

Spiritual Humility

There's no itemized strategy or list of resources to "do this" or "review that" in order to provide optimal spiritual care. Spiritually sensitive caregiving is patient-centered, patient-informed, and patient-prioritized. It requires a humble orientation of *not knowing*.[2] Spiritual humility is other-centered rather than self(ish)-centered. Whatever my view of spirituality is can't, shouldn't, and mustn't overflow and interfere with my beingness and caring for any patient. Spiritual humility doesn't require additional or special boundaries or a code of ethics per se because *spiritual humility is its own boundary* as it honors your *you*, without pushing my *me*.

We often can't and don't see our blind spots because it's so much who and what we are that we can't and don't see it. It's just there. It's just us. To begin really seeing what we're not seeing in ourselves, which impacts our interactions with others (including patients), we're called to come to a place of such blunt honesty about the good, the bad, and the ugly within, so we can acknowledge all this and give ourselves permission to set it aside and let it go. It includes honesty about healthcare inequity and slurs against difference (see Chapter 6).[3] The litany of contributing factors that harm human dignity directly interconnect with the contributing factors of spirituality as *all of me*. We need to honestly confront our own baggage and bias and embrace personal cultural humility, which moves toward spiritual maturity.

A Black male nurse in his mid-fifties who supervises nurses in a large metropolitan hospital in the Pacific Northwest and who's a practicing Christian, said what guides his calling is what's termed the Greatest Commandment (Matthew 22:36–40). The first or greatest is to love God, with the second part of the greatest commandment "to love your neighbor as yourself." He said it's this call to love others as yourself that keeps him focused on caring for patients: body, mind, and spirit. He explained, "If I'm working with a child molester, I've got to lean on God. I've got small children. My flesh doesn't want to care compassionately for someone when they've done something egregious." He added, "You might be presented with a wife beater, or a wife who beats her spouse. When that's who's my patient, that's when I have to lean on God. It comes down to remembering that people are not to judge others. That's up to God. People are not to be the judges."[4] Listening, acceptance, grace through difference, and internal (mis)judgment are ever-present challenges in a provider-patient *mis*balanced power dynamic.

Revisiting Cultural Humility

Cultural humility is intertwined with spiritual humility by owning up to the intersectionality of each human being: body, mind, spirit contextually situated in a particular cultural orientation. What disregards, disrespects, or disses one aspect directly impacts the others. As a Black male octogenarian who was hospitalized for hip surgery bluntly observed earlier, "I can spot a phony." Cultural humility isn't a "fake it 'till you make it" orientation. Patients notice when they're not being received, not being welcomed, and not being cared for because of whatever difference. Patients aren't stupid! Without even a spoken word communicated from provider to patient, it's readily evident whether or not there's genuine care, genuine compassion, and genuine unbiased regard.

For example, an Indigenous male who shared his mother's experience as a patient in an upper Midwestern hospital explained how cultural humility created an overall better experience for his mother when she was hospitalized with COPD and doesn't have much longer to live:

> *My mother is an old native lady. It's very common for older native people to do everything possible to avoid a hospital, for good reason, as the past has not treated us well. Cultural humility of the doctors and nursing staff has now changed my mother's mind about going into the hospital when she's feeling under the weather. She's now more willing to go to the hospital, which is significantly more likely to extend her life expectancy.[5]*

His native mother wouldn't have agreed to hospital care without the cultural humility that respects who she is as a unique individual.

Patient-Centered Holistic Caregiving: Body, Mind, Spirit

When medical care focuses all of its attention on fixing the physically broken aspect of the body, without noticing or caring about how the body is directly interconnected with the same person's internal and often invisible spiritual and emotional well-being, it short-circuits holistic caregiving. Care shouldn't be limited to part of me. It must include *all of me*. Patients don't leave their essence of being at home. The full person rides along in the ambulance or car. The full person is treated in urgent care and/or admitted to a hospital. It's never part of the person's essence of being. Every part of who they are is languishing in an ER waiting room, strapped to a gurney, or anxiously trying to doze in a hospital bed. When this full humanity isn't acknowledged and respected, their essence of being suffers.

Finding Your Spiritual Center

You won't and can't find your spiritual center by running around with your head cut off from task to task and activity to activity. When you're too busy to be, it's impossible to *be*, and *being time* is the heart of spirituality, whatever that being time is for you. A nursing student said quietude helps her to recenter from the overly structured and hectic life as a mother, wife, student, and nurse. Referring to the first chapter in *Our Greatest Gift*, when Nouwen discusses how he intends to stay for five weeks in his friend's apartment for the purpose of being quiet, meditating on death and dying, and writing, she said the nursing school has afforded her almost no quiet time. She said she'd "been making an effort to show up early at the hospital to stop in the chapel for a few minutes before running off to my twelve-hour shift" and also that she'd been "intending to show up earlier so that I have longer to pray before my shift, be quiet a moment, and center myself." She said, unfortunately, many days she simply stopped for around a minute or so because she didn't show up early enough. She reflected, "It is my goal to improve on this, and to actually show up earlier to really take some time to pray and be quiet."[6] She added,

> *Mother Teresa has been my hero since childhood. Before heading out into the streets of Calcutta, the Missionaries of Charity sisters always spend one hour of prayer before the Blessed Sacrament, and Mother Teresa herself often spent two hours praying. She credited her work to her prayer time. I think of how busy she must have been, way busier than myself, but she still made time to pray every day. Mother Teresa frequently said, "We are contemplatives in action." It's my goal as a future nurse, to take the time to pray and ground myself before every shift so that I can offer better care to my patients.*[7]

Referring to when Nouwen discusses the benefit of being quiet and the ways in which we avoid it in his reflection, "The stillness is purifying. Strange as it may seem, the outer quietude quickly reveals the inner restlessness. What am I going to do when there is nothing to do?"[8] The soon-to-graduate nursing student added, "I believe in the benefits of quiet and solitude, but I too find it much easier to keep running, running, and running. When I truly take the time to be quiet, I'm grateful that I did, but it is all too easy to find excuses to avoid it." It's easier to remain too busy to be still, but it's through the stillness that it becomes possible to find your spiritual center. Recentering provides the spiritual fortitude to continue with the larger issues of life. Instead of living for bread alone, as Dorothee Soelle describes the success and the busyness of the rat race to worldly success in *Death by Bread Alone*, intentionally pausing to reclaim your spiritual center prioritizes the meaningful moments of being time.[9]

Mindfulness (or Centering Prayer)

Mindfulness (or centering prayer) is helpful for reclaiming your spiritual center. Intentionality with mindfulness helps caregivers to be agents of compassion. Mindfulness also helps to quiet, or at least to refocus, the noisy inner voice that's each person's incessant noisy conversation partner. Mindfulness stills the otherwise nonstop internal voice that narrates every moment, almost like an "inner roommate."[10] What a Jewish mother described as "the God within" becomes a guidon through stillness, through listening, through being. Whether through mindfulness, contemplative prayer, or a deep silence, it's this intentional silence that facilitates spiritual centering.[11] There are a bazillion books and YouTube videos on mindfulness (and also prayer), including genres, techniques, and benefits. Here, I'll briefly highlight a few insights of Vietnamese Buddhist guru Thich Nhat Hanh.

Thich Nhat Hanh on Mindfulness

First, the Four Noble Truths of Buddhism revolve around suffering, including (1) life is suffering; (2) desire causes suffering; (3) it's possible to end suffering; and (4) there's a path to follow that will end suffering. With this primacy of suffering in view, Thich Nhat Hanh believes through mindfulness it's possible to understand pain and also to soothe suffering.[12] When someone's unable to practice mindfulness themselves because of their ill or distraught state, this person can draw their peace and support from others who practice mindfulness (or prayer) on their behalf.[13] Hanh advises, "If we face our unpleasant feelings with care, affection, and nonviolence, we can transform them into the kind of energy that is healthy and has the capacity to nourish us. By the work of mindful observation, our unpleasant feelings can illuminate so much for us, offering us insight and understanding into ourselves and society."[14] This Buddhist guru describes the daily practice of mindfulness "practice[ing] resurrection.... With an in-breath, you bring your mind back to your body. In this way, you become alive in the here and now. Joy, peace, and happiness are possible. You have an appointment with life, an appointment that is in the here and now."[15] It's this being fully present in the moment that engenders spiritual centering.[16]

Mantra Repetition

Another contemplative practice is "frequent repetition of a single chosen holy name," a spiritual centering practice that's commonly used in Protestantism and Roman Catholicism, though it's applicable to any religious or nonreligious spirituality for centering.[17] The point of mantra repetition is to slow down to a single directional focus "for calming the mind, body, and spirit."[18] It "provides a 'short pause,' putting enough space between the triggering event and the individual's reaction to enable him or her to choose how or whether to respond to a stressful situation."[19] It's a portable spiritual practice to facilitate a calming presence anytime and anywhere.[20]

Expanding the Spiritual Practice Options

Prayer and mindfulness are almost stereotypical spiritual practices that also tend to come with religious connotations or affiliations. However, there are a myriad of possibilities for what could be a spiritual practice and source of centering, depending on what contributes to your spirituality and calm within a storm. Part of spiritual self-care is recognizing which practices bring you centeredness, including activities you might not name as being spiritual practices, such as the melanoma patient who went rock climbing after his cancer treatments.

Creative Spiritual Practice Examples

Finding your spiritual center moves forth from your self-understanding of the contributing factors to what spirituality is for you. Nature? Treadmill? Art? Music? Silence? Solitude? People? When you're overstructured and too busy to do whatever brings you spiritual centeredness, you're too busy to be *you*. My spiritual center is restored when I take time to read, do art for art's sake, journal, garden, play clarinet, and/or sit quietly beside the ocean. Even pounding out miles on the treadmill is one of my spiritual practices because, unlike most of the people at this gym, I use this time to be unplugged and offline as I center through internal reflective prayer. I also practice contemplative photography, where I view the beauty of nature through the lens of my iPhone. For example, in 2020, when the world was in lockdown with the Covid-19 pandemic, I took several hundred photographs of the giant sunflowers we'd planted in our backyard. I later used these photographs for contemplative art as spiritual care (see Illustration 14.1). A spiritual practice could be sitting on the floor and playing with your child or grandchild or reading them a bedtime story. Spiritual practices support centeredness by shifting the focus off of being productive and doing, to appreciating the essence of being. They're also central to what Audre Lorde calls "living a considered life."

Living a Considered Life

As Lorde experienced in her spiritual journey through breast cancer and a single mastectomy, "The need to look death in the face and not shrink from it, yet not ever to embrace it too easily, was a developmental and healing task for me that was constantly being sidelined by the more practical and immediate demands of hurting too much. . . ."[21] Lorde's answer is the recommendation "to live a considered life."[22] Living a considered life includes being intentional about actions, interactions, and choices in how we live and respond to the stressors that come with living in a fast-paced, a/religious, and often a/spiritual world. We can't control or shape exactly what's going to happen to us on any given day, but as Frankl learned, we can choose our response, which then shapes our spirituality of living a considered life through *responsibleness*.

Responsibleness

We've come full circle to the intersection of spirituality and the meaning of life. Spirituality isn't part of me, it's *all of me*. The existential meaning of life is one (important) contributing factor, but only one. It's *part* of me, but it's not *all of me*. Spirituality also includes the world around me. Life is what Frankl terms *responsibleness*, which emphasizes personal agency for how each person responds to what happens to them during this short life.[23] Patient-centered spirituality for holistic caregiving asks caregivers for a responsibleness in

Illustration 14.1 *Sunflower in Bloom* watercolor with ink example of art as spiritual (self-) care. © Helen T. Boursier

compassionate caring which respects the agency of each patient, including attentiveness to their spiritual well-being. Responsibleness discovers what my nursing and social work students consistently have remarked on their last day of class: "Spirituality doesn't mean what I thought it meant." Spirituality isn't part of me. It's *all of me*.

Notes

Introduction

1 See, Viktor E. Frankl, *Man's Search for Meaning*, foreword by Harold S. Kushner (Boston: Beacon Press, 1959, 2006). For an example refuting healthcare's inaccurate view of spirituality, see, Guy Harrison, ed., *Psycho-spiritual Care in Health Care Practice* (London: Jessica Kingsley Publishers, 2017), 178–9.

3 Patient demographics include three LGBTQIA, three Black females, two Black males, three Hispanic females, one Hispanic male, three Jewish American females, ten white females, and five white males. Ages include young adults in their twenties and thirties, a few middle-aged adults, approximately half of the participants in their sixties and seventies, and one "super senior" octogenarian. Approximately half of these research participants have no religious affiliation, eleven are loosely affiliated with a Protestant church, four are Roman Catholic, and three are semi-practicing Jews.

4 For the role of testimony as an authentic witness to justice/injustice, see, Rebecca S. Chopp, "Theology and the Poetics of Testimony," in *Converging on Culture: Theologians in Dialogue with Cultural Analysis and Criticism*, ed. Delwin Brown, Sheila Greeve Davaney, and Kathryn Tanner (Oxford: Oxford University Press, 2001), 56–65; bell hooks (Gloria Watkins), *Talking Back: Thinking Feminist, Thinking Black* (Boston: South End Press, 1989); and Judith Herman, *Trauma and Recovery: The Aftermath of Violence from Domestic Abuse to Political Terror* (New York: Perseus Books, 1992, 1997, 2015). For grounded theory in qualitative research, see, Juliet Corbin and Anselm Strauss, *Basics of Qualitative Research*, 3rd ed. (Thousand Oaks, CA: Sage Publications, Inc., 2008).

Chapter 1

1. In contrast to this being a season of "spiritual disorientation," as argued by David N. Elkins, L. James Hedstrom, Lori L. Hughes, J. Andrew Leaf, and Cheryl Saunders, "Toward a Humanistic-Phenomenological Spirituality," *Journal of Humanistic Psychology* 28, no. 4 (fall 1988): 5–14 (p. 7). doi:10.1177/0022167888284002.

2. See, Wesley Carr, "Spirituality and Religion: Chaplaincy in Context," in *Spirituality in Health Care Contexts*, ed. Helen Orchard, 21–32 (London: Jessica Kingsley Publishers, 2001), 27; Mathew Guest, "In Search of Spiritual Capital: The Spiritual as a Cultural Resource," in *A Sociology of Spirituality*, ed. Kieran Flanagan and Peter C. Jupp, 181–200 (Farnham: Ashgate Publishing: 2009), 181; Ivan Varga, "Georg Simmel: Religion and Spirituality," in *An Ethic of Care: Feminist and Interdisciplinary Perspectives*, ed. Peter C. Jupp and Kieran Flanagan, 145–60 (London: Routledge, 1993), 145; see also, David Voas and Steve Bruce, "The Spiritual Revolution: Another False Dawn for the Sacred," in *A Sociology of Spirituality*, ed. Kieran Flanagan and Peter C. Jupp, 43–61 (Farnham: Ashgate Publishing, 2009), 145; Kieran Flanagan, Introduction to *A Sociology of Spirituality* (Farnham: Ashgate Publishing, 2009), 5; Ryan P. Burge, *The Nones: Where They Came From, Who They Are, and Where They Are Going* (Minneapolis, MN: Fortress Press, 2021); and Charles Taylor, *A Secular Age* (Cambridge, MA: Belknap Press of Harvard University Press, 2007), 513.

3. Ernest Kurtz and Katherine Ketcham, *The Spirituality of Imperfection: Storytelling and the Search for Meaning* (New York: Bantam Books, 1992), 31.

4. Kurtz and Ketcham, *Spirituality of Imperfection*, 19.

5. Nina Redl, "What Can You Do for Me?: David, A Mid-sixties Jewish Man with Stage IV Pancreatic Cancer," in *Spiritual Care in Practice*, ed. George Fitchett and Steve Nolan, 223–41 (Jessica Kingsley Publishers, 2015), 236–7.

6. See, Roger Haight, *Spiritual and Religious: Explorations for Seekers* (Maryknoll, NY: Orbis Books, 2016), 19.

7. See, Haight, *Spiritual and Religious*, xiii–xvi.

8. Jonathan Haidt, "Religion, Evolution, and the Ecstasy of Self-transcendence," *TED Talk*, March 14, 2012. https://www.youtube.com/watch?v=2MYsx6WArKY&t=11s.

9. See, Christina Puchalski and Betty Ferrell, *Making Health Care Whole: Integrating Spirituality into Patient Care* (West Conshohocken, PA: Templeton Press, 2010), 21.

10 See, Elkins, Hedstrom, Hughes, Leaf, and Saunders, "Humanistic-Phenomenological Spirituality," 16.

11 See, Gian Carlo M., Ledesma, Marc Eric S. Reyes, and Clarissa F. Delariarte, "Meaning in Life, Death Anxiety, and Spirituality in the Lesbian, Gay, and Bisexual Community: A Scoping Review," *Sexuality & Culture* 27, no. 2 (April 2023): 636–58 (p. 638). doi:10.1007/s12119-022-10032-4.

12 See, Evelyn Underhill, *Evelyn Underhill: The Best Works. 1. Practical Mysticism (1914), 2. Mysticism: A Study in Nature and Development of Spiritual Consciousness (1911). 3. The Essentials of Mysticism (1920)* (New York: Vintage Books, 2003), 3.

13 See, Giuseppe Giordan, "Spirituality: From a Religious Concept to a Sociological Theory," in Flanagan and Jupp, *A Sociology of Spirituality*, 166.

14 Spring 2024.

15 Spring 2024.

16 See, Helen T. Boursier, *Willful Ignorance: Overcoming the Limitations of (Christian) Love for Refugees Seeking Asylum* (Lanham, MD: Rowman and Littlefield, 2022), 24–5.

17 Haight, *Spiritual and Religious*, 5.

18 See, Helen T. Boursier, *Precious Precarity: A Spirituality of Borders* (Minneapolis, MN: Fortress Press, 2024), xix–xxi.

19 See, Meredith Gould, *Desperately Seeking Spirituality: A Field Guide to Practice* (Collegeville, MN: Liturgical Press, 2016), xii.

20 Roger S. Gottlieb, *A Spirituality of Resistance: Finding a Peaceful Heart and Protecting the Earth* (Lanham, MD: Rowman & Littlefield, 2003), 137.

21 See, Haidt, "Ecstasy of Self-transcendence," (06:17); and L. Ross, "The Nurse's Role in Assessing and Responding to Patients' Spiritual Needs," *International Journal of Palliative Nursing* (January 1, 1997): 37–41 (p. 38). ISSN: 1357-6321.

22 Kurtz and Ketcham, *Spirituality of Imperfection*, 17.

23 Kurtz and Ketcham, *Spirituality of Imperfection*, 16.

24 For spirituality as a part of a person's whole health, see, National Center for Complementary and Integrative Health (NCCIH), NCCIH Strategic Plan FY 2021–2025: Mapping the Pathway to Research on Whole Person Health, Accessed December 2, 2021, https://fles.nccih.nih.gov/ nccih-strategic-plan-2021-2025 .pdf; and A. B. Newberg, "The Neuroscientifc Study of Spiritual Practices," *Frontiers in Psychology* 5 (2014): 215. doi:10.3389/fpsyg.2014.00215.

25 See, Edward R. Canda and Leola Dyrud Furman, *Spiritual Diversity in Social Work Practice: The Heart of Helping.* 2nd ed. (Oxford: University of Oxford Press. 2019), 66.

26 Harold G. Koenig, "Religion, Spirituality, and Health: Understanding the Mechanisms," in *Spiritual Dimensions of Nursing Practice*, rev. ed., ed. Verna Benner Carson and Harold G. Koenig, 33–61 (West Conshohocken, PA: Templeton Press, 2008), 39.

27 Koenig, "Understanding the Mechanisms," 39.

28 See, Flanagan, Introduction to *A Sociology of Spirituality*, 25.

29 See, Duncan S. Ferguson, *Exploring the Spirituality of the World Religions: The Quest for Personal, Spiritual, and Social Transformation* (London: Bloomsbury Academic, 2010).

30 See, Heidegger, *Being and Time*, trans. John Macquarrie and Edward Robinson, forward by Taylor Carman (New York: Harper and Row, 1962, 2008), 480.

31 See, Boursier, *Precious Precarity*, 5–8.

32 Summer 2023.

33 See, Boursier, *Willful Ignorance*, 23–53; and Boursier, *Precious Precarity*, 5–8.

34 Redl, "What Can You Do for Me," 237.

35 See, Kathleen S. Isaac, Jennifer L Hay, and Erica I. Lubetkin, "Incorporating Spirituality in Primary Care," *Journal of Religion and Health* 55, no. 3 (June 2016): 1065–77 (p. 1065). doi:10.1007/s10943-016-0190-2.

36 Andre E. De La Porte, "Spirituality and Holistic People-Centered Healthcare: A South African Model," in *Proceedings of the 2nd Biennial South African Conference on Spirituality and Healthcare*, ed. André de la Porte, Nicolene Joubert and Annemarie Oberholzer, 70–89 (Cambridge Scholars Publishing, 2018), 70.

37 De La Porte, "Spirituality and Holistic People-Centered Healthcare," 73. See, World Health Organization (WHO), 1998, *WHOQOL and Spirituality, Religiousness and Personal Beliefs: Report on WHO Consultation* (Geneva, 2010). "Key Components of a Well-functioning Health System," https://www.paho.org/derechoalaSSR/wp-content/uploads/Documentos/Bloques-Basicos-de-un-Sistema-de-Salud-OMS.pdf; and World Health Organization (WHO), "WHO Definition of Health," 2003, https://www.publichealth.com.ng/world-health-organizationwho-definition-of-health/.

38 Christina M. Puchalski, "The Role of Spirituality in the Care of Seriously Ill, Chronically Ill, and Dying Patients," in *A Time for Listening and Caring: Spirituality and the Care of the Chronically Ill and Dying*, ed. Christina M. Puchalski, 5–26 (Oxford: Oxford University Press, 2006), 22.

39 Wilfred McSherry, et al., "Preparing Undergraduate Nurses and Midwives for Spiritual Care: Some Developments in European Education Over the Last Decade," *Journal for the Study of Spirituality* 10, no. 1 (2020): 56, doi:10.1080/20440243.2020.1726053.

40 Fall 2023.
41 See, Shri K. Mishra, Elizabeth Togneri, Byomesh Tripathi, and Bhavesh Trikamji, "Spirituality and Religiosity and Its Role in Health and Diseases," *Psychological Exploration* 56 (2017): 1282–3, doi:10.1007/s 10943-015-0100-z.
42 Barbara Ganim, *Art and Healing: Using Expressive Art to Heal Your Body, Mind, and Spirit* (US: Echo Point Books & Media, 1999, 2013), 44.
43 See Canda and Furman, *Spiritual Diversity in Social Work Practice*, 60–3.
44 For spirituality as nonreligious religion, see, Paul Heelas and Linda Woodhead with Benjamin Seel, Bronislaw Szerszynski and Karin Tusting, *The Spiritual Revolution: Why Religion Is Giving Way to Spirituality* (Oxford: Blackwell Publishing. 2005); and Giselle Vincent and Linda Woodhead, "Spirituality," in *Religions in the Modern World: Traditions and Transformations*, 3rd ed., ed. Linda Woodhead, Christopher Partridge, and Hiroko Kawanami (London: Routledge, 2016), 323–44.

Chapter 2

1 See, Boursier, *Willful Ignorance*, 161–7; Eboo Patel, "Building Bridges: Religions' Role in Our Societies," *TEDx Chicago*, December 10, 2021, https://www.youtube.com/watch?v=GYLesUKHPGc&t=2s; and James Mohr and John Nicols, eds., "Life Expectancy 1850-2000," *Mapping History, University of Oregon*, https://mappinghistory.uoregon.edu/english/US/US39-01.html. Accessed March 16, 2024.
2 Wilfred McSherry and Peter Draper, "The Debates Emerging from the Literature Surrounding the Concept of Spirituality as Applied to Nursing," *Journal of Advanced Nursing* (Wiley-Blackwell) 27, no. 4 (1998): 687, doi:10.1046/j.1365-2648.1998.00585.x.
3 McSherry and Draper, "Debates . . . Concept of Spirituality," 687.
4 McSherry and Draper, "Debates . . . Concept of Spirituality." See also, A. Bradshaw, "The Legacy of Nightingale," *Nursing Times* 92, no. 6 (1996): 42–3. ISSN: 09960207.
5 For holistic or whole person health, see, National Center for Complementary and Integrative Health (NCCIH) NCCIH Strategic Plan FY 2021–2025, https://fles.nccih.nih.gov/nccih-strategic-plan-2021-2025.pdf; and Newberg, "Neuroscientifc Study of Spiritual Practices," 5, 215.
6 The proliferation of academic literature on spirituality in nursing led one journal article to suggest, "nurses are pioneers in the field of spirituality and related

concepts." See, Fateme Eshghi, Lida Nikfarid, and Armin Zareiyan, "An Integrative Review of Defining Characteristic of the Nursing Diagnosis 'Spiritual Distress,'" *Nursing Open* 10, no. 5 (May 2023): 2838, doi:10.1002/nop2.

7   There's a large body of literature on spirituality in healthcare. For this particular project, space doesn't permit me to explore the nursing and physician literature in great detail. Instead, refer to the endnotes for recommended reading. For an example on refuting healthcare's inaccurate view of spirituality, see, Harrison, ed., *Psycho-spiritual Care,* 178–9. Among many others on spirituality in healthcare, see, Puchalski and Ferrell, *Making Health Care Whole*; Gillian White, *Talking About Spirituality in Health Care Practice: A Resource for Multi-Professional Health Care Team* (Jessica Kingsley Publishers, 2008); Association of American Medical Colleges (AAMC), *Report III: Contemporary Issues in Medicine: Communication in Medicine* (Washington, DC: AAMC, 1999). https://gwish.smhs.gwu.edu/sites/g/files/zaskib1011/files/2022-08/msop_iii_report_2.pdf; and World Health Organization https://www.who.int/. For a social work perspective on spirituality, see, Canda and Furman, *Spiritual Diversity in Social Work Practice*; and Fiona Gardner, *Critical Spirituality: A Holistic Approach to Contemporary Practice* (Surrey: Ashgate Publishing Limited, 2011). For the role of Clinical Pastoral Education (CPE) in preparing for chaplaincy, see, Wendy Cadge, *Paging God: Religion in the Halls of Medicine* (Chicago, IL: University of Chicago Press, 2013); Wendy Cadge and Shelly Rambo, eds., *Chaplaincy and Spiritual Care in the Twenty-First Century: An Introduction* (University of North Carolina Press, 2022); George Fitchett, *Assessing Spiritual Needs: A Guide for Caregivers* (Academic Renewal Press, 2002); and Fitchett and Nolan, eds., *Spiritual Care in Practice*. For a nursing perspective, see, Doreen, A. Westera, *Spirituality in Nursing Practice: The Basics and Beyond* (New York: Springer Publishing Company, 2017); Mary Elizabeth O'Brien, *Spirituality in Nursing: Standing on Holy Ground*, 6th ed. (Jones and Bartlett Learning, 2017); and Wilfred McSherry, "Spiritual Crisis? Call a Nurse," in Orchard, *Spirituality in Health Care Contexts*, 107–17. For a medical imaging view, see, Zainul Ibrahim Zainuddi, "Aligning Islamic Spirituality to Medical Imaging," *Journal of Religio Health* 56 (June 2015): 1605–19. doi:10.1007/sl0943-015-0074-x. See also, Harvard University. Initiative on Health, Spirituality, and Religion, https://projects.iq.harvard.edu/rshm/home?fbclid=IwAR0Eu6QIOKH1fW2hKXK4PBL-Z0cn8aRZ2BuOjFJoO6wyiSAVFtJLV9S1bD4.

8   Frankl, *Man's Search for Meaning*, 49–50.

9   Frankl, *Man's Search for Meaning*, 139.

10   Frankl, *Man's Search for Meaning*, 135. See also, Viktor Frankl, *Viktor Frankl: Self-Actualization is Not the Goal*, Noetic Films, YouTube, September 20, 2019, https://www.youtube.com/watch?v=OL8DyVusLeE, (07:25).

11   Frankl, *Man's Search for Meaning*, 135.

12 See, Bradshaw, "Legacy of Nightingale," 42; and Puchalski, "Spirituality in the Care of Seriously Ill," 11; and Christina M. Puchalski, "Spirituality: Implications for Healing," *New Theology Review* 18, no. 4 (2021): 77–81. Puchalski and Ferrell, *Making Health Care Whole*, 25.

13 See, Bonnie Weaver Batty, "Perspectives of Spiritual Care for Nurse Managers," *Journal of Nursing Management* 20 (2012): 1013, [Blackwell Publishing]. doi:10.1111/j.1365-2834.2012.01360.x.

14 Janet K. Shim, *Heart-Sick: The Politics of Risk, Inequality, and Heart Disease* (New York: New York University Press, 2014), 18–19. On the concept of black boxes in science and technology studies, see, Bruno Latour, *Science in Action: How to Follow Scientists and Engineers Through Society* (Cambridge, MA: Harvard University Press, 1987); and Bruno Latour and Steve Woolgar, *Laboratory Life: The Construction of Scientific Facts*, introduction by Jonas Salk (Princeton: Princeton University Press, 1986), as cited by Shim.

15 Shim, *Heart-Sick*, 18–19.

16 For information on how nurses view spirituality and spiritual care, see, Wilfred McSherry and Steve Jamieson, "The Qualitative Findings from an Online Survey Investigating Nurses' Perceptions of Spirituality and Spiritual Care," *Journal of Clinical Nursing* (John Wiley & Sons, Inc.) 22, no. 21–22 (November 2013): 3170–82. doi:10.1111/jocn.12411.

17 Bradshaw, "Legacy of Nightingale," 42.

18 Bradshaw, "Legacy of Nightingale," 42.

19 For spirituality as meaning in life in healthcare, see, Fitchett, *Assessing Spiritual Needs*, 16.

Chapter 3

1 See, Puchalski and Ferrell, *Making Health Care Whole*, 11.

2 Puchalski and Ferrell, *Making Health Care Whole*, 12.

3 Anne Fadiman, *The Spirit Catches You and You Fall Down: A Hmong child, Her American Doctors, and the Collision of Two Cultures* (New York: Farrar, Straus and Giroux, 1977, 2012), 274–5.

4 Fadiman, *The Spirit Catches You*, 274–5. See also, Mark D. Sullivan, *The Patient as Agent of Health and Health Care* (Oxford: Oxford University Press, 2017), 77.

5 See, Charles Taylor, *The Malaise of Modernity* (Canada: House of Anansi Press Ltd., 1991), 8; Charles Taylor, *The Ethics of Authenticity* (Cambridge, MA: Harvard University Press, 1991), 10; and James K. A. Smith, *How (Not) to be Secular:*

Reading Charles Taylor (Grand Rapids, MI: William B. Eerdmans Publishing Co., 2014), 20–1.

6 See, Smith, *How (Not) to be Secular*, 21.
7 Taylor, *A Secular Age*, 265–6.
8 See, Hamish Ferguson-Stuart, "Discourses of Spiritual Healthcare," in *Critical Care*, 30.
9 See, Taylor, *A Secular Age*, 38–9, 47; and Smith, *How (Not) to be Secular*, 29.
10 Sullivan, *Patient as Agent*, 76.
11 See, Cadge, *Paging God*, 145.
12 O'Brien, *Standing on Holy Ground*, 3.
13 Patricia Grayhall, *Making the Rounds: Defying Norms in Love and Medicine* (Berkeley, CA: She Writes Press, 2022), 153.
14 Grayhall, *Making the Rounds*, 153–4.
15 Grayhall, *Making the Rounds*, 155.
16 Grayhall, *Making the Rounds*, 154–5.
17 Grayhall, *Making the Rounds*, 155.
18 On aloofness, see, Henri J. M. Nouwen, *The Wounded Healer: In Our Own Woundedness, We Can Become a Source of Life for Others* (New York: Doubleday, 1979), 72.
19 On being summarily ignored, see, *The Couch Trip*, directed by Michael Ritchie (MGM, Orion Pictures, 1988); see also, Ken Kolb, *The Couch Trip* (New York: Dell, 1970, 1971).
20 See, John Paley, "Spirituality and Secularization: Nursing and the Sociology of Religion," *Journal of Clinical Nursing* 17, no. 2 (January 2008): 175–86 (p. 179).

Chapter 4

1 See, Albert Bandura, "Moral Disengagement in the Perpetration of Inhumanities," *Personality and Social Psychology Review* 3, no. 3 (July 1, 1999): 193–209. doi:10.1207/s15327957pspr0303_3; and Albert Bandura, *Moral Disengagement: How People Do Harm and Live with Themselves* (New York: Worth Publishers, 2016).
2 Nursing student, Fall 2023.
3 See, Caroline Young and Cyndie Koopsen, *Spirituality, Health, and Healing* (Sudbury, MA: Jones and Bartlett, 2005), 4.

4   Katarzyna Kotfis, Annachiara Marra, and Eugene Wesley Ely, "ICU Delirium - a Diagnostic and Therapeutic Challenge in the Intensive Care Unit," *Anaesthesiology Intensive Therapy* 50, no. 2 (2018): 160–7. doi:10.5603/AIT.a2018.0011. See also, Anil K. Malik, Dalim K. Baidya, Rahul K. Anand, and Rajeshwari Subramaniam, "A New ICU Delirium Prevention Bundle to Reduce the Incidence of Delirium: A Randomized Parallel Group Trial," *Indian Journal of Critical Care Medicine* 25, no. 7 (July 2021): 754.

5   See, Iris Murdoch, *The Sovereignty of Good*, Routledge Classics (New York: Routledge, 1970), 89.

6   Young and Koopsen, *Spirituality, Health, and Healing*, 10.

7   William F. May, "The Patient as Person: Beyond Ramsey's Beecher Lectures," in *The Patient as Person: Explorations in Medical Ethics*, 2nd ed., ed. Paul Ramsey, xxix–xliii (New Haven, CT: Yale University Press, 1970, 2002), xxxvii.

8   See, Sullivan, *Patient as Agent*, 94.

9   On assumptions, inequality, and justice in healthcare, see, J. Paul Kelleher, "Health Inequalities and Relational Egalitarianism," in *Understanding Health Inequalities and Justice: New Conversations Across Disciplines*, ed. Mara Buchbinder, Michele Rivkin-Fish, and Rebecca L. Walker, 88–111 (Chapel Hill, NC: University of North Carolina Press, 2016), 127.

Chapter 5

1   Heidegger, *Being and Time*, 391.

2   Boursier, *Precious Precarity*, 151.

3   Heidegger, *Being and Time*, 391; italics his.

4   Boursier, *Precious Precarity*, 151.

5   See, Boursier, *Willful Ignorance*, 92–5.

6   Paul Tillich, *The Courage to Be* (New Haven, CT and London: Yale University Press, 1952), 35. See also, Boursier, *Precious Precarity*, 157–8.

7   Tillich, *Courage to Be*, 156.

8   See, Philip Yancy, *Where Is God When It Hurts?* (Grand Rapids: Zondervan, 1977, 1990), 176.

9   Catriona Mackenzie, Wendy Rogers, and Susan Dodds, "Introduction: What is Vulnerability, and Why Does It Matter for Moral Theory?" in *Vulnerability: New Essays in Ethics and Feminist Philosophy*, ed. Catriona Mackenzie, Wendy Rogers,

and Susan Dodds., 1–29, Studies in Feminist Philosophy (Oxford and New York: Oxford University Press, 2014), 1.

10 On a patient's hope amidst a grim prognosis, see, Marilyn Smith-Stoner and Amy Lynn Frost, "How to Build Your 'Hope Skills,'" *Nursing*, 29, no 9 (September 1, 1999): 48.

11 The Principle of Autonomy specifies that "rational individuals should be permitted to be self-determining. There is a duty of others to respect the inherent worth of all." Debra Shearer, "Colliding Cultures in Delivery of Health Services: The Role of Cultural Competency in Health," White Paper. Maryville University, March 2013, 7–8. See also, Puchalski and Ferrell, *Making Health Care Whole*, 42.

12 See, "Health Insurance Portability and Accountability Act of 1996 (HIPAA)," Centers for Disease Control and Prevention (CDC), U.S. Department of Health and Human Services, updated June 27, 2022, https://www.cdc.gov/phlp/publications/topic/hipaa.html. See also, Puchalski and Ferrell, *Making Health Care Whole*, 149.

13 See, Judith Butler, "Rethinking Vulnerability and Resistance," in *Vulnerability in Resistance*, ed. Judith Butler, Zeynep Gambetti and Leticia Sabsay, 12–27 (Durham and London: Duke University Press, 2016), 15.

14 Regarding confidentiality and gaining patient permission, see Puchalski and Ferrell, *Making Health Care Whole*, 148.

15 For various types of consent, see, Peter Speck, *Being There: Pastoral Care in Time of Illness* (London: SPCK, 1988), 135.

16 Errin C. Gilson, *The Ethics of Vulnerability: A Feminist Analysis of Social Life and Practices*, Routledge Studies in Ethics and Moral Theory (London and New York: Routledge, 2014), 3.

17 See, Gilson, *Ethics of Vulnerability*, 4–5.

18 Due to space limitations and content focus, ethical parameters are only briefly addressed here. For excellent resources in medical ethics see, Tom L. Beauchamp and James F. Childress, *Principles of Biomedical Ethics*, 8th ed. (Oxford: Oxford University Press, 2019); Pamela J. Grace and Melissa K. Uveges, *Nursing Ethics and Professional Responsibility in Advanced Practice*, 4th ed. (Jones and Bartlett Learning, 2022); and Ronald Munson, *Intervention and Reflection Basic Issues in Medical Ethics*, 8th ed. (Belmont, CA: Thomson Wadsworth, 2008, 2004).

19 See, Westera, *Spirituality in Nursing Practice*, 189–90. For prohibition against proselytizing in a clinical setting, see also, Puchalski and Ferrell, *Making Health Care Whole*, 45.

20 See, Gilson, *Ethics of Vulnerability*, 27.

Chapter 6

1 See, Emmanuel Levinas, *Otherwise Than Being—Or Beyond Essence*, trans. Alphonso Lingis (Pittsburgh, PA: Duquesne University Press, 1981, 1997), 18; and Helen T. Boursier, *The Ethics of Hospitality: An Interfaith Response to U.S. Immigration Policies* (Lanham, MD: Lexington Books, 2019), 52–4.

2 Jacque Derrida, *Positions*, trans. and annotated by Alan Bass (Chicago, IL: University of Chicago Press, 1981), xvi; See also, Jacque Derrida, *The Gift of Death*, trans. David Wills (Chicago, IL: University of Chicago Press, 1995); Kevin Hart, *The Trespass of the Sign: Deconstruction, Theology, and Philosophy* (New York: Fordham University Press, 2000), 37.

3 Fall 2023. For an argument on plurality in spirituality in a healthcare context, see, Pam McCarroll, Thomas St. James O'Conner, and Elizabeth Meakes, "Assessing Plurality in Spirituality Definitions," in *Spirituality and Health: Multidisciplinary Explorations*, ed. Augustine Meier, Thomas St. James O'Connor, and Peter L. VanKatwyk, 43–59 (Waterloo, ON: Wilfrid Laurier University Press, 2005), 43.

4 See, Miranda Fricker, *Epistemic Injustice: Power and the Ethics of Knowing* (Oxford: Oxford University Press, 2007), 1.

5 Bandura, *Moral Disengagement*, 84.

6 Bandura, *Moral Disengagement*, 84.

7 See, Fricker, *Epistemic Injustice*, 1.

8 See, Judith Butler, *Gender Trouble: Feminism and the Subversion of Identity* (London: Routledge, 2006).

9 Judith Butler, *Undoing Gender* (London: Routledge, 2004), 53.

10 See, bell hooks, *Feminist Theory: From Martin to Center* (New York: Routledge, 2015), 28; See also, bell hooks, *Feminism is for Everybody: Passionate Politics* (New York: Routledge, 2015), 47; and Valarie Kaur, *See No Stranger: A Memoir and Manifesto of Revolutionary Love* (New York: Random House, 2020), 95.

11 See, hooks, *Feminist Theory*, 37.

12 Simone de Beauvoir, *The Second Sex*, introduction by Judith Thurman, trans. Constance Borde and Sheila Malovany-Chevallier (New York: Vintage Books, Random House, 1949, 2009), 283.

13 See, Boursier, *Precious Precarity*, 31–2.

14 See, Herman, *Trauma and Recovery*, 65.

15 See, Boursier, *Willful Ignorance*, 23–53. See also, Audre Lorde, *Sister Outsider: Essays and Speeches by Audre Lorde* (Berkley, CA: Crossing Press, 1984, 2007),

115–23; and Toni Morrison, "Home," in *The House that Race Built: Original Essays by Toni Morrison, Angela Y. Davis, Cornel West, and Others on Black Americans and Politics in America Today*, ed. Wahneema Lubiano, 3–12 (New York: Vintage Books, 1998), 3.

16 See, Morrison, "Home," in Lubiano, *House that Race Built*, 3.

17 Lorde, "Age, Race, Class, and Sex," in *Sister Outsider*, 117.

18 See, Jamie T. Phelps, "Joy Came in the Morning Risking Death for Resurrection: Confronting the Evil of Social Sin and Socially Sinful Structures," in *Embracing the Spirit: Womanist Perspectives on Hope, Salvation and Transformation*, ed. Emilie M. Townes, 48–70 (Maryknoll, NY: Orbis Books, 1997), 49.

19 See, Rebecca L. Walker, Michele Rivkin-Fish, and Mara Buchbinder, Introduction to *Understanding Health Inequalities and* Justice, 1–30.

20 Vivian Chávez, director/producer, "Cultural Humility," YouTube, 03:36, 2012, https://www.youtube.com/watch?v=SaSHLbS1V4w.

21 hooks, *Feminist Theory*, 15. For a (bad) example which supports this false narrative about "strong Black women," see, Ann M. Callahan, "Key Concepts in Spiritual Care for Hospice Social Workers: How an Interdisciplinary Perspective Can Inform Spiritual Competence," *Social Work & Christianity* 42, no. 1 (March 2015): 43–62 (p. 45). For examples which reinforce this racist belief, see also, Barbara Baele Vincensi and Elizabeth Burkhard, "Spiritual Distress," in *Nursing Diagnosis Handbook: An Evidence-Based Guide to Planning Care. Reprint with 2021-2023 NANDA-I Updates*, 12th ed., ed. Betty J.Ackley, Gail B. Ladwig, Mary Beth Flynn Makic, Marina Martinez Kratz, and Melody Zanotti, 844–7 (St. Louis, MO: Elsevier, Inc., 2022), 846.

22 Summer 2023.

23 Summer 2023.

24 Summer 2023; responding to Anjeanette Allen's, "Do Not Pass Me By: A Womanist Reprise and Responses to Health Care's Cultural Dismissal and Erasure of Black Women's Pain," in *The Rowman and Littlefield Handbook of Women's Studies in Religion*, ed. Helen T. Boursier, 61-74 (Lanham, MD: Rowman and Littlefield, 2021, 2023); and Lorde's, *The Cancer Journals*, foreword by Tracy K. Smith (New York: Penguin Books, Random House, 1980, 2020). See also, Diana L. Hayes, *No Crystal Stair: Womanist Spirituality* (Maryknoll, NY: Orbis Books), 2016.

25 See also, Michele Norris, *Our Hidden Conversations: What Americans Really Think About Race and Identity* (Simon & Schuster), 1–5. Kindle Edition.

26 Bruce D. Rumbold, *Helplessness and Hope: Pastoral Care in Terminal Illness* (Harrisburg, PA: Trinity Press International, 1996), 69.

27 American Counts Staff, Oregon Population 4.2 Million in 2020, Up 10.6% from 2010. U.S. Census Bureau. August 25, 2021. https://www.census.gov/library/stories/state-by-state/oregon-population-change-between-census-decade.html.
28 Joan Chittister, *The Gift of Years: Growing Older Gracefully* (Katonah, NY: BlueBridge, 2010), 22–3.
29 Lorde, "Age, Race, Class, and Sex," in *Sister Outsider*, 114–15.
30 See, Walker, Rivkin-Fish, and Buchbinder, Introduction to *Understanding Health Inequalities and Justice*, 1–30.

Chapter 7

1 Puchalski and Ferrell, *Making Health Care Whole*, 34. See also, Young and Koopsen, *Spirituality, Health, and Healing*, 116–18.
2 Vincensi and Burkhard, "Spiritual Distress," 844–7; 847; 848 and 845–51 respectively.
3 Young and Koopsen, *Spirituality, Health, and Healing*, 118.
4 See, Marta Illueca, Ylisabyth S Bradshaw, and Daniel B Carr, "Spiritual Pain: A Symptom in Search of a Clinical Definition," *Journal of Religion and Health* 62, no. 3 (June 2023): 1920–32 (p. 1930). doi:10.1007/s10943-022-01645-y; and Amy Rex Smith, "Using the Synergy Model to Provide Spiritual Nursing Care in Critical Care Settings," *Critical Care Nurse* 26 no. 4 (2006): 41–7 (p. 45). doi:10.4037/ccn2006.26.4.41.
5 Vincensi and Burkhard, "Spiritual Distress," 844.
6 Vincensi and Burkhard, "Spiritual Distress," 196–7. Brien, *Standing on Holy Ground*.
7 Vincensi and Burkhard, "Spiritual Distress," 844–7.
8 Vincensi and Burkhard, "Spiritual Distress," 844–5.
9 See, Michelle A. Lemiesz, "The Spiritual Care of the Hospitalized Patient: A Nursing Perspective." *Journal of Religion, Disability and Health* 3, no. 1 (1999): 75–97 (p. 87).
10 See, Speck, *Being There*, 33–6; see also, Zach Cooper, "Spirituality in Primary Care Settings: Addressing the Whole Person through Christian Mindfulness," *Religions* 13, no. 346 (April 2022). doi:10.3390/rel13040346.
11 April 3, 2024.
12 See, Cadge, *Paging God*, 20–1.

13 For an analysis of different patient responses to the "same" diagnosis, see, David J. Zucker and Bonita E. Taylor, "Spirituality, Suffering, and Prayerful Presence within Jewish Tradition," in Puchalski, *A Time for Listening and Caring*, 193–214, 195.

14 See, Cooper, "Christian Mindfulness."

15 For the fascination with fixing through measuring spirituality to facility "fixing" spiritual distress in a clinical setting see, Philip Austin, Jessica Macdonald, and Roderick MacLeod, "Measuring Spirituality and Religiosity in Clinical Settings: A Scoping Review of Available Instruments," *Religions* 9, no. 70 (2018): 1–14. Basel, Switzerland: MDPI. doi:10.3390/rel9030070. See also, Wendy Cadge and Julia Bandini, "The Evolution of Spiritual Assessment Tools in Healthcare," *Society* 52, no. 5 (2015): 430–7. doi:10.1007/s12115-015-9926-y; Westera, *Spirituality in Nursing Practice*, 169; and Lemiesz, "Spiritual Care of the Hospitalized Patient," 75–97.

16 O'Brien, *Standing on Holy Ground*, 109. See also, P. Burnard, "Spiritual Distress and Nursing Response: Theoretical Considerations and Counseling Skills," *Journal of Advanced Nursing* 12, no. 3 (1988): 377–82, cited in ibid.

17 See, Katarzyna Kotfis, Annachiara Marra, and Eugene Wesley Ely, "ICU Delirium," and Thomas DeChant, Lauren Smith, and Jose Chavez, "Recognizing and Reducing Delirium in the Intensive Care Unit," *Critical Care Nurse Quarterly* 46, 3 (2023): 277–81. doi:10.1097/CNQ. 0000000000000465; and Malik, et al, "ICU Delirium Prevention Bundle," 7.

18 See, Kotfis, Marra, and Ely, "ICU Delirium," 134.

19 Milos Forman, director, *Hair* (Tribe Entertainment Group, 1979).

Chapter 8

1 For how patients, nurses, and chaplains understand and define what spiritual needs are and how these can be responded to, see, Julia Emblen and Lois Halstead, "Spiritual Needs and Interventions: Comparing the Views of Patients, Nurses, and Chaplains," *Clinical Nurse Specialist* 7, no. 4 (July 1993): 175–82. Journals@Ovid Full Text. Web. 10 October 2023. http://ovidsp.ovid.com/ovidweb.cgi?T=JS&PAGE=reference&D=ovfta&NEWS=N&AN=00002800-199307000-00005.

2 See, Brenda Cole, Ethan Benore, and Kenneth Pargament, "Spirituality and Coping with Trauma," in *Spirituality, Health, and Wholeness: An Introductory Guide for Health Care Professionals*, ed. Siroj Sorajjakool and Henry Lamberton (New York: Routledge, 2004), 53–4.

3   See, Young and Koopsen, *Spirituality, Health, and Healing*, 15. For spiritual health see also, Azita Jaberi, Marzieh Momennasab, Shahrzad Yektatalab, Abbas Ebadi, and Mohammad Ali Cheraghi, "Spiritual Health: A Concept Analysis," *Journal of Religion and Health* 58, no. 5 (2019): 1537–60 (p. 1540). doi:10.1007/s10943-017-0379-z.

4   Duncan Mac Laren, "All Things to All People? The Integrity of Spiritual Care in a Plural Health Service," *Health & Social Care Chaplaincy* 9, no. 1 (January 2021): 27–41 (p. 31). doi:10.1558/hscc.40568.

5   Philip Sheldrake, "Spirituality and Healthcare," *Practical Theology*, 3, no. 3 (2010): 373, doi:10.1558/prth.v3i3.367. Caring for the infirmed, ailing, aging, and lonely is imbued in the sacred text. See, Zechariah 7:10; Matthew 25: 31–36.

6   See, Maclaren, "All Things to All People?" 31.

7   See, Young and Koopsen, *Spirituality, Health, and Healing*, 118. For examples on spiritual assessment and spiritual care, see 103–16 in ibid. For definitions, descriptions, and an explanation on the focus or purpose of spiritual assessment, including a clinical analysis, see, Westera, *Spirituality in Nursing Practice*, 126–40; and Cadge, and Bandini, "Evolution of Spiritual Assessment," 430–7. For examples of how to use measurement tools, or scales to assess spirituality, see, Craig. W. Ellison, "Spiritual Well-Being: Conceptualization and Measurement," *Journal of Psychology and Theology* 11, no. 4 (1983): 330–8.

8   See, Fitchett, *Assessing Spiritual Needs*, 20–1. For a chaplain's view of spiritual assessment, see, Dagmar Grefe and Pamela McCarroll with Bilal Ansari, "Meaning Making in Chaplaincy Practice: Presence, Assessment, and Interventions," in Cadge and Rambo, *Chaplaincy and Spiritual Care*, 66–89.

9   See, Grefe and McCarroll with Ansari, "Meaning Making," 78.

10 See Puchalski and Ferrell, *Making Health Care Whole*, 112; and Young and Koopsen, *Spirituality, Health, and Healing*, 17.

11 Linda F. Pitrowski, "Advocating and Educating for Spiritual Screening Assessment and Referrals to Chaplains," *Omega* 67, no. 1–2 (2013): 189. doi:10.2190/OM.67.1-2.v.

12 See, Eshghi, Nikfarid, and Zareiyan, "Defining Characteristic of the Nursing Diagnosis 'Spiritual Distress,'" 2839.

13 For an analysis of why patients say they don't want or expect spiritual care while they're in a hospital, see, Nicolas Pujol, Guy Jobin, and Sadek Beloucif, "'Spiritual Care Is Not the Hospital's Business': A Qualitative Study on the Perspectives of Patients about the Integration of Spirituality in Healthcare Settings," *Journal of Medical Ethics* 42, no. 11 (2016): 733–7. http://www.jstor.org/stable/44606002.

14 See, Heidegger, *Being and Time*, 172.

15 Heidegger, *Being and Time*, 422.

16 See, Grefe and McCarroll with Ansari, "Meaning Making," 77–8.

17 See, Kimberly Matas, "Benjamin Schultz: Pharmacist Improved Medical Care Nationwide," *Arizona Daily Star*, May 25, 2009, https://tucson.com/news/science/health-med-fit/benjamin-schultz-pharmacist-improved-medical-care-nationwide/article_34516976-dded-5c1d-94ab-d8e470322df8.html.

18 December 2023.

19 December 2023.

20 December 2023.

21 December 2023.

22 December 2023.

23 December 2023.

24 December 2023.

25 December 2023.

26 On the role of reflective practice in spiritual caregiving see, Sheldrake, "Spirituality and Healthcare," 375.

Chapter 9

1 Boursier, *Precious Precarity*, xii.

2 See, Boursier, *Precious Precarity*, xxii, 2, 108. For finitude in a postmodern perspective, see, B. Keith Putt, *Gazing through a Prism Darkly: Reflections on Merold Westphal's Hermeneutical Epistemology*, ed. B. Keith Putt (New York: Fordham University Press, 2009), 8.

3 See, Steve Nolan, *Spiritual Care at the End of Life: The Chaplain as 'Hopeful Presence'* (Jessica Kingsley Publishers, 2011), 66. See also, Dorothee Soelle, *The Mystery of Death* (Minneapolis, MN: Fortress Press, 2007).

4 See, Boursier, *Precious Precarity*, 1–2.

5 Heidegger, *Being and Time*, 307.

6 See, Yancy, *Where Is God?*, 189.

7 See, Rumbold, *Helplessness and Hope*, 83.

8 Hans-Georg Gadamer, *The Enigma of Health: The Art of Healing in a Scientific Age* trans. Jason Gaiger and Nicholas Walker (Sanford, CA: Stanford University Press,

1993), 62. See also, Michel Foucault, *The Birth of the Clinic: An Archaeology of Medical Perception* (Vintage Press, 1994).

9   Gadamer, *Enigma of Health*, 62.
10 Gadamer, *Enigma of Health*, 65.
11 Henri J. M. Nouwen, *Our Greatest Gift: A Meditation on Dying and Caring* (San Francisco: HarperCollins, 1995), xvi.
12 August 14, 2023.
13 See, Paley, "Spirituality and Secularization," 121.
14 Nouwen, *Our Greatest Gift*, 47.
15 Nouwen, *Our Greatest Gift*, 97.
16 Nouwen, *Our Greatest* Gift, 51.
17 Nouwen, *Our Greatest Gift*, 58.
18 Nouwen, *Our Greatest Gift*, 103.
19 Nouwen, *Our Greatest Gift*, 31
20 August 19, 2023.
21 August 19, 2023.
22 See, Nouwen, *Our Greatest Gift*, 80–1.
23 Elisabeth Kübler-Ross, *On Death and Dying: What the Dying Have to Teach Doctors, Nurses, Clergy and Their Own Families*, foreword by Ira Byock, 50th anniv. ed. (New York: Scribner, 1969, 2019), 27.
24 Ramsey, *Patient as Person*, 134.
25 See, Boursier, *Precious Precarity*, 1–2, 85, 105–6, 215.
26 Ray S. Anderson, *On Being Human: Essays in Theological Anthropology* (Pasadena, CA: Fuller Seminary Press, 1982), 213–14.
27 August 20, 2023.
28 August 31, 2023.
29 Nouwen, *Our Greatest Gift*, xvi.
30 Nouwen, *Our Greatest Gift*, 6.
31 Nouwen, *Our Greatest Gift*, 26–7.
32 Nouwen, *Our Greatest Gift*, 20–1.
33 Sushila Blackman, ed. *Graceful Exits: How Great Beings Dies; Death Stories of Hindu, Tibetan, Buddhist, and Zen Masters* (Boston: Shambhala, 2005), 13.
34 Blackman, ed., *Graceful Exits*, 17.
35 Blackman, ed., *Graceful Exits*, 18.

36 Nouwen, *Our Greatest Gift*, 13–14.

37 August 16, 2023.

38 For the steps and definitions that characterize a spiritual quest, see, Harry R. Moody and David Carroll, *The Five Stages of the Soul: Charting the Spiritual Passages that Shape our Lives* (New York: Anchor Books, Random House, 1997), 31–4.

39 August 20, 2023.

40 Richard Rohr, *Falling Upward: A Spirituality for the Two Halves of Life* (San Francisco: Jossey-Bass, 2011), 101.

41 December 2023.

42 December 2023.

43 December 2023.

Chapter 10

1 See, Elie Wiesel, "The Perils of Indifference," YouTube, April 12, 1999, https://www.youtube.com/watch?v=JpXmRiGst4k. On defining humanity in relationship to justice, see Judith Butler, *Precarious Life: The Powers of Mourning and Violence* (London and New York: Verso, 2004, 2006), 91–2.

2 American Nurses Association, *Code of Ethics with Interpretative Statements*, 2002, https://www.nursingworld.org/practice-policy/nursing-excellence/ethics/code-of-ethics-for-nurses/. Cited by nursing student.

3 Summer 2023.

4 See, Chávez, "Cultural Humility," 01:24–02:56, https://www.youtube.com/watch?v=SaSHLbS1V4w. See also, Melanie Tervalon and Jann Murray-García, "Cultural Humility versus Cultural Competence: A Critical Distinction in Defining Physician Training Outcomes in Multicultural Education," *Journal of Health Care for the Poor and Underserved* 9, no. 2 (1988). doi:10.1353/hpu.2010.0233.

5 Merold Westphal, *Overcoming Onto-Theology: Toward a Postmodern Christian Faith* (New York: Fordham University Press, 2001), 128; cited in Boursier, *Ethics of Hospitality*, ix.

6 Boursier, *Ethics of Hospitality*, ix.

7 See, Chávez, "Cultural Humility," 01:24–02:56.

8 See, Chávez, "Cultural Humility," 24:56.

9 See, Thich Nhat Hanh, *Peace Is Every Step: The Path of Mindfulness in Everyday Life* (New York: Bantam Books, 1991), 43.

10 Thich Nhat Hanh, *You Are Here: Discovering the Magic of the Present Moment* (Boston: Shambhala, 2010), 61.

11 Hanh, *Magic of the Present Moment*, 62.

12 Kaur, *See No Stranger*, 143. For tips on how to listen, see, Elizabeth Johnston Taylor, *What Do I Say? Talking with Patients about Spirituality*, foreword by Christina M. Puchalski, MD (Philadelphia: Templeton Foundation Press, 2007), 31–6.

13 Taylor, *What Do I Say?*, 29.

14 Hanh, *Magic of the Present Moment*, 92.

15 Spring 2024.

16 Fricker, *Epistemic Injustice*, 27.

17 See also, Nel Noddings, *Caring: A Feminine Approach to Ethics and Moral Education*, 2nd ed. (Berkley: University of California Press, 1984, 2003), 65.

18 See, Canda and Furman, *Spiritual Diversity in Social Work Practice*, 215.

19 Kübler-Ross, *On Death and Dying*, 8.

20 Martin Luther King, Jr., *Strength to Love* (Minneapolis, MN: Fortress Press, 1963), 27 as cited by a nursing student, Summer 2023.

21 Brené Brown on Empathy. YouTube. Retrieved August 5, 2023 from https://www.youtube.com/watch?v=1Evwgu369Jw&t=0s; cited by student.

22 King, Jr., *Strength to Love*, 26 as cited by a nursing student, Summer 2023.

23 See, Canda and Furman, *Spiritual Diversity in Social Work Practice*, 30.

24 Nancy Rue, *The Value of Compassion* (New York: Rosen Publishing, 1991), 13.

25 Rue, *Value of Compassion*, 14.

26 Hanh, *Peace Is Every Step*, 77.

27 For dimensions in caring which include family members, see, O'Brien, *Standing on Holy Ground*, 12–15.

28 Barbara Stevens Barnum, *Spirituality in Nursing: The Challenges of Complexity*, 3rd ed. (Springer Publishing Col., 2010), 10.

29 See, Westera, *Spirituality in Nursing Practice*, 43.

30 See, Philippians 2:7.

Chapter 11

1. See, Abdul S. Majid and Lance D. Laird, "Encountering God, Accompanying Others: Spirituality and Theology among Muslim Health Care Chaplains," *Spirituality in Clinical Practice* 10, no. 1 (2023): 80, doi:10.1037/scp0000315.
2. See, Hannah Arendt, *The Human Condition,* 2nd ed., introduction by Margaret Canovan (Chicago, IL: University of Chicago Press, 1958, 1998), 183–4.
3. See, Barbara Pesut, "Critical Response to Palliative Case Studies: A Nurse's Perspective," in Fitchett and Nolan, *Spiritual Care in Practice*, 277.
4. Nouwen, *Our Greatest Gift*, 74.
5. August 18, 2023.
6. August 17, 2023.
7. Nouwen, *Our Greatest Gift*, 55.
8. August 17, 2023.
9. For prayers offered visibly and invisibly, see, Cadge, *Paging God*, 3, 156.
10. Quoted in Hannah Morrissey, "Living to the Maxx: A Mother and Daughter's Courageous Tête-à-Tête with Cancer," Meaning Making. [Blog] April, 2023, Austin, TX: Eterneva, Accessed October 10, 2023, https://www.eterneva.com/resources/living-to-the-maxx.
11. Quoted in, Morrissey, "Living to the Maxx."
12. Quoted in, Morrissey, "Living to the Maxx."
13. Quoted in, Morrissey, "Living to the Maxx."
14. On what's "better than" as it intersects with choice to inform spirituality, see, Boursier, *Precious Precarity*, 123–4.
15. See, Carol J. Farran, Kaye A. Herth, and Judith Popovich, *Hope and Hopelessness: Critical Clinical Constructs* (London: Sage Publications, 1995), 24.
16. On hopelessness, see, Farran, Herth, and Popovich, *Hope and Hopelessness*, 24–34.
17. See, Frankl, *Man's Search for Meaning*, 96–7.
18. For the difference between wishing, optimism, coping, and hope see, Farran, Herth, and Popovich, *Hope and Hopelessness*, 11–20; and Puchalski, "Spirituality in the Care of the Seriously Ill," 19–20.
19. For hope rising up through lament see, Emilie M. Townes, *Breaking the Fine Rain of Death: African American Health Issues and a Womanist Ethic of Care* (Eugene, OR: Wipf & Stock Publishers, 1998), 179; and Boursier, *Precious Precarity*, 225–6. For sources on hope in caregiving, see, E. Benzein and B. I. Saveman. "One Step

towards the Understanding of Hope: A Concept Analysis," *International Journal of Nursing Studies* 35, no. 6 (January 1, 1998): 322–9; Eve Garrard and Anthony Wrigley, "Hope and Terminal Illness: False Hope versus Absolute Hope," *Clinical Ethics* 4, no. 1 (March 2009): 38–43, doi:10.1258/ce.2008.008050; GC Chi, "The Role of Hope in Patients with Cancer," *Oncology Nursing Forum*, 34, no. 2 (2007): 415–24. doi:10.1188/07.ONF.415–24; and Clare M. Butt, "Hope in Patients with Cancer Transitioning to Survivorship: The Mid-Life Directions Workshop as a Supportive Intervention," *Oncology Nursing Forum* 39, no. 3 (May 2012): E269–74. doi:10.1188/12.ONF.E269-E274.

20 Howard W. Stone and Andrew Lester, "Helping Parishioners Envision the Future," in *Strategies for Brief Pastoral Counseling*, ed. Howard W. Stone, 46–60 (Minneapolis: Fortress Press, 2001), 46. No source given.

21 Stone and Lester, "Helping Parishioners Envision the Future," 46–60.

22 Stone and Lester, "Helping Parishioners Envision the Future," 46–60.

23 Stone and Lester, "Helping Parishioners Envision the Future," 46.

24 Frankl, *Man's Search for Meaning*, 98.

Chapter 12

1 On how to use art as spiritual care for a ministry of presence, see, Helen T. Boursier, *Art as Witness: A Practical Theology of Arts-Based Research* (Lanham, MD: Lexington Books, 2021).

2 For a chaplaincy perspective, see, Cadge, *Paging God*, 93–5; and Jim Browning and Jim Spivey. *The Heart of a Chaplain: Exploring Essentials for Ministry* (Dallas: BH Carroll Theological Institute, 2022), 35.

3 On accompaniment as spiritual care, see, Puchalski and Ferrell, *Making Health Care Whole*, 10.

4 See, Sheldrake, "Spirituality and Healthcare," 375–6.

5 For a survey of the spiritual care in nursing, see, Loralee Sessanna, Deborah Finnell, and Mary Ann Jezewski, "Spirituality in Nursing and Health-Related Literature: A Concept Analysis," *Journal of Holistic Nursing* 4, no. 25 (2007): 252–62. doi:10.1177/0898010107303890. For philosophical approaches see, Susan T. Tinley and Anita Y. Kinney, "Three Philosophical Approaches to the Study of Spirituality," *Advances in Nursing Science* 30, no. 1 (2007): 71–80. doi:10.1097/00012272-200701000-00008. For articles which address analyses and debates regarding spirituality and nursing, see, Barbara Pesut, Marsha Fowler, Sheryl Reimer-Kirkham, Elizabeth Johnston Taylor, and Rick Sawatzky,

"Particularizing Spirituality in Points of Tension: Enriching the Discourse," *Nursing Inquiry* 16, no. 4 (December 2009): 337–46. doi:10.1111/j.1440-1800.2009.00462.x; Janice Clarke, "A Critical View of How Nursing Has Defined Spirituality," *Journal of Clinical Nursing* (Wiley-Blackwell) 18, no. 12 (2009): 1666–73, doi:10.1111/j.1365-2702.2008.02707.x.; and McSherry and Draper, "Debates . . . Concept of Spirituality." For models of spirituality which have been applied to nursing research and practice, see, Douglas A. MacDonald, "Studying Spirituality Scientifically: Reflections, Considerations, Recommendations," *Journal of Management, Spirituality and Religion* 8, no. 3 (2011): 195–210, doi:10.1080/14766086.2011.599145; and Amy Rex Smith, "Using the Synergy Model to Provide Spiritual Nursing Care in Critical Care Settings," *Critical Care Nurse* 26, no. 4 (2006): 41–7, doi:10.4037/ccn2006.26.4.41.

6 On caring presence in healthcare, see also, Helen Orchard, "Being There? Presence and Absence in Spiritual Care Delivery," in Orchard, *Spirituality in Health Care Contexts*, 147–59, 147; and James E. Miller and Susan C. Cutshall, *The Art of Being a Healing Presence: A Guide for Those in Caring Relationships* (Willowgreen Publishing, 2001, 2012).

7 See, Sheldrake, "Spirituality and Healthcare," 375–6.

8 On living in the present, see, Ronald Rolheiser, *Sacred Fire: A Vision for a Deeper Human and Christian Maturity* (New York: Penguin Random House, 2014), 274.

9 See, Nolan, *Spiritual Care at the End of Life*, 111.

10 See, Paley, "Spirituality and Secularization," 37. For caring presence in nursing, see, Emmerential DuPleissis, Kathleen Froneman, Khumoetsile Shopo, Babalwa Tau, and Sipho Sojane, "Promoting Caring Presence in Nursing: Initial Findings," in *Proceedings of the 2nd Biennial South African Conference on Spirituality and Healthcare*, ed. André de la Porte, Nicolene Joubert and Annemarie Oberholzer (Cambridge Scholars Publishing, 2018), 155.

11 December 2023, citing, Nouwen, *Our Greatest Gift*, 6.

12 See, Miller and Cutshall, *Healing Presence*, 15.

13 On *caring together with* in a healthcare setting, see, Nolan, *Spiritual Care at the End of Life*, 73.

14 Summer 2023.

15 Nolan, *Spiritual Care at the End of Life*, 76.

16 Nolan, *Spiritual Care at the End of Life*, 78.

17 Nouwen, *Our Greatest Gift*, 61.

18 Spring 2024.

19 Nouwen, *Our Greatest Gift*, 93.

20 Nouwen, *Our Greatest Gift*, 93.
21 On disarming fear amidst suffering, see, Yancy, *Where Is God?*, 178-80. See also Dorothee Soelle, *Suffering*, trans. Everett R. Kalin (Philadelphia: Fortress Press, 1975).
22 Yancy, *Where Is God?*, 210.
23 Ram Dass [Richard Alpert] *Remember: Be Here Now*, Hanuman Foundation (New York: Harmony House, 1971), 326.
24 William and Nancy Martin, *The Caregiver's Tao Te Ching: Compassionate Caring for Your Loved Ones and Yourself* (Novato, CA: New World Library, 2011), 50.
25 Martin, *Caregiver's Tao Te Ching*, 50.
26 See, Martin, *Caregiver's Tao Te Ching*, 75.
27 For how a Muslim trusts in Allah during illness or end-of-life, see, Imam Yusuf Hasan and Yusef Salaam, "Faith and Islamic Issues at the End of Life," in Puchalski, *A Time for Listening and Caring*, 183–92.
28 On dying as being very lonely, see, Kübler-Ross, *On Death and Dying*, 8.

Chapter 13

1 See, Dorothee Soelle, *Against the Wind: Memoir of a Radical Christian*, trans. Barbara and Martin Rumscheidt (Minneapolis, MN: Fortress Press, 1999), 83.
2 Lorde, *The Cancer Journals*, 13.
3 Summer 2023.
4 Summer 2023.
5 See, Paul Ricoeur, *Figuring the Sacred: Religion, Narrative, and Imagination* trans. David Pellauer, ed. Mark I Wallace (Minneapolis: Fortress Press, 1995), 207.
6 For an excellent argument on how to use power from the periphery for advocacy and agency, see, Rosita deAnn Mathews, "Using Power from the Periphery: An Alternative Theological Model for Survival in Systems," in *A Troubling in My Soul: Womanist Perspectives on Evil and Suffering*, ed. Emilie, M. Townes, vol. 8 of The Bishop Henry McNeal Turner Studies in North American Black Religion (Maryknoll, NY: Orbis Books, 1993), 93.
7 Heidegger, *Being and Time*, 318.
8 Kaur, *See, No Stranger*, 133.
9 Traci C. West, *Solidarity and Defiant Spirituality: Africana Lessons on Religion, Racism, and Ending Gender Violence* (New York: New York University Press, 2019), 223.

10 See, King, Jr. *Strength to Love*, 23.
11 King, Jr. *Strength to Love*, 35.
12 Frankl, *Man's Search for Meaning*, 65–6.
13 For choice in relationship to something being "better than" another, see, Boursier, *Precious Precarity*, 123–4.

Chapter 14

1 See, Stephen Pattison, *Alive and Kicking: Towards a Practical Theology of Illness and Healing* (London: SCM Press, 1989); and James Woodward and Stephen Pattison, eds., *The Blackwell Reader in Pastoral and Practical Theology* (Oxford: Blackwell Publishing, 2000).
2 See, bell hooks, *All About Love: New Visions* (New York: HarperCollins, 2000), 80.
3 See, Shim, *Heart-Sick*, 8.; and Janet K. Shim, "Cultural Health Capital: A Theoretical Approach to Understanding Health Care Interactions and the Dynamics of Unequal Treatment," *PubMed* 51, no. 10 (March 2010): 1–15, doi:10.1177/0022146509361185.
4 See, Fricker, *Epistemic* Injustice, vii.
5 Spring 2024.
6 August 2023.
7 August 2023.
8 Nouwen, *Our Greatest Gift*, 3 as cited by a nursing student, August 2023.
9 See, Dorothee Soelle, *Death by Bread Alone: Texts and Reflections on Religious Experience* trans. David L. Scheidt (Philadelphia: Fortress Press, 1978), 3–4.
10 Michael A. Singer, *The Untethered Soul: The Journey Beyond Yourself* (Oakland, CA: New Harbinger Publications, Inc., 2007), 59.
11 For contemplative prayer through music in the style of Taizé see, Taizé Prayer, Taizé, YouTube, September 5, 2020, https://www.youtube.com/watch?v=5OG6WGpk-Tg&t=13s; and Kathryn Shirey, Prayer Plus Possibilities, March 12, 2015, https://www.prayerandpossibilities.com/taize-prayer-meditative-prayer-through-music/.
12 Thich Nhat Hanh, *No Mud, No Lotus: The Art of Transforming Suffering* (Berkeley, CA: Parallax Press, 2014), 32.
13 Hanh, *No Mud, No Lotus*, 74–5.
14 Hanh, *Peace Is Every Step*, 52.

15 Hanh, *Magic of the Present Moment*, 9.

16 See, Thich Nhat Hanh, "Introduction to Mindfulness/Tranquility Meditation," Wind Tree Studios, YouTube, 2018, https://www.youtube.com/watch?v=b5gMJ1BovQ0.

17 See, Doug Oman and Joseph D. Driskell, "Holy Name Repetition as a Spiritual Exercise and Therapeutic Technique," *Journal of psychology and Christianity* 22, no. 1 (2003): 5–19 (p. 7). ISSN - 07334273.

18 Luc R. Pelletier and Jill E. Bormann, "Evidence-Based Portable Mindful Strategies for Well-Being," in *Healing with Spiritual Practices: Proven Techniques for Disorders from Addictions and Anxiety to Cancer and Chronic Pain*, ed. Thomas Plante (Praeger, 2018), 43.

19 Pelletier and Bormann, "Portable Mindful Strategies," 44.

20 See Table 4.1 for mantra examples for Christianity, Hinduism, Buddhism, Judaism, Native American, and Islam. Pelletier and Bormann, "Evidence-Based Portable Mindful Strategies," 45–6.

21 Lorde, *Cancer Journals*, 39.

22 Lorde, *Cancer Journals*, 50–1.

23 Frankl, *Man's Search for Meaning*, 131–2.

Bibliography

Ackley, Betty J., Gail B. Ladwig, Mary Beth Flynn Makic, Marina Martinez Kratz, and Melody Zanotti, eds. *Nursing Diagnosis Handbook: An Evidence-Based Guide to Planning Care. Reprint with 2021-2023 NANDA-I Updates*. 12th ed. St. Louis, MO: Elsevier, Inc., 2022.

Allen, Anjeanette. "Do Not Pass Me By: A Womanist Reprise and Responses to Health Care's Cultural Dismissal Land Erasure of Black Women's Pain." In *The Rowman and Littlefield Handbook of Women's Studies in Religion,* edited by Helen T. Boursier, 61–74. Lanham, MD: Rowman and Littlefield, 2021, 2023.

American Nurses Association. *Code of Ethics for Nurses with Interpretive Statements*. 2nd ed. American Nurses Association, 2015. https://www.nursingworld.org/practice-policy/nursing-excellence/ethics/code-of-ethics-for-nurses/.

Anderson, Ray S. *On Being Human: Essays in Theological Anthropology*. Pasadena, CA: Fuller Seminary Press, 1982.

Arendt, Hannah. *The Human Condition*. 2nd ed. Introduction by Margaret Canovan. Chicago, IL: University of Chicago Press, 1958, 1998.

Association of American Medical Colleges (AAMC). *Report I: Learning Objectives for Medical Student Education: Guidelines for Medical Schools*. Washington, DC: AAMC, 1999. https://webcampus.med.drexel.edu/professionalism/AAMCMedicalSchoolObjectivesProject.pdf.

Association of American Medical Colleges (AAMC). *Report III: Contemporary Issues in Medicine: Communication in Medicine*. Washington DC: AAMC, 1999. https://gwish.smhs.gwu.edu/sites/g/files/zaskib1011/files/2022-08/msop_iii_report_2.pdf.

Augustine Meier, Thomas St. James O'Connor, and Peter L. VanKatwyk, eds. *Spirituality and Health: Multidisciplinary Explorations*. Waterloo, ON: Wilfrid Laurier University Press, 2005.

Austin, Philip, Jessica Macdonald, and Roderick MacLeod. "Measuring Spirituality and Religiosity in Clinical Settings: A Scoping Review of Available Instruments." *Religions* 9, no. 70 (2018): 1–14. Basel, Switzerland: MDPI. doi:10.3390/rel9030070.

Bandura, Albert. *Moral Disengagement: How People Do Harm and Live with Themselves.* New York: Worth Publishers, 2016.

Bandura, Albert. "Moral Disengagement in the Perpetration of Inhumanities." *Personality and Social Psychology Review* 3, no. 3 (July 1, 1999): 1088–8683.

Barnum, Barbara Stevens. *Spirituality in Nursing: The Challenges of Complexity.* 3rd ed. New York: Spring Publishing Company, 2010.

Batty, Bonnie Weaver. "Perspectives of Spiritual Care for Nurse Managers." *Journal of Nursing Management* 20 (2012): 1012–20. [Blackwell Publishing] doi:10.1111/j.1365-2834.2012.01360.x

Beauchamp, Tom L., and James F. Childress. *Principles of Biomedical Ethics.* 8th ed. Oxford: Oxford University Press, 2019.

Beauvoir, Simone de. *The Ethics of Ambiguity.* New York: Open Road Integrated Media, 1947, 2018.

Beauvoir, Simone de. *The Second Sex.* Introduction by Judith Thurman. Translated by Constance Borde and Sheila Malovany-Chevallier. New York: Vintage Books, Random House, 1949, 2009.

Benzein, E., and B. I. Saveman. "One Step towards the Understanding of Hope: A Concept Analysis." *International Journal of Nursing Studies* 35, no. 6 (January 1, 1998): 322–9.

Blackman, Sushila, ed. *Graceful Exits: How Great Beings Dies; Death Stories of Hindu, Tibetan, Buddhist, and Zen Masters.* Boston: Shambhala, 2005.

Bloechl, Jeffrey, ed., *The Face of the Other and the Trace of God: Essays on the Philosophy of Emmanuel Levinas.* New York: Fordham University Press, 2000.

Boursier, Helen T. *Art as Witness: A Practical Theology of Arts-Based Research.* Lanham, MD: Lexington Books, 2021.

Boursier, Helen T. *Desperately Seeking Asylum: Testimonies of Trauma, Courage, and Love.* Lanham, MD: Rowman & Littlefield, November 2019.

Boursier, Helen T. *Precious Precarity: A Spirituality of Borders.* Minneapolis, MN: Fortress Press, 2024.

Boursier, Helen T., ed. *The Rowman and Littlefield Handbook of Women's Studies in Religion.* Lanham, MD: Rowman & Littlefield, 2021.

Boursier, Helen T. *Willful Ignorance: Overcoming the Limitations of (Christian) Love for Refugees Seeking Asylum.* Lanham, MD: Lexington Books, 2022.

Bradshaw, A. "The Legacy of Nightingale." *Nursing Times* 92, no. 6 (1996): 42–3. ISSN: 09960207.

Brown, Delwin, Sheila Greeve Davaney, and Kathryn Tanner, eds. *Converging on Culture: Theologians in Dialogue with Cultural Analysis and Criticism*. Oxford: Oxford University Press, 2001.

Browning, Jim, and Jim Spivey. *The Heart of a Chaplain: Exploring Essentials for Ministry*. Dallas: BH Carroll Theological Institute, 2022.

Buchbinder, Mara, Michele Rivkin-Fish, and Rebecca L. Walker. *Understanding Health Inequalities and Justice: New Conversations Across Disciplines*. Chapel Hill, NC: University of North Carolina Press, 2016.

Burge, Ryan P. *The Nones: Where They Came From, Who They Are, and Where They Are Going*. Minneapolis, MN: Fortress Press, 2021.

Butler, Judith. *Precarious Life: The Powers of Mourning and Violence*. London: Verso, 2004, 2006.

Butler, Judith. *Undoing Gender*. London: Routledge, 2004.

Butler, Judith, Zeynep Gambetti, and Leticia Sabsay, eds. *Vulnerability in Resistance*. Durham and London: Duke University Press, 2016.

Butt, Clare M. "Hope in Patients with Cancer Transitioning to Survivorship: The Mid-Life Directions Workshop as a Supportive Intervention." *Oncology Nursing Forum* 39, no. 3 (May 2012): E269–74. doi:10.1188/12.ONF.E269-E274.

Cadge, Wendy. *Paging God: Religion in the Halls of Medicine*. Chicago, IL: University of Chicago Press, 2013.

Cadge, Wendy, and Julia Bandini. "The Evolution of Spiritual Assessment Tools in Healthcare." *Society* 52, no. 5 (2015): 430–7. doi:10.1007/s12115-015-9926-y.

Cadge, Wendy, and Shelly Rambo, eds. *Chaplaincy and Spiritual Care in the Twenty-First Century: An Introduction*. University of North Carolina Press, 2022.

Callahan, Ann M. "Key Concepts in Spiritual Care for Hospice Social Workers: How an Interdisciplinary Perspective Can Inform Spiritual Competence." *Social Work & Christianity* 42, no. 1 (March 2015): 43–62.

Canda, Edward R., and Furman, Leola Dyrud. *Spiritual Diversity in Social Work Practice: The Heart of Helping*. 2nd ed. Oxford: University of Oxford Press. 2019.

Carr, Wesley. "Spirituality and Religion: Chaplaincy in Context." In *Spirituality in Health Care Contexts*, edited by Helen Orchard, 21–32. London: Jessica Kingsley Publishers, 2001.

Chávez, Vivian, Director/producer. "Cultural Humility." YouTube. 2012. https://www.youtube.com/watch?v=SaSHLbS1V4w.

Chi, G. C. "The Role of Hope in Patients with Cancer." *Oncology Nursing Forum* 34, no. 2 (2007): 415–24. doi:10.1188/07.ONF.415-424.

Chittister, Joan. *The Gift of Years: Growing Older Gracefully*. Katonah, NY: BlueBridge, 2010.

Chopp, Rebecca S. "Theology and the Poetics of Testimony." In *Converging on Culture: Theologians in Dialogue with Cultural Analysis and Criticism*, edited by Delwin Brown, Sheila Greeve Davaney, and Kathryn Tanner, 56–65. Oxford: Oxford University Press, 2001.

Clarke, Janice. "A Critical View of How Nursing Has Defined Spirituality." *Journal of Clinical Nursing* (Wiley-Blackwell) 18, no. 12 (2009): 1666–73. doi:10.1111/j.1365-2702.2008.02707.x.

Cole, Brenda, Ethan Benore, and Kenneth Pargament. "Spirituality and Coping with Trauma." In *Spirituality, Health, and Wholeness: An Introductory Guide for Health Care Professionals*, edited by Siroj Sorajjakool and Henry Lamberton, 49–76. New York: Routledge, 2004.

Cooper, Zach. "Spirituality in Primary Care Settings: Addressing the Whole Person through Christian Mindfulness." *Religions* 13 (April 2022): 346. https://doi.org/10.3390/rel13040346.

Corbin, Juliet, and Anselm Strauss. *Basics of Qualitative Research*. 3rd ed. Thousand Oaks, CA: Sage Publications, 2008.

Dass, Ram [Richard Alpert]. *Remember: Be Here Now*. Hanuman Foundation. New York: Harmony House, 1971.

DeChant, Thomas, Lauren Smith, and Jose Chavez. "Recognizing and Reducing Delirium in the Intensive Care Unit." *Critical Care Nurse Q* 46, no. 3 (2023): 277–81. doi:10.1097/CNQ. 0000000000000465.

Derrida, Jacques. *The Gift of Death*. Translated by David Wills. Chicago, IL: University of Chicago Press, 1995.

Derrida, Jacques. *Positions*. Translated and annotated by Alan Bass. Chicago, IL: University of Chicago Press, 1981.

Elkins, David N., L. James Hedstrom, Lori L. Hughes, J. Andrew Leaf, and Cheryl Saunders. "Toward a Humanistic-Phenomenological Spirituality." *Journal of Humanistic Psychology* 28, no. 4 (fall 1988): 5–14. doi:10.1177/0022167888284002.

Ellison, Craig W. "Spiritual Well-Being: Conceptualization and Measurement." *Journal of Psychology and Theology* 11, no. 4 (1983): 330–8.

Emblen, Julia, and Lois Halstead. "Spiritual Needs and Interventions: Comparing the Views of Patients, Nurses, and Chaplains." *Clinical Nurse Specialist* 7, no. 4 (July 1993): 175–82. Journals@Ovid Full Text. Web. 10 October. 2023. http://ovidsp.ovid.com/ovidweb.cgi?T=JS&PAGE=reference&D=ovfta&NEWS=N&AN=00002800-199307000-00005.

Eshghi, Fateme, Lida Nikfarid, and Armin Zareiyan. "An Integrative Review of Defining Characteristic of the Nursing Diagnosis 'Spiritual Distress.'" *Nursing Open* 10, no. 5 (May 2023): 2831–41. doi:10.1002/nop2.1574.

Fadiman, Anne. *The Spirit Catches You and You Fall Down: A Hmong Child, Her American Doctors, and the Collision of Two Cultures*. Later printing edition. Farrar, Straus and Giroux, April 24, 2012.

Farran, Carol J., Kaye A. Herth, and Judith Popovich. *Hope and Hopelessness: Critical Clinical Constructs*. Sage Publications, 1995.

Ferguson, Duncan S. *Exploring the Spirituality of the World Religions: The Quest for Personal, Spiritual and Social Transformation*. London: Bloomsbury Academic, 2010.

Fitchett, George. *Assessing Spiritual Needs: A Guide for Caregivers*. Academic Renewal Press, 2002.

Fitchett, George, and Steve Nolan, eds. *Spiritual Care in Practice*. Jessica Kingsley Publishers, 2015.

Flanagan, Kieran, and Peter C. Jupp, eds. *A Sociology of Spirituality*. Farnham: Ashgate Publishing, 2009.

Foucault, Michel. *The Birth of the Clinic: An Archaeology of Medical Perception*. Vintage Press, 1994.

Frankl, Viktor E. *Man's Search for Meaning*. Foreword by Harold S. Kushner. Boston: Beacon Press, 1959, 1984, 2006.

Frankl, Viktor E. "Viktor Frankl: Self-Actualization is Not the Goal." Noetic Films. YouTube, September 20, 2019. https://www.youtube.com/watch?v=OL8DyVusLeE.

Fricker, Miranda. *Epistemic Injustice: Power and the Ethics of Knowing*. Oxford: Oxford University Press, 2007.

Gadamer, Hans-Georg. *The Enigma of Health: The Art of Healing in a Scientific Age*. Stanford, CA: Stanford University Press, 1996.

Ganim, Barbara. *Art and Healing: Using Expressive Art to Heal your Body, Mind, and Spirit*. US: Echo Point Books & Media, 1999, 2013.

Gardner, Fiona. *Critical Spirituality: A Holistic Approach to Contemporary Practice*. Surrey: Ashgate Publishing Limited, 2011.

Garrard, Eve, and Anthony Wrigley. "Hope and Terminal Illness: False Hope versus Absolute Hope." *Clinical Ethics* 4, no. 1 (March 2009): 38–43. doi:10.1258/ce.2008.008050.

Gilson, Errin C. *The Ethics of Vulnerability: A Feminist Analysis of Social Life and Practices*. Routledge Studies in Ethics and Moral Theory. London and New York: Routledge Taylor & Francis Group, 2014.

Gottlieb, Roger S. *A Spirituality of Resistance: Finding a Peaceful Heart and Protecting the Earth*. Lanham, MD: Rowman & Littlefield, 2003.

Gould, Meredith. *Desperately Seeking Spirituality: A Field Guide to Practice*. Collegeville, MN: Liturgical Press, 2016.

Grace, Pamela J., and Melissa K. Uveges. *Nursing Ethics and Professional Responsibility in Advanced Practice*. 4th ed. Jones and Bartlett Learning, 2022.

Grayhall, Patricia. *Making the Rounds: Defying Norms in Love and Medicine*. Berkeley, CA: She Writes Press, 2022.

Guest, Matthew. "In Search of Spiritual Capital: The Spiritual as a Cultural Resource." In *A Sociology of Spirituality*, edited by Kieran Flanagan and Peter C. Jupp, 181–200. Farnham: Ashgate Publishing, 2009.

Haidt, Jonathan. "Religion, Evolution, and the Ecstasy of Self-transcendence." TED Talk, March 14, 2012. https://www.youtube.com/watch?v=2MYsx6WArKY&t=11s.

Haight, Roger. *Spiritual and Religious: Explorations for Seekers*. Maryknoll, NY: Orbis Books, 2016.

Hạnh, Thích Nhất. *No Mud, No Lotus: The Art of Transforming Suffering*. Berkeley, CA: Parallax Press, 2014.

Hạnh, Thích Nhất. *Peace Is Every Step: The Path of Mindfulness in Everyday Life*. New York: Bantam Books, 1991.

Hạnh, Thích Nhất. *You Are Here: Discovering the Magic of the Present Moment*. Boston: Shambhala, 2010.

Harrison, Guy, ed. *Psycho-Spiritual Care in Health Care Practice*. London: Jessica Kingsley Publishers, 2017.

Harvard University. Initiative on Health, Spirituality, and Religion. https://projects.iq.harvard.edu/rshm/home?fbclid=IwAR0Eu6QlOKH1fW2hKXK4PBL-Z0cn8aRZ2Bu OjFJoO6wyiSAVFtJLV9S1bD4.

Hayes, Diana L. *No Crystal Stair: Womanist Spirituality*. Maryknoll, NY: Orbis Books, 2016.

Heelas, Paul and Linda Woodhead with Benjamin Seel, Bronislaw Szerszynski, and Karin Tusting. *The Spiritual Revolution: Why Religion is Giving Way to Spirituality*. Oxford: Blackwell Publishing, 2005.

Herman, Judith. *Trauma and Recovery: The Aftermath of Violence from Domestic Abuse to Political Terror*. New York: Perseus Books, 1992, 1997, 2015.

hooks, bell. *All About Love: New Visions*. New York: HarperCollins, 2000.

hooks, bell. *Feminism is for Everybody: Passionate Politics*. New York: Routledge, 2015.

hooks, bell. *Feminist Theory: From Martin to Center*. New York: Routledge, 2015.

hooks, bell. *Talking Back: Thinking Feminist, Thinking Black*. Boston: South End Press, 1989.

Illueca, Marta, Ylisabyth S Bradshaw, and Daniel B Carr. "Spiritual Pain: A Symptom in Search of a Clinical Definition." *Journal of Religion and Health* 62, no. 3 (June 2023): 1920–32. doi:10.1007/s10943-022-01645-y.

Isaac, Kathleen S, Jennifer L. Hay, and Erica I. Lubetkin. "Incorporating Spirituality in Primary Care." *Journal of Religion and Health* 55, no. 3 (June 2016): 1065–77. doi:10.1007/s10943-016-0190-2.

Jaberi, Azita, Marzieh Momennasab, Shahrzad Yektatalab, Abbas Ebadi, and Mohammad Ali Cheraghi. "Spiritual Health: A Concept Analysis." *Journal of Religion and Health* 58, no. 5 (2019): 1537–60. doi:10.1007/s10943-017-0379-z.

Jupp, Peter C., and Kieran Flanagan, eds. *A Sociology of Spirituality*. Surrey: Ashgate Publishing Limited, 2007, 2010.

Kaur, Valarie. *See No Stranger: A Memoir and Manifesto of Revolutionary Love*. New York: Random House, 2020.

Kelleher, J. Paul. "Health Inequalities and Relational Egalitarianism." In *Understanding Health Inequalities and Justice: New Conversations Across Disciplines*, edited by Mara Buchbinder, Michele Rivkin-Fish, and Rebecca L. Walker, 88–111. Chapel Hill, NC: University of North Carolina Press, 2016.

King, Martin Luther, Jr. *Strength to Love*. Philadelphia: Fortress Press, 1963.

Koenig, Harold G. "Religion, Spirituality, and Health: Understanding the Mechanisms." In *Spiritual Dimensions of Nursing Practice*. Rev. ed., edited by Verna Benner Carson, and Harold G Koenig, 33–61. West Conshohocken, PA: Templeton Press, 2008.

Kold, Ken. *The Couch Trip*. New York: Dell, 1970, 1971.

Kotfis, Katarzyna, Annachiara Marra, and Eugene Wesley Ely. "ICU Delirium - A Diagnostic and Therapeutic Challenge in the Intensive Care Unit." *Anaesthesiology Intensive Therapy* 50, no. 2 (2018): 160–7. doi:10.5603/AIT.a2018.0011.

Kübler-Ross, Elisabeth. *On Dying and Caring: What the Dying Have to Teach Doctors, Nurses, Clergy & Their Own Families*. 50th Anniv. ed. New York: Scribner, 1969, 2014.

Kurtz, Ernest, and Katherine Ketcham. *The Spirituality of Imperfection: Storytelling and the Search for Meaning*. New York: Bantam Books, 1992.

Larrabee, Mary Jeanne, ed. *An Ethic of Care: Feminist and Interdisciplinary Perspectives*. London: Routledge, 1993.

Ledesma, Gian Carlo M., Marc Eric S. Reyes, and Clarissa F. Delariarte. "Meaning in Life, Death Anxiety, and Spirituality in the Lesbian, Gay, and Bisexual Community: A Scoping Review." *Sexuality & Culture* 27, no. 2 (April 2023): 636–58. doi:10.1007/s12119-022-10032-4.

Lemiesz, Michelle A. "The Spiritual Care of the Hospitalized Patient: A Nursing Perspective." *Journal of Religion, Disability and Health* 3, no. 1 (1999): 75–97.

Levinas, Emmanuel. *Otherwise Than Being—Or Beyond Essence*. Translated by Alphonso Lingis. Pittsburgh, PA: Duquesne University Press, 1981, 1997.

Lorde, Audre. *The Cancer Journals*. Forward by Tracy K. Smith. New York: Penguin Books, Random House, 1980, 2020.

Lorde, Audre. *Sister Outsider: Essays and Speeches by Audre Lorde*. Berkley, CA: Crossing Press, 1984, 2007.

Lubiano, Wahneema, ed. *The House that Race Built: Original Essays by Toni Morrison, Angela Y. Davis, Cornel West, and Others on Black Americans and Politics in America Today*. New York: Vintage Books, 1998.

MacDonald, Douglas A. "Studying Spirituality Scientifically: Reflections, Considerations, Recommendations." *Journal of Management, Spirituality & Religion* 8, no. 3 (2011): 195–210. doi:10.1080/14766086.2011.599145.

Mackenzie, Catriona, Wendy Rogers, and Susan Dodds. *Vulnerability: New Essays in Ethics and Feminist Philosophy*. Studies in Feminist Philosophy. Oxford and New York: Oxford University Press, 2014.

Mac Laren, Duncan. "All Things to All People? The Integrity of Spiritual Care in a Plural Health Service." *Health & Social Care Chaplaincy* 9, no. 1 (January 2021): 27–41. doi:10.1558/hscc.40568.

Majid, Abdul S., and Lance D. Laird. "Encountering God, Accompanying Others: Spirituality and Theology among Muslim Health Care Chaplains." *Spirituality in Clinical Practice* 10, no. 1 (2023): 74–8. https://doi.org/10.1037/scp0000315.

Malik, Anil K., Dalim K. Baidya, Rahul K. Anand, and Rajeshwari Subramaniam. "A New ICU Delirium Prevention Bundle to Reduce the Incidence of Delirium: A Randomized Parallel Group Trial." *Indian Journal of Critical Care Medicine* 25, no. 7 (July 2021): 754.

Martin, William, and Nancy Martin. *The Caregiver's Tao Te Ching: Compassionate Caring for Your Loves Ones and Yourself*. New World Library, 2011.

Matas, Kimberly. "Benjamin Schultz: Pharmacist Improved Medical Care Nationwide." *Arizona Daily Star*, May 25, 2009. https://tucson.com/news/science/health-med-fit/benjamin-schultz-pharmacist-improved-medical-care-nationwide/article_34516976-dded-5c1d-94ab-d8e470322df8.html.

Mathews, Rosita deAnn. "Using Power from the Periphery: An Alternative Theological Model for Survival in Systems." In *A Troubling in My Soul: Womanist Perspectives on Evil and Suffering*, edited by M. Townes Emilie, 82–95. Maryknoll, NY: Orbis Books, 1993.

May, William F. "The Patient as Person: Beyond Ramsey's Beecher Lectures." In *The Patient as Person: Explorations in Medical Ethics*. 2nd ed., edited by Paul Ramsey, xxix–xliii. New Haven, CT: Yale University Press, 1970, 2002.

McCarroll, Pam, Thomas St. James O'Conner, and Elizabeth Meakes. "Assessing Plurality in Spirituality Definitions." In *Spirituality and Health: Multidisciplinary Explorations,* edited by Augustine Meier, Thomas St. James O'Connor, and Peter L. VanKatwyk, 43–59. Waterloo, ON: Wilfrid Laurier University Press, 2005.

McGuire, Meredith B. *Religion: The Social Context*. 5th ed. Belmont, CA: Wadsworth Group, 2002.

McSherry, Wilfred. "Spiritual Crisis? Call a Nurse." In *Spirituality in Health Care Contexts*, edited by Helen Orchard, 107–17. London: Jessica Kingsley Publishers, 2001.

McSherry Wilfred and Peter Draper. "The Debates Emerging from the Literature Surrounding the Concept of Spirituality as Applied to Nursing." *Journal of Advanced Nursing* (Wiley-Blackwell) 27, no. 4 (1998): 683–91. doi:10.1046/j.1365-2648.1998.00585.x.

McSherry, Wilfred, and Steve Jamieson. "The Qualitative Findings from an Online Survey Investigating Nurses' Perceptions of Spirituality and Spiritual Care." *Journal of Clinical Nursing* (John Wiley & Sons, Inc.) 22, no. 21–22 (November 2013): 3170–82. doi:10.1111/jocn.12411.

McSherry, Wilfred, Linda Ross, Josephine Attard, René van Leeuwen, Tove Giske, Tormod Kleiven, and Adam Boughey. "Preparing Undergraduate Nurses and Midwives for Spiritual Care: Some Developments in European Education over the Last Decade." *Journal for the Study of Spirituality* 10, no. 1 (2020): 55–71. doi:10.1080/20440243.2020.1726053. [CSS Library ordered 10/15/23].

Meier, Augustine. Thomas St. James O'Connor, and Peter L. VanKatwyk. 2005. *Spirituality and Health: Multidisciplinary Explorations*. Waterloo, ON: Wilfrid Laurier University Press.

Miller, James E., and Susan C. Cutshall. *The Art of Being a Healing Presence: A Guide for Those in Caring Relationships*. Willowgreen Publishing, 2001, 2012.

Mishra, Shri K., Elizabeth Togneri, Byomesh Tripathi, and Bhavesh Trikamji. "Spirituality and Religiosity and Its Role in Health and Diseases." *Psychological Exploration*. 56 (2017): 1282–301. doi:10.1007/s 10943-015-0100⁻z.

Mohr, James, and John Nicols, eds. "Life Expectancy 1850-2000." Mapping History. University of Oregon. Accessed March 16, 2024. https://mappinghistory.uoregon.edu/english/US/US39-01.html.

Moody, Harry R., and Carroll, David. *The Five Stages of the Soul: Charting the Spiritual Passages that Shape our Lives.* New York: Anchor Books, Random House, 1997.

Morrison, Toni. *The Source of Self-Regard: Selected Essays, Speeches, and Meditations.* New York: Penguin Random House LLC, Vintage Books, 2019.

Morrissey, Hannah. "Living to the Maxx: A Mother and Daughter's Courageous Tête-à-Tête with Cancer." Meaning Making. [Blog] Austin, TX: Eterneva (n.d.). Accessed October 10, 2023, https://www.eterneva.com/resources/living-to-the-maxx.

Munson, Ronald. *Intervention and Reflection Basic Issues in Medical Ethics.* 8th ed. Belmont, CA: Thomson Wadsworth, 2008, 2004.

Murdoch, Iris. *The Sovereignty of Good.* Routledge Classics. New York: Routledge, 1970.

National Center for Complementary and Integrative Health (NCCIH). NCCIH Strategic Plan FY 2021–2025. https://fles.nccih.nih.gov/nccih-strategic-plan-2021-2025.pdf.

Noddings, Nel. *Caring: A Feminine Approach to Ethics and Moral Education.* 2nd ed. Berkley: University of California Press, 1984, 2003.

Nolan, Steve. "Searching for Identity in Uncertain Profession Territory: Psycho-spirituality as Discourse for Non-Religious Spiritual Care." In *Psycho-Spiritual Care in Health Care Practice*, edited by Guy Harrison. London: Jessica Kingsley Publishers, 2017.

Nolan, Steve. *Spiritual Care at the End of Life: The Chaplain as "Hopeful Presence".* Jessica Kingsley Publishers, 2011.

Nouwen, Henri J. M. *Our Greatest Gift: A Meditation on Dying and Caring.* San Francisco: HarperCollins, 1995.

Nouwen, Henri J. M.. *The Wounded Healer: In Our Own Woundedness, We Can Become a Source of Life for Others.* New York: Doubleday, 1979.

O'Brien, Mary Elizabeth. *Spirituality in Nursing: Standing on Holy Ground.* 6th ed. Jones and Bartlett Learning, 2017.

Oman, Doug, and Joseph D. Driskell. "Holy Name Repetition as a Spiritual Exercise and Therapeutic Technique." *Journal of psychology and Christianity* 22, no. 1 (2003): 5–19. ISSN - 07334273.

Orchard, Helen, ed. *Spirituality in Health Care Contexts.* London: Jessica Kingsley Publishers, 2001.

Otto, Rudolf. *The Idea of the Holy.* Translated by John W. Harvey. Oxford: Oxford University Press, 1923.

Paley, John. "Spirituality and Secularization: Nursing and the Sociology of Religion." *Journal of Clinical Nursing* 17, no. 2 (January 2008): 175–86.

Patel, Eboo. "Building Bridges: Religions' Role in Our Societies." TEDx Chicago, December 10, 2021. https://www.youtube.com/watch?v=GYLesUKHPGc&t=2s.

Pattison, Stephen. *Alive and Kicking: Towards a Practical Theology of Illness and Healing*. London: SCM Press Ltd., 1989.

Pesut Barbara, Marsha Fowler, Sheryl Reimer-Kirkham, Elizabeth Johnston Taylor, and Rick Sawatzky. "Particularizing Spirituality in Points of Tension: Enriching the Discourse." *Nursing Inquiry* 16, no. 4 (December 2009): 337–46. doi:10.1111/j.1440-1800.2009.00462.x.

Phelps, Jamie T. "Joy Came in the Morning Risking Death for Resurrection: Confronting the Evil of Social Sin and Socially Sinful Structures." In *Embracing the Spirit: Womanist Perspectives on Hope, Salvation and Transformation*, edited by Emilie M. Townes, 48–70. Maryknoll, NY: Orbis Books, 1997.

Pitrowski, Linda F. "Advocating and Educating for Spiritual Screening Assessment and Referrals to Chaplains." *Omega* 67, no. 1–2 (2013): 185–92. doi:10.2190/OM.67.1-2.v

Plante, Thomas, ed. *Healing with Spiritual Practices: Proven Techniques for Disorders from Addictions and Anxiety to Cancer and Chronic Pain*. Praeger, 2018.

Porte, André de la, Nicolene Joubert, and Annemarie Oberholzer, eds. *Proceedings of the 2nd Biennial South African Conference on Spirituality and Healthcare*. Cambridge: Cambridge Scholars Publishing, 2018.

Puchalski, Christina M., ed. *A Time for Listening and Caring: Spirituality and the care of the Chronically Ill and Dying*. Foreword by His Holiness the Dalai Lama. Oxford: Oxford University Press, 2006.

Puchalski, Christina M. "The Role of Spirituality in Health Care." *Baylor University Medical Proceedings* 14, no. 4 (2005): 352–7. doi:10.1080/08998280.2001.11927788.

Puchalski, Christina M. "Spirituality: Implications for Healing." *New Theology Review* 18, no. 4 (2021): 77–81.

Puchalski, Christina M., and Betty Ferrell. 2010. *Making Health Care Whole: Integrating Spirituality into Patient Care*. West Conshohocken, PA: Templeton Press.

Pujol, Nicolas, Guy Jobin, and Sadek Beloucif. "'Spiritual Care Is Not the Hospital's Business': A Qualitative Study on the Perspectives of Patients about the Integration of Spirituality in Healthcare Settings." *Journal of Medical Ethics* 42, no. 11 (2016): 733–7. http://www.jstor.org/stable/44606002.

Putt, B. Keith, ed. *Gazing through a Prism Darkly: Reflections on Merold Westphal's Hermeneutical Epistemology*. Perspectives in Continental Philosophy. New York: Fordham University Press, 2009.

Ramsey, Paul. *The Patient as Person: Explorations in Medical Ethics*. 2nd ed. New Haven, CT: Yale University Press, 1970, 2002.

Ricoeur, Paul. *Figuring the Sacred: Religion, Narrative, and Imagination*. Minneapolis, MN: Augsburg Fortress Press, 1995.

Ritchie, Michael, director. *The Couch Trip*. Orion Pictures Films, 1988.

Rohr, Richard. *Falling Upward: A Spirituality for the Two Halves of Life*. San Francisco: Jossey-Bass, 2011.

Rolheiser, Ronald. *Sacred Fire: A Vision for a Deeper Human and Christian Maturity*. New York: Penguin Random House, 2014.

Roof, Wade Clark. *Spiritual Marketplace: Baby Boomers and the Remaking of American Religion*. Princeton, NJ: Princeton University Press, 1999.

Rue, Nancy. *The Value of Compassion*. New York: Rosen Publishing, 1991.

Rumbold, Bruce D. *Helplessness and Hope: Pastoral Care in Terminal Illness*. Harrisburg, PA: Trinity Press International, 1996.

Sessanna, Loralee, Deborah Finnell, and Mary Ann Jezewski. "Spirituality in Nursing and Health-Related Literature: A Concept Analysis." *Journal of Holistic Nursing* 4, no. 25 (2007): 252–62. doi:10.1177/0898010107303890.

Shearer, Debra. "Colliding Cultures in Delivery of Health Services: The Role of Cultural Competency in Health." White Paper. Maryville University, March 2013.

Sheldrake, Philip. "Spirituality and Healthcare." *Practical Theology*, 3, no. 3 (2010): 367–79. doi:10.1558/prth.v3i3.367.

Shim, Janet K. "Cultural Health Capital: A Theoretical Approach to Understanding Health Care Interactions and the Dynamics of Unequal Treatment." *PubMed*. 51, no. 10 (March 2010): 1–15. doi:10.1177/0022146509361185.

Shim, Janet K. *Heart-Sick: The Politics of Risk, Inequality, and Heart Disease*. New York: New York University Press, 2014.

Singer, Michael A. *The Untethered Soul: The Journey Beyond Yourself*. Oakland, CA: New Harbinger Publications, Inc., 2007.

Smith, Amy Rex. "Using the Synergy Model to Provide Spiritual Nursing Care in Critical Care Settings." *Critical Care Nurse* 26, no. 4 (2006): 41–7. doi:10.4037/ccn2006.26.4.41.

Smith-Stoner, Marilyn, and Amy Lynn Frost. "How to Build Your 'Hope Skills.'" *Nursing* 29, no. 9 (September 1, 1999): 48–9.

Soelle, Dorothee. *Against the Wind: Memoir of a Radical Christian*. Translated by Barbara and Martin Rumscheidt. Minneapolis, MN: Fortress Press, 1999.

Soelle, Dorothee. *Death by Bread Alone: Texts and Reflections on Religious Experience*. Translated by David L. Scheidt. Philadelphia: Fortress Press, 1978.

Soelle, Dorothee. The Mystery of Death. Minneapolis, MN: Fortress Press, 2007.

Soelle, Dorothee. *Suffering*. Translated by Everett R. Kalin. Philadelphia: Fortress Press, 1975.

Sorajjakool, Siroj, and Henry Lamberton, eds. *Spirituality, Health, and Wholeness: An Introductory Guide for Health Care Professionals*. New York: Routledge, 2004.

Speck, Peter. *Being There: Pastoral Care in Times of Illness*. SPCK Publishing, March 1988.

Stone, Howard W., and Andrew Lester. "Helping Parishioners Envision the Future." In *Strategies for Brief Pastoral Counseling*, edited by Howard W. Stone, 46–60. Minneapolis: Fortress Press, 2001.

Strauss, Anselm, and Juliet Corbin. *Basics of Qualitative Research: Techniques and Procedures for Developing Grounded Theory*, 2nd ed. Los Angeles, CA: Sage Publications, Inc., 1998.

Sullivan, Mark D. *The Patient as Agent of Health and Health Care*. Oxford: Oxford University Press, 2017.

Taylor, Charles. *A Secular Age*. Cambridge, MA: Belknap Press of Harvard University Press, 2007.

Taylor, Charles. *The Ethics of Authenticity*. Toronto: House of Anansi Press, Ltd., 1991.

Taylor, Charles. *The Malaise of Modernity*. Toronto: House of Anansi Press, Ltd., 1991.

Taylor, Charles. *Sources of the Self: The Making of the Modern Identity*. Harvard: Harvard University Press, 1992.

Taylor, Elizabeth Johnston. *What Do I Say? Talking with Patients about Spirituality*. Forword by Christina M. Puchalski, MD. Philadelphia: Templeton Foundation Press, 2007.

Tervalon, Melanie, and Jann Murray-García. "Cultural Humility versus Cultural Competence: A Critical Distinction in Defining Physician Training Outcomes in Multicultural Education." *Journal of Health Care for the Poor and Underserved* 9, no. 2 (1988). doi:10.1353/hpu.2010.0233.

Tillich, Paul. *The Courage to Be*. New Haven, CT: Yale University Press, 1952.

Tinley, Susan T., and Anita Y. Kinney. "Three Philosophical Approaches to the Study of Spirituality." *Advances in Nursing Science* 30, no. 1 (2007): 71–80. doi:10.1097/00012272-200701000-00008.

Townes, Emilie M., ed. *A Troubling in My Soul: Womanist Perspectives on Evil and Suffering*. The Bishop Henry McNeal Turner Studies in North American Black Religion, Vol. 8. Maryknoll, NY: Orbis Books, 1993.

Townes, Emilie M. *Breaking the Fine Rain of Death: African American Health Issues and a Womanist Ethic of Care*. Eugene, OR: Wipf & Stock Publishers, 1998.

Townes, Emilie M., ed. *Embracing the Spirit: Womanist Perspectives on Hope, Salvation & Transformation*. Maryknoll, NY: Orbis Books, 1997.

Townes, Emilie M. *Womanist Ethics and the Cultural Production of Evil*. New York: Palgrave MacMillan, 2006.

Underhill, Evelyn. *Evelyn Underhill: The Best Works. 1. Practical Mysticism (1914), 2. Mysticism: A Study in Nature and Development of Spiritual Consciousness (1911). 3. The Essentials of Mysticism (1920)*. New York: Vintage Books, 2003.

U.S. Census Bureau. *American Counts Staff, Oregon Population 4.2 Million in 2020, Up 10.6% from 2010*. August 25, 2021. https://www.census.gov/library/stories/state-by-state/oregon-population-change-between-census-decade.html.

U.S. Department of Health and Human Services. *Health Insurance Portability and Accountability Act of 1996 (HIPAA)*. Center for Disease Control and Prevention. Updated June 27, 2022. https://www.cdc.gov/phlp/publications/topic/hipaa.html.

Varga, Ivan. "Georg Simmel: Religion and Spirituality." In *An Ethic of Care: Feminist and Interdisciplinary Perspectives,* edited by . Peter C. Jupp and Kieran Flanagan, 145–60. London: Routledge, 1993.

Vincensie, Barbara Baele, and Elizabeth Burkhard. "Spiritual Distress." In *Nursing Diagnosis Handbook: An Evidence-Based Guide to Planning Care. Reprint with 2021-2023 NANDA-I Updates*. 12th ed., edited by Betty J.Ackley, Gail B. Ladwig, Mary Beth Flynn Makic, Marina Martinez Kratz, and Melody Zanotti, 844–7. St. Louis, MO: Elsevier, Inc., 2022.

Vincent, Giselle, and Linda Woodhead. "Spirituality." In *Religions in the Modern World: Traditions and Transformations*. 3rd ed., edited by Linda Woodhead, Christopher Partridge, and Hiroko Kawanami, 323–44. London: Routledge, 2016.

Voas, David, and Steve Bruce. "The Spiritual Revolution: Another False Dawn for the Sacred." In *A Sociology of Spirituality*. edited by Kieran Flanagan and Peter C. Jupp, 43–61. Farnham: Ashgate Publishing, 2009.

West, Cornel. *Race Matters*. New York: Vintage Books, Random House, 1993, 2001.

West, Traci C. *Solidarity and Defiant Spirituality: Africana Lessons on Religion, Racism, and Ending Gender Violence*. New York: New York University Press, 2019.

Westera, Doreen, A. RN, MscN, Med. 2017. *Spirituality in Nursing Practice: The Basics and Beyond*. New York: Springer Publishing Company.

Westphal, Merold. *Overcoming Onto-Theology: Toward a Postmodern Christian Faith.* New York: Fordham University Press, 2001.

White, Gillian. *Talking About Spirituality in Health Care Practice: A Resource for Multi-Professional Health Care Team.* Jessica Kingsley Publishers, 2008.

Wiesel, Elie. "The Perils of Indifference." YouTube. April 12, 1999. https://www.youtube.com/watch?v=JpXmRiGst4k.

Woodward, James, and Stephen Pattison, eds. *The Blackwell Reader in Pastoral and Practical Theology.* Oxford: Blackwell Publishing, 2000.

World Health Organization (WHO). 2003. "WHO Definition of Health." https://www.publichealth.com.ng/world-health-organizationwho-definition-of-health/.

Yancy, Philip. *Where is God When it Hurts?* Anniv. ed. Zondervan, 2002.

Young, Caroline, and Cyndie Koopsen. *Spirituality, Health, and Healing.* Sudbury, MA: Jones and Bartlett, 2005.

Zainuddi, Zainul Ibrahim. "Aligning Islamic Spirituality to Medical Imaging." *Journal of Religio Health* 56 (June 2015): 1605–19. doi:10.1007/sl0943-015-0074-x.

Index

Note: Page numbers followed by 'n' denotes note numbers, while numbers in *italics* represent figures.

abandoned (patients feel)   21, 31, 64
acceptance
   in caring   115, 124, 127, 174
   Emmanuel Levinas on   69
   patients on health status   84, 156
   and spirituality   20
   unconditional   107, 122
accompaniment   149, 201
actuality (Kierkegaard)   146
Addison's disease   31, 41, 48, 92, 93, 163
admission process   58, 78, 81
advocacy (patient)
   BYO advocate   161–2
   chaplain perspective   203 n.6
   as choice   172
   covenant relationships and   163
   "divine rage" (Kaur)   169
   "holy boldness" (clergy)   170
   presence obligates   168
   provider for patients   164, 171
   self-education as   166
   spirituality and   169
   teaching self-advocacy   165–6
   voice as   167–8
ageism   77
agency (patient)
   advocacy for   161
   autonomy and   63, 128–9
   choice and   172
   disrespect of   33, 67–8, 90, 94, 98
   example of   32, 33, 166
   of hope   146
   moral   168–9
   from periphery   203 n.6

personal   179
   and spirituality   20, 49, 89, 106, 169
all of me (spirituality as)   20, 149, 179–80
   all-encompassing   106
   care including   95, 172, 175
   and meaning in/of life   18–19, 179
   patient example   *20*
   self-assessment (caregiver)   173.
      See also spiritual; spiritual care;
      spirituality
Allah   10, 203 n.27
Allen, Anjeanette   40, 98, 137–8, 145
aloofness (Nouwen)   33, 188 n.18
American College of Physicians   11
anxiety
   of caregivers   157
   and courage   58
   and death   112–13, 115, 157
   of families   131–2, 140
   and fear   57
   of patients   19–20, 58, 78
   and spirituality   20. *See also* courage,
      death; risk, spiritual distress,
      vulnerability
a/religious   9, 26, 95, 179
art (as spiritual care)   *60*, *114*, 201 n.1
Art as Witness: A Practical Theology of Arts-
      Based Research (Boursier)   201 n.1
assessment
   admissions   58–9
   chaplaincy on   87–8, 95, 195 n.8
   clinical   166
   patient perspectives   96–7
   spiritual   83–4, 87, 96, 173, 195 n.7

assumptions
  bias of   72–3, 125
  cause harm   53, 72, 127
  examples of   53, 84
  in healthcare   189 n.9
  racist   74
  spiritual maturity and   121
  and spirituality   20, 106
attitude reorientation   123, 126
autonomy (patient)
  advocacy for   167–8
  empowerment of   63
  lack of   53
  principle of   190 n.11
  and spirituality   20, 34, 89–90, 98, 106, 108, 128
avoidance medicine   12

Beauchamp, Tom L.   190 n.18
Beauvoir, Simone de   73
being present   8, 23, 117, 153, 157, 202 n.6
being there   99, 128, 154
being together with   150, 152, 202 n.13
beingness   6, 82, 149, 153, 173. *See also* caring presence
belief/belief system
  acceptance of   106
  equity and   106
  in higher power   5
  and hope   146
  religious   8, 9, 11, 107, 157
  spiritual   10
  and spirituality   5, 20, 84, 106, 108
  superimposing   85–6
"beloved child of God" (Nouwen)   153
black boxes   17, 187 n.14
Boursier, Helen T.   183 n.16, 183 n.18, 184 n.33, 196 n.2
Brown, Brené   129
Buddha   10
Buddhist   125, 131, 177
busy-ness   22, 119, 150. *See also* being-ness
Butler, Judith   72, 190 n.13, 191 n.9, 198 n.1

calling
  and advocacy   169
  chaplaincy as   170

nursing as   99–100, 134, 138, 140
  spiritual   169
The Cancer Journals (Lorde)   164
candy striper   139
care
  and bias   19–20, 74–5, 78–9
  compassionate   63, 108, 130, 131, 139
  for dying   115–16
  example of   *155*
  as excellent   48, 101–2, 140, 157
  for families   158–9
  and gender   72–3
  harmful   76–7, 97, 171
  holistic   12, 37, 175, 179
  lack of   40, 105
  long-term   13
  miscare   104
  model of   29
  and nonjudgementalism   124
  palliative   11
  pastoral   11, 88
  patient-centered   30, 103, 149
  and power differentials   72
  as practical   155–6
  racist   74–7
  and spiritual care   123
  and spirituality   7, 8, 99–100, 176
  unbiased   175
  whole-person   15. *See also* caring presence; caring together with; comforting presence; non-anxious presence; spiritual care
The Caregiver's Tao Te Ching: Compassionate Caring for Your Loves Ones and Yourself (Martin and Martin)   157
caregiving
  anxiety and   115
  compassionate   69
  ego and   76
  as holistic   12, 27, 95, 172–3, 179–80
  hope in   200 n.19
  "ministry of touch" (nurse)   22
  as overtasked   29
  patient-centered   123, 175
  practical   125. *See also* care; caring together with; listening
caring presence (in a clinical context)   202 nn.6, 10

as calming   119
caring together with   152
as comforting presence   *155*, 156
defining   150–1
with family   158
not as "fixing"   154
as healing presence   151–2
as practical   158–9
with the dying   156–8
caring together with   152–3, 202 n.13
caring together with   152, 202 n.13
"caring well" (Nouwen)   116–17
case studies (spirituality as all of me)
    Addison's disease   31, 48, 92, 93, 163
    cancer care   33, 48–9, 60–6, 89–90, 98, 112, 117, 130, 141–2, *142*
    Covid-19   97, 104
    dying daughter (cancer)   141–2, *142*
    dying daughter (eating disorders and alcohol abuse)   135, 143–4, 157–9
    father in maternity   131–2]
    hip replacement   20–4, 35–6, 90, 98, 134–5, 161–2
    long-distance parent   62–4
    lupus patient   51–6, 70–2, 84, 90, 97
    maternity   97, 131–4, 140
    mother with chronic obstructive pulmonary disease (COPD)   118–19, 153–4, 175
    octogenarian   134–5, 161–2, 175
    potential amputation   66–7, 128
    thyroid storm   100–1
    transgender   19–*20*, 49–51, 78–9, 97, 127–8
centering prayer   139, 177, 202 n.11
chaplaincy (healthcare)
    on boundaries   87–8, 154–5
    preparation for   154–5, 186 n.7
    on spiritual distress   85
    on spirituality   201 n.2
    as patient advocate   167–8
"chocolate or vanilla" (patient)   71–2
choice   147, 179
    agency as   172
    "chocolate or vanilla" (patient)   71–2
    courage and   58
    lack of   133
    nonchoice   103

spirituality and   20, 67, 108. See also advocacy; agency; freedom (Kierkegaard)
Chopp, Rebecca S.   181 n.4
Christian church   95
Christian/Christianity   10, 19, 135, 143–4, 174
chronic illness   19, *20*, 27, 70, 108, 166
chronic obstructive pulmonary disease (COPD)   118–19, 153–4, 175
Code of Ethics (American Nurses Association)   124, 198 n.2
cognitive dissonance   25–6
comforting presence   153–4
communication
    disconnects   47
    importance of   156
    miscommunication   48
    as therapeutic   80, 109
compassion
    Brené Brown on   129
    characteristics of   69
    lack of   74, 81, 90
    Nancy Rue on   130
    and nursing   134
    spirituality and   106–8
    and spiritual maturity   121, 122
    vs. sympathy   130
    value of   130. *See also* caring presence; compassionate care
compassionate care
    "absolute best" (patient experience)   133
    caring comes first   134–5
    chaplaincy perspective   85
    dignity as   69, 156
    informs caregiving   106
    in maternity   131–2. *See also* spiritual care
compassionate listening (Thich Nhat Hanh)   126
condescending (attitude)   33, 35–6, 90, 96
confidentiality (patient)   190 n.14. *See also* HIPAA
coping   84, 200 n.18
courage   58, 121. *See also* anxiety, risk, vulnerability

covenant relationships (respect for)   163–4
Covid-19, 113, 178–9
crisis (medical)
    caregiver response to   116, 170–1
    patient experience of   *41*, 66, 104–5
cultural humility   124–5, 127, 174–5
cultural competency   190 n.11
"The 'cure' is actually worse than the process of the disease itself" (patient)   56

Dass, Ram   156
death (and dying)
    Audre Lorde on   179
    befriending   114–15
    death watch   158–9
    clergy and chaplain reflections on   118, 157–8
    denial of   114–15
    embracing life   117–20
    "good death" (Nouwen)   119–21
    as Great Divide   111
    as Grim Reaper   111
    Henri Nouwen on   119–21, 176
    hiddenness   113
    ignoring   118
    as liberation   119–20
    as lonely   157–8, 203 n.28
    preparing for   117–18
    spirituality and   *20*, 108
    to tell (or not to tell)   116–17
    as Ultimate Equalizer   112. *See also* spiritual distress
death anxiety   112–13
    caring well   115–16
    "dying well" (Nouwen)   113
    embracing life   113, *114*
    reducing anxiety by naming death   114–15
Death by Bread Alone (Soelle)   177
Death Stories of Hindu, Tibetan, Buddhist, and Zen Masters (Blackman)   120
"defiant spiritualty" (West)   169
dehumanization   81
dementia   29, 52–3, 77
demographics (research)   1–2, 181 n.2
denial   112, 115

depression   114
Derrida, Jacque   69
despair   7, 25, 83, 146–7
diagnosis   92, 97, 155, 157, 165, 167, 169–71. *See also* spiritual distress
différance (Derrida)   69
dignity
    chaplaincy and   84
    and justice   69
    nursing perspective   70, 71, 124
    patient perspective   70
    psychiatric   79–80
    and spirituality   *20*, 106, 108, 174. *See also* compassionate care; spiritual distress
disaffiliation   5, 10, 26
disbelief   54, 70
disenchantment   26
dismissiveness   47, 53
dissociation (of caregivers)   25
distrust of caregivers (by patients)   56, 77
diversity   1–2, 115, 164
"divine rage" (Kaur)   169
"don't take it personal" (nurse manager)   134
drug seeker. *See* "frequent flier"
"dying is like being born into another phase" (grandfather)   144

efficiency (medical)
    just a number   49
    patient example (transgender top surgery)   49–50
emergency room (ER)   *41*, 53–6, 59, 66–7. *See also* anxiety; hospital systems
"emotional skin-thickening" (Fadiman)   25
empathic listening   125
empathy   70, 81, 129–31, 167. *See also* patient-centered care; holistic caregiving
end of life. *See* death (and dying)
Energizer Bunny   149, 155
"entering a second childhood" (Nouwen)   120–1
Epistemic Injustice: Power and the Ethics of Knowing (Fricker)   191 n.4

essence of being   6–8, 12, *20*, 27, 127, 143, 149, 173, 175. *See also* spiritual care; spirituality
ethics
   American Nurses Association Code of Ethic   124, 198 n.2
   as boundary   174
   committee   167–8
   medical   34, 190 n.18
   and spirituality   *20*, 105, 108. *See also* spiritual care; spiritual humility
"everydayness" (Heidegger)   99

Fadiman, Anne   29
faith   99, 118, 139, 143–4
family members   6–7, *20*, 45, 47, 63, 73, 100, 108, 116, 117, 133–4, 199 n.27. *See also* death (and dying)
fear
   of controversy   164
   disarming   58, 153–4, 169, 203 n.21
   of going to ER   57–8
   Heidegger on   57
   of patients   30, 139, 153–4
   and spirituality   *20*, 106, 108. *See also* death (and dying); spiritual distress
finitude (human)   111, 117–18, 196 n.2. *See also* death (and dying)
"fixing" (caregivers)   25, 154–5, 175, 194 n.15
"forever peace" (father)   157
forgiveness   84, 137
Ft. Davis Army Hospital (Boursier)   *16*
freedom
   Søren Kierkegaard on   146–7
   spirituality and   *20*, 106, 108
   Viktor Frankl on   16. *See also* agency; choice
Freezing Cold in ER (Boursier)   *41*
"frequent fliers"   168
   chaplain on   70–1
   "drug users"   70–1, 169
   nurse on   70–1
Fricker, Amanda   191 n.4

gender bias   72–4
generic spiritual care   95
Get Me Out of Here (Boursier)   *114*

God   10, *20*, 26, 40, 69, 115, 120, 143, 170, 174
God is ↔ God isn't   26
God within   141, 177
gold standard   16–17
"good death" (Nouwen)   113, 119, 120
Goodbye Mommy (Boursier)   143, *144*
Grayhall, Patricia, MD   27–8
greater good   121
Greatest Commandment (Mt. 22:36–40)   174
guilt (feelings of)   32, 82

Haidt, Jonathan   6
hallucinations   73–4, 92–4, 97. *See also* ICU delirium
Hanh, Thich Nhat   125–6, 131, 177
Harrison, Guy   181 n.1
healing
   acceptance and   155
   vs. curing   12
   spirituality and   *20*, 108, 137
   and wholeness   25. *See also* spirituality
healing presence   149, 151–2
Health Insurance Portability and Accountability Act (HIPAA). *See* HIPAA
Heidegger, Martin   9, 18, 57, 99, 111, 168
helplessness   59
hermeneutical injustice   69–70
higher calling   141
higher power   5, 8, *20*, 84, 108
HIPAA   63–5, 190 n.12
Historical Hospital Ward (Boursier)   *16*
Holding Hands (Boursier)   *155*
holistic caregiving   12, 37, 95, 123, 175, 179. *See also* caring; compassion; empathy
holy boldness   169–71
holy ground   137–8, 142
hope
   agency of   145–6, 169
   as false   201 n.19
   hoping for a (better) future   137, 146, 147
   through lament   200 n.19
   loss of   84

vs. optimism   200 n.18
Søren Kierkegaard on   146
spiritual distress and   84
spirituality and   7, *20*, 107, 108. *See also* defiant spirituality (West)
hopefulness   146–7
hopelessness   59, 85, 145–6, 200 n.18
hospice   11, 119, 135, 142, 145, 154. *See also* chaplaincy
hospitals as systems (harm patient spirituality)
 communication (disconnects)   47
 efficiency and productivity   48–9
 freezing cold in ER   39–40, *41*
 ICU: no privacy   46–7
 internal (medical) miscommunication   48
 impossible to sleep   42–3
 just a number   49
 kitchen hours   43–4
 making the rounds   42
 maternity floor protocols   44–5
 shift change   104–5
human spirit   146
humility (cultural)   124–7, 174–5
humility (spiritual)   124–5, 173–4

"I can spot a phony" (patient)   175
ICU delirium   93–93, 97, 189 n.4
The Idea of the Holy (Otto)   137
"incomprehensible mystery" (Otto)   137
"indifference" (Wiesel)   124
inequality (in healthcare)   17, 76–7, 189 n.9
interconnectedness   6, 115, 127
injustice
 Audre Lorde on   164
 in healthcare   76–7, 189 n.9
 hermeneutical   69–70
 spirituality and   *20*, 108
 testimonial   69–72
 testimony (role of)   181 n.4
Inpatient 09 (Boursier)   58–9, *60*
Intensive Care Unit (ICU)   73–4, 92–3. *See also* ICU delirium; spiritual distress
Intimidating (Boursier)   *46*
is-ness of life   8
"I–Thou" (Buber)   115

James F. Childress   190 n.18
Jesus   10, 89, 90, 98, 157
Jewish   10, 32, 58, 101, 112, 141, 157, 177
Journal of Clinical Nursing   187 n.16, 188 n.20
"just a number" (patient)   49, 128
justice
 dignity and   69
 gender   72–4
 in healthcare   189 n.9
 patient advocacy and   161–3
 racial   74–5
 spiritual maturity and   121
 spirituality and   *20*, 108
 unconditional welcome as   69

Kaur, Valarie   126, 169
kenosis   135
Kierkegaard, Søren   18, 146;
 on actuality   147
 on freedom   147
 on possibility   147
King, Martin Luther, Jr. (MLK, Jr.)   129–30, 169
Kübler–Ross, Elisabeth   116, 129

Labor of Love (Boursier)   *134*
Lee and Maxx (Estridge)   *142*
LGBTQIA   164, 181 n.3. *See also* transgender; queer
liminal space   98, 137–8. *See also* sacred space
listening
 compassionate   7, 86–7, 156, 174
 deep   86, 125–6, 143, 177
 empathic   125
 not (listening)   33–4, 55, 89–90
 as spiritual practice   100, 101
 tips for   199 n.12
listening presence   145, 155
"living a considered life" (Lorde)   179
Lorde, Audre   164
love
 of caregivers   170
 as comforting presence   153
 God   21, 174
 and spirituality   8, *20*
 as unconditional   174

McSherry, Wilfred and Steve Jamieson   187 n.16
Manifest Destiny   8
Man's Search for Meaning (Frankl)   15
Martin, William and Nancy   157
maternity   44, 97, 131–2, 133–4. *See also* hospital systems
meaning in/of life   1, 16–19, 83, 96, 150–1
meaningful   26, 118, 131, 177
medical ↔ spiritual disjunctures (patient experiences of)   31–6
　agency   32
　being ignored   34–5, 188 n.19
　condescending   35–6
　"Look at me…" (patient to doctor)   35
　not doing their job   36–7
　not listening; not hearing   33–4
　not seeing; not respecting   33
Medical Power of Attorney   66
medical scavenger hunt   129
medicalized spiritual care   1, 15–16, 17. *See also* black boxes
medical/scientific ↔ spiritual divide   95
mindfulness   107, 125–6, 138, 150, 177–8
ministry of presence   150, 152, 201 n.1. *See also* caring presence
*mis*care (physical)   104
misdiagnosis   51–4
MLK (Jr.). *See* King, Martin Luther, Jr.
"monsters in my head" (patient)   93–4
moral/morals
　action   75
　agency   168–9
　choice   115, 147
　higher power and   7–8
　responsibility and   68
　spiritual maturity and   121, 122
　spirituality and   20, 108
music (as spirituality)   6, 20, 107, 139, 178, 204 n.11
Muslim   122, 127, 203 n.27
mystery   137

National Center for Complementary and Integrative Health (NCCIH)   183 n.24, 185 n.5

New Father: "It's All New to Me Too" (Boursier)   132
Nightingale, Florence   130
no privacy   46–7
non-anxious presence   149
nonjudgementalism   124
non-religious. *See* a/religious
North American Nursing Diagnosis Association (now NANDA International)   83
Nouwen, Henri   113–16, 118–21, 138–9, 150–4, 176–7. *See also* death (and dying)
not religious   10–11. *See also* a/religious
Nursing Diagnosis Handbook: An Evidence-Based Guide to Planning Care   84, 192 n.21

On Death and Dying (Kübler-Ross)   116
One Flew Over the Cuckoo's Nest (Forman)   127
"Other" (Levinas)   69
Otto, Rudolf   137
Our Greatest Gift (Nouwen)   150
"ownmost possibilities" (Heidegger)   168

pain (physical)
　acknowledgment of   127
　assessment   29, 69–70, 127, 153
　caregivers contribute to   21–2, 28, 44–5, 55–6
　impacts emotional and spiritual pain   21–2, 50–1, 55–6, 64, 123
　management of   12, 162, 167
　medication for   71, 91–2
　mindfulness and   177–8
　mismanagement of   69–70, 74–5, 89–90, 167
　racism and   74–5
　relief from   71
　respecting   69–70, 86–7, 97, 127
　spirituality and   20, 21, 106–8. *See also* risk, spiritual distress, spirituality, vulnerability   58–9, 62–3, 68
palliative care   11, 145. *See also* hospice; spiritual care
~~part~~ of me   95, 105, 123, 175, 179, 180
The Patient as Person (Ramsey)   116

Index   227

pastoral care 11, 88, 95–6, 190 n.15. See also spiritual care
patient recovery 40
paternalism 51–2, 54, 129
patient-centered care 98, 123, 149–50
  chaplain on 98–9
  spiritual care as 103–4, 173–4. See also spirituality
Peace Is Every Step: The Path of Mindfulness in Everyday Life (Thich Nhat Hanh) 125
permission (patient) 64–6, 156, 190 n.14. See also HIPAA
personhood 77
phlebotomist 102, 123
"politics of consequence" (nursing student) 123
possibility (Kierkegaard) 146–7
postmodern 26, 196 n.2
post traumatic stress disorder (PTSD) 161
"*potentiality*-for-Being-its-Self" (Heidegger) 168
power
  abuse of 34, 50–1, 79–81, 127
  differentials of 72
  and gender 72–4
  from periphery 203 n.6
  provider-patient misbalance 50–1, 125, 174
  psychiatric admissions process 79–81
  and race 74–5
  and sexual orientation 48–9, 78–9. See also humility (cultural)
Powers-That-Be 39, 169
practical presence 155–6
practical theology 2, 173, 201 n.1
prayer 87, 96, 98, 107, 139, 176–8, 200 n.9, 204 n.11, 205 n.20. See also mindfulness
precarious (life is) 11
pride (human)
  as negative 125
  as normative 124
Principle of Autonomy 190 n.11
productivity (medical). See efficiency (medical)

proselytizing 87–8, 90, 190 n.19
Puchalski, Christina M. 186 n.7, 200 n.18, 201 n.3, 203 n.27

quality of life 119
queer 20, 49, 78–9, 97, 127, 163–4

racism/racist
  examples 74–6
  "strong Black women" 75, 192 n.21
Ramsey, Paul 116–17
reflective practice 150, 196 n.26
"regulatory norm" (Butler) 72–3
*re*humanizing 82
religious spirituality. See spirituality, religious
respect. See spirituality, respect
responsibleness (Frankl) 179–8
risk 45, 56–8, 62–3. See also anxiety, courage, vulnerability
Rue, Nancy 130

sacred space 137–42, 144, 147, 202 n.8
sacredness 7, 142, 202 n.8
second opinion 53–4
The Second Sex (Beauvoir) 73
secularity 25–6
See No Stranger (Kaur) 126
self-care 178
self-esteem 20
self-understanding 20, 106, 127, 173, 178
sexism 72–3
sexual orientation 19, 20, 69–70, 78–9, 86, 106, 115. See also queer; transgender
shame feelings 23, 79, 164
shift change 40–1, 104–5
silence 66, 75, 116, 125, 153
sleeplessness 30, 41–5, 47, 73–4. See also ICU delirium
Soelle, Dorothee 177
solidarity 49, 116, 119–21, 132, 138, 149–51, 153, 159
soul 118, 127, 129, 141
specialization (medical) 27
spirit 118, 127, 129, 141
The Spirit Catches You and You Fall Down (Fadiman) 25

Spirit of God   115
spiritual. *See* spirituality
spiritual assessment   195 n.7
   chaplaincy perspective   85, 87–8, 198 n.8, 195 n.8
   nursing perspective   84, 194 n.15, 195 n.7
   patient perspective   84
spiritual care
   as accompaniment   149, 201 n.3
   art as   6, *20*, *60*, 107, *114*, 139, 178, 201 n.1, 204 n.11
   as being there   99–100, 128, 133, *134*, 154, 202 n.6
   Christian church and   95
   crossing the line   87–8
   ethical considerations   174
   healthcare literature   186 n.7
   interventions (clinical)   96, 98
   "know your edges" (chaplain)   86–7
   NANDA-I definition of   83
   and NANDA-I nursing diagnosis   83
   nursing views on   187 n.16, 201 n.5
   origins of   25, 95–6
   patients on   195 n.13
   physical care as   *20*, 99, 101–3, 123, 175, 179–80
   plurality of   191 n.3
   prayer   87, 90, 96, 98, 107, 139, 176–8, 200 n.9, 204 n.11, 205 n.20
   and religiosity   9. *See also* chaplaincy; holistic caregiving; listening; mindfulness
   respect and   *20*, 50–2, 63, 70, 106–7, 116, 121–3, 127–8, 161
   role of   87
spiritual disorientation   182 n.1
spiritual distress
   assessment   96
   chaplaincy perspective   85–6
   diagnosis of   83–4
   "Everybody's different"   91
   fixing   194 n.15
   hallucinations and visions in ICU   92–3
   healthercare literature   186 n.6
   hip replacement patient   91
   ICU delirium   93–93, 97, 189 n.4
   measuring   194 n.15
   North American Nursing Diagnosis Association (now NANDA International)   83
   nursing perspective   88
   "monsters in my head" (patient)   93–4
   pain and medication mismanagement   87, 89–90
   patient's perspective   88–94, 96–7
   "What can I do to help you today?"   90. *See also* spiritual care; spirituality
spiritual interventions (clinical)   96, 98
spiritual maturity (in a healthcare context)   109, 121–2, 140, 169, 174
spiritual needs
   as all of me   *20*
   nurses on   11, 194 n.1
spiritual (*not* religious)   10
spiritual practices
   centering prayer   177
   meditation   178
   mantra repetition   205 n.20
   mindfulness   177
   music   6, *20*, 107, 139, 178, 204 n.11
   prayer   177
   stacked journaling   *60*
   Thich Nhat Hanh   177–8
spiritual well-being   26, 45, 106–8, 180
spirituality
   and acceptance   122
   agency and   32, 48
   as all of me   1, *20*, 172–4, 179, 180
   as something more   6
   autonomy and   63
   chaplaincy literature on   186 n.7
   clergy/chaplains on   1
   in clinical context   12
   as defiant   169
   definition   1, 5–6
   dignity and   69
   as essence of being   1, *20*
   family and   133
   as God within   141
   and health   1, *20*, 172–4, 179, 180

healthcare literature on 181 n.1, 183 n.24, 185 n.6, 186 n.7
in healthcare setting 31–2
as holistic 11
hope and 7, 147
as indescribable 7
ineffable 6
intersectionality of 8
as is-ness 8
Jonathan Haidt on 8
Kurtz and Ketcham on 5
many forms of 1
measuring 193 n.15
medicalized view 15–17, 25, 44
misconceptions about 1, 15–17
nature of 1–3
nurses on 18, 22–4, 127, 187 n.16
nursing students on 5–7, 106–9, 121–2
patient autonomy and 108, 113, 167
as patient-centered 149
patients on 19–21, *20*
as a/religious 26–7, 185 n.44
vs. religion 9
as religious 9–11
respect and 33–6
as responsibleness 179
Roger Gottlieb on 8
as rudder 8
sacred and 137
(against) tolerance 121–2
World Health Organization (WHO) on 11. See also black boxes; compassion; death (and dying); gold standard; humility; meaning in/of life; spiritual maturity (in a healthcare context); spiritual care
spirituality of dignity 3
spirituality of finitude 111, 117
spirituality of perseverance 167
"strong Black woman" (racist belief) 192 n.21
sub*humanize* 71. *See also* dignity
Sullivan, Mark, MD 26
Sunflower in Bloom (Boursier) 180
suffering
acceptance of 127

addressing all dimensions of 11
Anne Fadiman on 25, 27–8
Buddhism on 177
caregiver dissociation from 25
disarming fear 203 n.21
meaning in/of 137
needless 27–8
patient views 194 n.13
Viktor Frankl on 15–16, 147. *See also* compassion; hospitals as systems; spiritual distress
surrender 101–2

"task bunny" (nurses as) 30, 165
testimonial injustice
definition of 69–70
example of 70–2
testimony (role of) 69, 181 n.4
thyroid storm 100–1
tolerance as "allowing" (nursing student) 121–2
top surgery (transgender) 19–*20*, 49–51, 78–9, 97, 127–8
transgender 19–*20*, 49–51, 78–9, 97, 127–8
trauma
childhood 86
emotional 28, 161–2
in healthcare 93–4, 161–2, 168
physical 28
spiritual 44, 72–3, 78, 86–7
spirituality and *20*
unnecessary 28, 168. *See also* ICU delirium; spiritual distress
"True Self" (Rohr) 121
trust 19, *20*, 67, 70, 76, 96, 97, 101–2, 121, 153

unconditional welcome 69

The Value of Compassion (Rue) 130
voice (agency) 164–5, 167. *See also* advocacy; witness
vulnerability 59, *60*, 68, 105
cancer diagnosis 60–1
estranged by distance 62–4
of families 62–3

and HIPAA 64–5
of patients 68, 114, 152. *See also*
anxiety, courage, risk, vulnerability

walk together with 138
Wiesel, Elie 124

"We're here until we're not" (cancer patient mantra) 141, 157
"We're not numbers" (patient) 128
West, Traci 169
World Health Organization (WHO) 11